The Art of Laurel and Hardy

The Art of
Laurel and Hardy

Graceful Calamity in the Films

Kyp Harness

Foreword by John V. Brennan and John Larrabee

McFarland & Company, Inc., Publishers
Jefferson, North Carolina, and London

LIBRARY OF CONGRESS CATALOGUING-IN-PUBLICATION DATA

Harness, Kyp, 1964–
   The art of Laurel and Hardy : graceful calamity in the films /
Kyp Harness ; foreword by John V. Brennan and John Larrabee.
      p.   cm.
   Includes bibliographical references and index.

   ISBN-13: 978-0-7864-2440-5
   softcover : 50# alkaline paper ∞

   1. Laurel, Stan — Criticism and interpretation.   2. Hardy,
   Oliver, 1892–1957 — Criticism and interpretation.   I. Title.
   PN2287.L285H37   2006
   791.4302'80922 — dc22   2006000207

British Library cataloguing data are available

Cover photograph: Stan Laurel and Oliver Hardy (Photofest)

Manufactured in the United States of America

McFarland & Company, Inc., Publishers
   Box 611, Jefferson, North Carolina 28640
   www.mcfarlandpub.com

For Arthur and Norvell

CONTENTS

FOREWORD

Whatever happened to Laurel and Hardy? They are no longer American cultural icons. Their influence on our comedy has dwindled to a point of near nonexistence. Certainly, there is little trace of Laurel and Hardy's dignity, gentility and humanity in films that pass for comedies today. Since the days when "the Boys" cavorted in front of movie cameras on Culver City backlots, comedy has devolved from the shock of recognition to mere shock for shock's sake. As Mr. Hardy said in *Helpmates,* one of the greatest comedies ever made, "It's enough to make a man burst out crying."

In an era when "stars," — or, to be more accurate, "marginally talented media curiosities"— demand the sort of diva treatment that Cleopatra would deem excessive, it is perhaps difficult to recall a time when two genuinely talented and humble gentlemen made funny little films for 48 weeks out of the year, expecting nothing in return but a comfortable salary and a bit of laughter. Kind and gentle men on and off screen, Laurel and Hardy were unpretentious souls in unpretentious times. As such, their broad lampooning of life's absurdities may seem tame today, when the absurdity of modern culture has outpaced the absurdity of what was once lampooned. We've gone from nice messes to scatological explosions, from witty dialogue to nonstop profanity, and from kicks in the rear to kicks in the groin.

Yet despite the odds and the seeming inhospitable environment of 21st-century pop culture, the comedy of Laurel and Hardy endures. It may be less ubiquitous on television and in video stores, but it is still capable of generating gales of laughter even from those weaned on a steady diet of Adam Sandler and Pauly Shore. Thanks to the collective genius of Mr. Arthur Stanley Jefferson and Mr. Oliver Norvell "Babe" Hardy, films that were sometimes criticized for being simple and slow-moving even in their day can still bring about the kind of joyful laughter, born of self-recognition, that eludes so many modern-day comic films. Long ago, people found Laurel and Hardy funny because they saw themselves and their neighbors in the sad-faced skinny one and his fat and fussy pal. Here we are, some

70-odd years after Laurel and Hardy's heyday, and things are still the same. Popular culture may have changed, but humanity? Not so much. Laurel and Hardy are still us, and we are still them, and thank God for that.

They rarely attempted farce or satire. Their films are not loaded with topical references, pun-filled wisecracks or zany costumes. They were not Chaplinesque heroes or Keatonesque idiot savants. They did not see the world through the surrealistic fish-eye lens of the Marx Brothers nor approach it with the jaundiced, "screw everybody but me" stance of W. C. Fields. Although their comedy was no less personal than that of their contemporaries, it was purer. Laurel and Hardy took the simplest situations — delivering a piano, repairing a boat, cleaning a house — and commenced exploring the innumerable ways such straightforward ventures could go horribly, hilariously wrong. In short, they adopted poet Robert Browning's line "man's reach should exceed his grasp" and transformed it into poetry in motion.

How did these two gentle souls, one from Lancashire, England, the other from Harlem, Georgia, create a style of comedy so uncomplicated and universally accessible? That is the question that our friend Kyp Harness goes a long way toward answering in *The Art of Laurel and Hardy*. As you travel through the book, reading Kyp's thoughts on the Boys' career, from their completely coincidental pairing in the silent The Lucky Dog through to the final not-so-nice mess of *Utopia,* you will come to know what it was that made Laurel and Hardy the supreme comedy team in motion picture history. It is a wonderful introduction to the world of Laurel and Hardy. Or, as the Boys themselves might say, "It's a pip!"

— John V. Brennan and John Larrabee
Laurel and Hardy Central
http://laurelandhardycentral.com

PREFACE

For me, they seem always to have been there.

From earliest memory I felt they were the funniest of clowns. But it was something beyond laughter that kept me coming back to them, through childhood into adulthood. There was and is something indefinable in their art, in its depiction of the uneasy but unbreakable bond between two opposite characters, that bound itself to me — but that always eluded explanation.

So I dove into their world of lunatic disaster, followed their threads of graceful calamity back to their origins— or as close as I could come to them, for they spring forth from and are part of a current of eternal clownery. By seeking out and watching their films in chronological order from their first foundling steps as a team through to their final, failing efforts, I sought to experience their art as it occurred, to behold the evolution of their partnership —for theirs was a partnership that germinated and developed entirely onscreen — and to trace the arc of their gentle and genial foolishness in the early half of the twentieth century. I watched their coming together as a team: their transition from silent films to sound, from shorts to features, from their artistic heyday to their stifled and dismal last efforts.

In the end, I'm no further ahead at explaining their comedy's peculiar hold on me, or why what's funny is funny. The answers to these questions must always lie beyond the realm of words. All that can be documented is the creation of their perplexing yet compelling world, which mirrors and mocks our own. All that can be done is to assess their contribution in service of humanity's crucial yet often unacknowledged need to laugh at itself.

As the most human of clowns, their art brings a jolt of intimate connection along with the amusement it provides. If we empathize with their strivings and their failures, we rejoice in the unsullied, if unfounded, optimism they have for their next enterprise. We celebrate with them the success and perfection of their relationship, which remains intact no matter what destruction fate rains down upon them. They fail, yet they endure.

Perhaps that comforting sentiment accounts for the attraction their art exerts. That, and the mysterious machinations of the laughter instinct itself, the inexplicable genius of two men gifted with the talent of sheer funniness, to the grateful amusement of millions of their fellow humans.

Anyone who writes about Laurel and Hardy is indebted to John McCabe, the author of four books on the team, most notably *Mr. Laurel and Mr. Hardy,* the first, and still overall the best, book on the comedians. His pioneering investigations inform much of what is written here.

The best book on the making of the films is the extensively researched *Laurel and Hardy: The Magic Behind the Movies,* by Randy Skretvedt, which provides information on the chronological order in which the films were made — as opposed to the order of their release, as is often cited. This information, along with much else Skretvedt has unearthed, has been crucial to the present volume.

It's been a labor of love for me to explore the history and the world of Laurel and Hardy. I hope that others, too, will find inspiration in this documentation of their astonishing yet utterly natural journey.

— K. H.

INTRODUCTION:
THE CLOWN ANGELS

Stan Laurel and Oliver Hardy, described by J. D. Salinger as "two Heaven-sent artists and men," described by Kurt Vonnegut as "two angels of my time," are known the world over as the world's greatest comedy team and the most recognizable comic icons this side of Chaplin. More important though, Stan and Ollie are characters who have entered into the vast mythology of the world's good-humored creations in the name of fun, along with Punch & Judy and Pop Goes the Weasel, along with Mickey Mouse and Oliver Twist, Jack and the Beanstalk, Sir Arthur Aguecheek, Santa Claus, and Popeye. As we get further away from them in history we are better able to appreciate the immensity of this achievement — an achievement that would have amazed, befuddled, yes, gladdened, but perhaps also embarrassed the two comedians who for the most part regarded themselves as a couple of journeyman workers. Far below the lofty heights of Chaplin and never knowing the intellectual critical acclaim of Keaton, Fields, or the Marx Brothers, Laurel and Hardy saw their star fade and diminish in their time, till they were cast off from Hollywood, unwanted, passé—forced to mount arduous tours through drafty theaters in the British provinces while in their sixties and in ill health.

Yet it is this very lack of presumption and pretension that makes their art like no others' in its simple purity, for there was a genuine humility about the two men. By all accounts there was an unaffected sweetness about them (a deeply rooted gentleness that can't be faked) that informed their screen creations. These were two bumbling nitwits undone by their good-heartedness, struggling through this world and flailing within its complexities as if enmeshed in an underwater net — setting chirpily off at the beginning of another two-reeler, beaming with innocent jubilation on a sunny black-and-white morning that could be the first morning of all the mornings of the world, then sitting dismally twenty minutes later within the reeking confines of another nice mess. Ollie's features would be pursed into an expression of frustrated, exasperated resignation: the dimples on his plump round cheeks arranging themselves into the quintessence of last-ditch despair; his tiny, tired eyes beseeching us and making their irresistible appeal for empathy and sympathy and communion with us all in the shared understanding of the mysterious force that wanders the world undoing all our most prized plans and hopeful endeavors. The force that leaves us sitting in the midst of the wreckage, grimly staring into the distance as brick after brick plunges down the chimney, one after the other in a meticulous rhythm and with impeccable timing, bonking and clonking on our heads until we heave a sigh and the cascade of bricks ceases for a moment. We peer hesitantly, fearfully upward, hoping with a tenuous hope that the last brick has fallen (could it be true?)—and get one more emphatic CLONK! square in the middle of the forehead for the effort (no, it is never for pity that Ollie stares at us, it is for understanding, an understanding that we share the basic knowledge of how unendurable life can be).

Stan, the architect of this disaster, the unthinking conduit of mayhem, this oblivious causer of catastrophe and insentient instigator of disharmony and disgrace, sits beside Ollie with his face screwed into a mask of horrified bewilderment: the corners of the mouth pointing in the direction of his shoes; his eyes, tiny slits of hysterical agony; gulping and weeping in his squeaky high-pitched voice, "Well, I couldn't help it!" Stan does not weep because he fears his situation but because he does not understand his situation and this makes him feel afraid: Stan weeps in confusion. How could it be that just a moment ago everything was going so fine and now all of a sudden they find themselves in this gigantic mud puddle/ridiculously misshapen car with our legs wrapped around our necks? How could it be and how did it happen?

And yet, only a few minutes later in the next two-reeler, we unspool scenes of Stan and Ollie again, their batteries apparently recharged, puttering down the road in their Model T, setting off on a brand-new endeavor with all the hope in the world on their faces, with not one scintilla of doubt in the pure souls of these two angels that fate will treat them kindly, that their heartfelt plan is destined for anything but the greatest possible success, that the future happiness that awaits them and which they believe in so thoroughly is eminent and just around this very next corner. And in the sublime confidence of this anticipation they grin and beam with excited goodwill at their fellow creatures: Stan smiles idiotically, his dull eyes half-closed, his lips curling up at either side of his nose, perhaps doffing his derby and scratching up the electrified patch of sagebrush on the top of his head. Ollie coyly bows his head down into the folds of his double chins,

grinning up at the world with coquettish embarrassment, delicately fingering his necktie and perhaps hazarding a slight simpering chuckle (hmmh!
hmmh! hmmh!) of abashed friendliness (and if ladies are present, maybe
even chancing a bit of daring blushing flirtation). In a moment Stan will
say, "Ollie," Ollie will say, "What, Stan?," and Stan will say, "I've just had
an idea...."

Like great folk and blues songs, the films of Laurel and Hardy revolve
around one basic structural premise (with the thudding and unvarying
inevitability of all great art): Stan and Ollie attempt to do something, and
they fail to do it, repeatedly, noisily, and finally, irrevocably. The execution
of the simplest of tasks can, in the hands of these two men, lead to earth-
shattering explosions, entire buildings being burnt to the ground, orgies of
destructive chaos apt to engulf and decimate an entire city block, not to
mention cars twisting and deforming into unspeakably bizarre perversions
of their former utilitarian selves. Stan has never had an idea that has not
flung them headlong into catastrophe yet Ollie never fails to consider each
of these ideas with the greatest sobriety, his forefinger disappearing into the
dimple in his chin as his face assumes the countenance of careful meditation: "That's a good idea!" he concludes and so it goes. That only a few
frames prior to this, Ollie had been asking us to join in his vehement disgust at being saddled with the world's stupidest man as his partner is apparently of no concern to Ollie. Stan now has an idea and it is only right that
it be heard out. If the idea is acceptable, which it invariably proves to be,
then it is only right that it be acted upon with the greatest possible alacrity.

No one becomes more excited, inspired, and industrious with the
arrival of a good idea than Ollie, and no one is left more crestfallen, disil-
lusioned, and heartbroken than he when it inevitably blows up in his face.
Stan's far more resilient — if their jalopy's dismembered he can at least
receive comfort from the fact that the horn's still in good working condition. If one of their misadventures culminated in their detonating an atom
bomb and blowing up the entire world, Stan, floating weightless in the ether
of the universe, would likely find some curious piece of unexploded matter wafting past him and begin toying with it, giddily celebrating the fact
that at least this has survived. In any case, Stan can walk away from any
failure not too much the worse for wear (chiefly because he does not comprehend the meaning of the concept), easily distracted by even the promise of his next meal, his flat clown's feet slapping against the floor, with that
ridiculous arm-swinging tread he uses to hoist himself from one scene to
the next. For Ollie there are no such consolations, no such distractions —
the hurt goes deeper for him.

Their situations have entered our collective memories like snatches of old songs, nursery rhymes, folktales, like the remnants of a farcical dream we share that mirrors the world we know and at the same time seems more real than the world it mirrors: a chronicle of human aspiration in reverse, a world that ends with a bang and a whimper as well as the seat of your pants set afire into the bargain. They move through a surly, miserable universe, trying only to do their best and make everything better, but only making everything worse until someone clobbers them on the head and then the whole film's pace slows to a snail's crawl. They then roll up their sleeves and enter into a leisurely round-robin of retribution, putting off their pretense of middle-class decorum at last and drenching the interloper with a bucket of water or ripping his coat up the back or shoving a plate of cottage cheese up his nose. All done at an excruciatingly unhurried pace, with, one might say, delicacy — a stately, royal formality; a somber politeness that one must assume as one has one's necktie amputated at one's collar while awaiting to perform the same action upon one's opponent. After all, as the world has Geneva Convention to ensure that countries can blow each other to bits in a civilized, gentlemanly manner, so do the denizens of the world of Laurel and Hardy have their codes and regulations to guarantee the civilized, gentlemanly manner by which acts of violence and humiliation will be exchanged. Their way is no crazier than ours— only seems to be, and laughably so, through the lens of comedy — in much the same way that our scuffles and conflagrations undoubtedly provide endless amusement for the Venusians.

Stan and Ollie are our friends, our brothers, our helpmates, our fellow accident victims, our coworkers, companions, and compatriots in this terrifying, out-of-control avalanche/mudslide that is called Life. They do not stand outside of society and thumb their nose at the cop like Charlie; like us, they try to appease the psychopathic cop in every way possible, they try to play the game again and again, for they believe in the game, but the game does not want them — it kicks them in the teeth every time. The game, lest we forget, is a rabid, insane, gyrating, foaming-at-the-mouth beast that no one except the beastly can ride. Stan and Ollie haven't received this information and they hasten toward the beast, still believing that good intentions, cordiality, and impeccable manners will win the day. Comedy is not tragedy plus time but rather tragedy taken to a level no one would dare take it in a mere tragedy — it's tragedy taken to the place where one has to laugh, otherwise the weeping, once begun, would never stop. Laurel and Hardy dance their intricate ballet on this precipice; they shuffle their tangle-footed minuet here on the gravesite of our crushed ambitions, the trickling follies we indulge in and are destroyed by, the delicate affectations and rituals that comfort us and make us all the more ridiculous. Yes, Stan and Ollie are here, they live, and they are us.

Here they are, advancing toward the door, Stan dumbly striding ahead with his witless blank expression, for the hundredth time trying to enter the door before Ollie, only to be preeempted by a pointed tap on the shoulder by his portly friend. Ollie's wry and condescending expression, the dismissive jerk of his thumb dispatching Stan back to the rear, and Ollie's magisterial air all freshly remind Stan of his true and rightful place in the world, a place to which he repairs with meek submission (and perhaps relief), a place that is always and everywhere behind Ollie, who can stride boldly ahead, having restored the proper balance and order of things, who now can draw himself up with sublime dignity and almost unimaginable pomposity, who can gather himself up imperially with the knowledge that all is right in his world and lead his friend confidently forward into disaster.

Though it is Stan who at first glance marshals our sympathies most directly — Stan the put-upon, Stan the beaten-down and pushed, Stan the silenced and the shoved, with his slight frail body and his sad face — it is always Ollie who in the end must break our hearts most completely. Ollie commands our loyalty most fiercely, for it is Ollie who believes in happiness ahead most fervently, who holds onto the tattered rags of his dignity amid the onslaught of humiliation, who most earnestly, desperately yearns for just one solitary thing to go right in his world, who appreciates and has a genuine thirst for order, symmetry, and, yes, beauty. It is Ollie who is the engine of despair and humanity in the act, the darker shadow that makes us look again, the big heart, the counterpoint and counterweight to the airy hilarity of Stan.

Yet why divide them anyhow? They are united as one and united they fall. Born to be clowns, born to clown together, born to join and mirror the world and make it laugh by doing so, so seamlessly do they fit together — like egg and yolk, yin and yang, each one entirely complementary to the other, perfectly formed, like a pistachio nut, one of God's good works. They are bound inseverably by love. Ollie bemoans Stan's stupidity yet never thinks once of going without him; Stan suffers under Ollie's bossiness, yet life without him is an incomprehension. Each other is all they got, for better or worse, so they muddle on, thereby expressing something profound and tender about all human relationships. Their marvel and their miracle is the utter rightness and potency of their partnership — the simple fact that a comic from Ulverston, England, and a comic from Georgia in the United States would come together to form a comic entity so complete and holistic to set the world awash in laughter, for as long as we have hearts and mouths to laugh with. If fate kept them unduly underappreciated in their lifetimes, perhaps it was just to preserve that sweetness in them as men and artists — the sweetness of the genuinely humble and the thoughtful, the gentleness of the ones who know better than to take anything for granted, who are so very rarely heard from and who, like most of us, are more acquainted with failure than success, the patient and the kind ones who are always being asked by the world to wait (yet for whom no one waits), the meek who are supposed to inherit the earth — and to transmit and express that sweetness into their films so as to make them sunny documents of that portion of humanity for all time to come. They are funny and endlessly lovable. Who could doubt these clowns are angels?

1

STAN (1890–1965)

Eyewitnesses throughout Stan Laurel's life attested to the one thing that remained constant over the course of an often highly troubled and unpredictable existence: his laughter. Fellow employees at the Roach studios remarked on hearing him crowing with delight as he watched the rushes of each day's filming, reserving his most hysterical outbursts for the antics of his partner. John McCabe noted when he met Stan in a British music hall in the 1950s his "refined horse laugh."[1] A friend at the end of Stan's life recalled him laughing so much that they were afraid he was going into a life-threatening spasm.[2]

He was a man who enjoyed laughter, had few peers in creating laughter, who lived for laughter. "I can't think of a better life than creating comedy," he said.[3] His screen character laughed with the same sort of unbridled merriment, a high-pitched unrestrained cackle that conveyed utter gasping, side-aching abandonment to pure, delicious joy. The moments when the Stan of the movies becomes transported into this hysteria exist in stark contrast to the character's customary deadpan, dim-witted demeanor. Yet these moments occur often enough that we may be led to believe that they are the natural state of the character, that this pure magical joy is where Stan is most at home, and from whence perhaps comes his occasional transgressions of material reality, his otherworldly walking the world without ever being in it, or of it. There is a maniacal quality to Stan's laughter, that of one gleefully sabotaging what we call reality.

Then, as quickly as it appears, it is gone, and he is back to stumbling over the carpet, overturning the water pitcher, sheepishly suffering under the enraged gaze of his good friend, Mr. Hardy.

The road of laughter called to Stan early on. As a boy in boarding school, the masters found him so amusing they woke him up at night to entertain them in their chambers as they relaxed. Later, his father, himself an actor, writer and theatrical impresario, hoped the boy would find safe haven in the administrative side of the business. But it was too late–Stan had already fallen under the spell of Little Tich, Nipper Lane, Dan Leno, who were the traveling clowns of British music hall. These remained idols of Stan's for the rest of his days, and in retirement he spent many hours making tapes of the ancient recordings he had of them, sending them to friends.

So it was that young Arthur Stanley Jefferson donned the baggy pants himself — actually a pair of his father's best trousers — and made his debut. In his later screen incarnation we see all the hallmarks of the British music hall clown at the turn of the century — the befuddled, witless, vague tramp lost in the world; the foolish, asinine grin; the stumbling bumbler who somehow still possesses a strange grace and a battered elegance; an unfading idiosyncratic beauty that is set against the gray conforming brutalizing forces of reality and that triumphs over them, because of its guilelessness, its innocence. The hair standing on end like a lightning rod for all the absurdity of the universe was brought fresh from the fright wigs of clowns from time immemorial, and he brought the derby, as Chaplin had, across the ocean as the preferred headwear of all the comics that trod the boards. The fine, frothy enjoyment of silliness for silliness's sake is what calls to us from Stan's performances in the films, and it calls to us through him from the herky-jerky music and eccentric soft-shoe dances upon the stages of another time and another place that doesn't and can't exist anymore.

Success came late to Stan and so he never quite grew comfortable with it. Having spent most of his young adult life touring hectically in vaudeville while making occasional, abortive attempts to establish himself in films, he was 37 when he paired with Hardy and "made it" artistically as well as financially. His long apprenticeship must have seemed galling especially when compared with the incredible success attained by his friend and former roommate Charlie Chaplin during the same period (he and Stan came over to America as part of the same music hall troupe and were roommates during the tour). Certainly we know that Stan came to detest the seemingly endless series of rooming houses and train travel that the constant touring in vaudeville meant, and many a time it must have seemed to him that the road would last forever. At one time his act consisted of his impersonation of the suddenly famous Little Tramp character his onetime roommate had created. We can imagine Stan wondering when his turn was coming, or if it was even on the way at all.

But it is important to note that there is little reason to doubt that Stan ever wavered, from the time he first met Chaplin to the end of his life, in his admiration of Charlie as "the best there ever was or ever will be." Every quoted word of Stan about Chaplin glows with awed adoration, with the enraptured enthusiasm of the true disciple. When Laurel and Hardy were at their height, Stan made several attempts to attain the same type of artistic and financial independence that Chaplin had, but he lacked Chaplin's canniness, his pragmatism and boldness. And, of course, Laurel and Hardy were never the phenomenon, culturally or commercially, that Chaplin was.

A key example of the difference between Laurel and Chaplin may be seen in the way they presented their work to the world and invited acknowledgment for it. It's common knowledge that Chaplin wrote, directed, produced and starred in all of his movies, composing the music when sound came in and even, according to bystanders, styling the hair of his leading ladies. In the credits to his movies his name appears repeatedly in various capacities to an almost humorous degree. Stan, while not involved in his work in all the myriad ways that Chaplin was in his, is known to have contributed actively to the writing of all the vintage Laurel and Hardy films, and it is generally accepted that in most cases he was the de facto director of the comedies, that it was he who was in effective artistic control, regardless of who nominally sat in the director's chair. Even his producer Hal Roach, who had an often combative relationship with Stan, had to admit: "Hell, if you listed his name in terms of everything he did on the film, Laurel's name would be up there ten times."[4]

Yet in the credits of most of the movies, Stan's name appears only once — as star comedian. For whatever reasons, it wasn't important to Stan to receive formal acknowledgment for all his contributions. Apparently, all that was important to him was the quality of what appeared on the screen, regardless of who received official credit for it.

Perhaps there was the sense that in openly declaring Stan to be the "auteur" or prime creator of the team's work it would have taken away from the perceived unity of the team as a team, the sense of balance and equality between them that goes to the heart of the identity of Laurel and Hardy. Stan would have no doubt been the first to admit that their work came to full strength when it ventured furthest into the collaborative realm, that if he was the originator of the ideas, these ideas could only come to life within the magical interplay of the talents of Hardy and himself: an interplay within which both men were equal creators of their art. Often, as has been well documented, prepared scripts went by the wayside as the two men improvised as the cameras rolled, creating comedy out of the air with each other that neither would have been capable of producing on their own. Perhaps it was Stan's recognition of that fact, as well as his genuine modesty, that kept him from being concerned about being publicly identified as the main writer-director of the Laurel and Hardy comedies.

In any case, there is a possibility that this sort of reticence of the ego may have hurt him later on, when the team left Hal Roach Studios for

Twentieth Century Fox and MGM. At these larger facilities the subtle realities of Stan's artistic control, his uncredited role as being the "director
behind the director," and his quiet, guiding hand were quite lost — what
was not acknowledged before could not now be insisted upon, and so he
was stripped of half of his creative self, treated as just more raw material
to be ruthlessly forced through the system's machinery, at the mercy of
bureaucratic mediocrities whose only god was (is) the bottom line. The
result is a succession of some of the most horrible films ever associated with
any of the classic comedians, and to see Stan's performances in them is to
know this must have been one of the unhappiest periods of his life.

    A casual study of Stan's biographies shows us that aside from living a
part of his life in the direct shadow of Chaplin (the most formidable clown
in history and true originator and trailblazer in the medium Stan would
soon adopt as his own), there was something in Stan's character throughout his life that had a predilection to being dominated by a stronger figure,
or, if not actively dominated, something that was most comfortable being
subdominant in any given relationship. At various periods in his life, Stan
lived in the shadow of a more forceful personality.

    We see this first of all, naturally enough, in his relationship with his
father, whom Stan revered and honored all his life, judging by his descrip-
tions of him, and who, as an actor, writer and owner of several theaters,
must have seemed all-powerful to the young Stan trying to make his way
in show business. Then there was Chaplin, before whose miraculous talent
he had to humbly bow and kneel (he was Chaplin's understudy in the
troupe). And then there was Mae Laurel, the common-law wife and vaudeville partner he toured with for ten years, with whom he fought constantly,
who sabotaged Stan's early attempts to break into films by insisting on
appearing in them, who showed her displeasure with him by literally claw-
ing his face, and with whom Stan's alcoholism flourished to the degree that
he was considered untouchable by prospective film companies.

    It was only after a movie producer who had contracted Stan's services
paid for Mae's ticket back to Australia so that the comedian could work
productively on the films he was hired to do that Stan was out of Mae's grip.
We get the impression he never could have left her on his own. Somebody
else had to step in and make the arrangement. And it was only after this
that Stan's career would begin to take off, and though ten years later he
repeated the same pattern by marrying a woman who voiced objection by
hitting him over the head with a frying pan (he blessedly attained domestic contentment and true love in the last 20 years of his life), it was shortly
after this first marriage that Stan met Hardy, and together they created the
world's most famous relationship of the dominant and the dominated.

In the early Stan Laurel solo films we see a man of immense talent doing funny things, but they seem to be the wrong funny things for him to be doing. He is a comic in the Chaplin mode: all energy and vigor, his face wickedly mobile, flinching and flickering several emotions at once, his arms and legs are akimbo, he's a man on the move, a Jim Carrey, a Jerry Lewis. But all of his acrobatics, though amusing, don't add up to anything; they don't touch the heart. And this isn't for lack of talent, it's because the character, the vessel of the hijinks, simply doesn't ring true.

The character Chaplin created and played for 25 years affected the world so overwhelmingly because it rang so completely true — and Chaplin's genius shone through simply because in an essential way he was that character, an energetic little scuffler fighting his way out of obscene poverty with nothing but his wits and the sheer magic of his being so much more alive than anyone else. Chaplin took the central truth of his life, which in his case was the tragedy of his life — abandonment by his alcoholic father as a child, then becoming homeless from the institutionalization of his mentally ill mother — and fashioned it into a figure of joy and humor, a symbol of laughter throughout the world.

It was only after he was free of Mae that Stan could transmute his truth into art and his tragedy into comedy when he met Oliver Hardy. They made films that are an exploration of the dominant and the dominated, and how those two terms flow into and become one another over and over again, as the delicate balance of power shifts from side to side, until they're both rendered meaningless by the reality of loyalty and love.

Beyond Laurel's genius for clowning and his great pantomimic skills, beyond his genius as an inventor of gags and situations, is his gift for manifesting utter vulnerability and communicating complete, innocent mental blankness, which is singular and inimitable — as is proven by the failures of those who either attempt to imitate him directly or by the scores of comedians who have sought to continue in his tradition. No one has conveyed the sense of pure, helpless, otherworldly submissiveness so completely as did Stan Laurel.

The character is a man from nowhere, with no identity. It's fitting that Peter Sellers, when trying to find a voice for his character in *Being There*— who was a cipher who had no contact with the world other than through television, a blank slate on which all other characters project their own presumptions— settled on Stan Laurel's voice.[5] Stan is a fright-wig-haired clown shambling through the world confounding reality itself, enraging humanity in general and his good friend Mr. Hardy in particular.

A casual observer of the Laurel–Hardy relationship would likely note that it consists mainly of the larger Hardy bullying the smaller Laurel and blaming him for all misfortunes. A closer examination reveals that it fulfills an intricate network of needs on both sides. Ollie needs Stan because he needs someone to feel superior to, to bully and boss, as well as to protect. He never learns that Stan will only wreak havoc over all his carefully made plans. Or perhaps he does realize this but stoically accepts it as the price of his need to feel superior. Stan needs Ollie because he needs someone to protect him, to connect him with the world at large, because he knows his own limitations and believes Ollie is more intelligent than he is. Ollie believes this as well, despite the overwhelming evidence that Ollie is at least as brainless as Stan, if not more. Stan suffers Ollie's bullying because of his need to be protected; Ollie meets with disaster because of his need to feel superior. Ollie blames Stan entirely for all misfortunes and Stan seems to accept the blame, crying profusely. Yet the reality is that much of the time Stan isn't to blame at all, that at the very least they share the blame equally. But, Ollie seems convinced that Stan alone is entirely to blame — and if Stan does not completely concur with this opinion, he at least is willing to bear the punishment it engenders, for the sake of the relationship. Symptomatic of this, of course, is that all of these intersections of need are underlied, and intertwined with, the deep genuine love and warmth the two characters seem to have for each other.

Stan's character is in many ways the opposite of the Chaplin clown. He does not pirouette but can barely transport himself from one end of the room to the other without injuring someone nearby. He floats through the world in a bubble of infantile helplessness. Whereas Chaplin's eyes express emotion and cunning, Stan Laurel's eyes express utter vacuity. Without the leadership and protection of his friend, he is quite aware, he would be utterly lost. If Chaplin is the magician who triumphs over reality, Stan knows he has lost even before he left home — he is completely overwhelmed by reality.

Such a character could only develop and exist within the context of a partnership — certainly the Stan character on his own could never motivate a plot or keep a story moving. We get an unsettling vision of Stan alone in *Block-Heads* (1938), when he is separated from his partner and patrols a foxhole for 20 years after the end of World War I. Treading decisively as he marches soberly back and forth in his little rutted path, indenting the ground at each end where he turns smartly, flattening the earth with the same movement in the same place innumerable times over the past two decades, it's an eerie nightmare vision of the senseless repetition of a pointless act, an autistic loop Stan would fall into without his good friend Mr. Hardy to inspire him and promote him to higher endeavors

Stan is lost in the world. He is unable to understand the simplest of instructions, the most pedestrian figures of speech and metaphors. If Ollie says that "they have to get up pretty early in the morning to catch a Hardy," Stan must ask, "How early?" (*Sons of the Desert*, 1933). If Ollie asks Stan to retrieve a pitcher with which to procure some ice cream, Stan returns with a picture ("Come Clean," 1931). He is thoroughly unable to conform with social convention: when Ollie asks him why he can't bring him a box of chocolates during his stay in the county hospital, Stan replies that Ollie didn't pay him for the last one he brought ("County Hospital," 1932). He is confounded by societal roles, his own as well as others, as shown by his habit displayed in several films of addressing policemen as "ma'am" ("Another Fine Mess," 1930; *Bonnie Scotland*, 1935), or, in several of the "married films," of kissing Ollie's wife instead of his own. It isn't entirely that Stan is dumb — his mind is capable of making connections, sometimes inspired, surprising, unexpected connections. But they are always the wrong connections.

Likewise, there is ample evidence that Stan is lost even within his own body. Like his mental processes, his movements tend to be loose and flailing, the prime example of this being his walk, in which his legs throw themselves out before him like the grasping arms of a nonswimmer desperately approaching the side of the pool. Stan has difficulty at times in commanding his body to obey him, as shown in his inability to fold his arms without them slipping loose as in *Pardon Us* (1931) or by his frustrated attempts to unlock his feet from the curb in "The Music Box" (1932) — though at other times he is capable of a sudden magical dexterity. He often confuses his various body parts with one another, as when he hits his head on an attic beam in *Sons of the Desert* and frenziedly rubs his posterior to quell the pain. In *Way Out West* (1937), Ollie threatens to strap the palm of Stan's hand with a rope end — when Stan turns away, cringing and wincing with expected pain, Ollie relents, striking him on the top of his derby. Still, Stan rubs and blows on his hand as though it had been struck with uncompromised force.

Stan is the ultimate scapegoat. If Laurel and Hardy are the lowest on the pecking order in the world they inhabit in any given film, then between them Stan is lowest on the totem pole again, being bullied around by the second most powerless man in the world. He doesn't seem particularly to mind, however.

Yet, like the Chaplin character, Stan and Ollie's characters are heroic figures, because they keep coming back and trying again, against all odds. The graciousness and humility with which Stan steps aside, and stays behind, alone, would make Stan a heroic figure. The sheer delight of Stan's grin triumphs over the inequity of his situation. Stan is dumber than us, clumsier than us, but ultimately he is freer than us, for he can weep openly if something frightens him; he can retaliate immediately if someone's bothering him; he can surrender to waves of crippling hysteria.

And, of course, as every Laurel and Hardy fan knows, if Stan suffers under Ollie's bullying, it is not he who suffers most in any given film. No one has been more punished for presumptuous pomposity than Oliver Hardy and no one has had more transoms crashed over the head, more streams of water in the face, more internments in massive gaping mud holes than Oliver Hardy. Stan seems less punished by fate because he expects less, presumes less. Though he is as equally as stupid as Ollie, he is many ways wiser. He is quite open to the concept of making do, making the best of whatever comes along. Ollie is not — he has ideals he must stubbornly pursue and societal goals he must attain.

Stan is capable of flashes of intelligence, insight and inspiration that flicker, then sputter out like faulty light bulbs. He is capable of conceiving and articulating a plan but can only hold it whole in his mind for a moment before it dissolves like a snowflake into nothingness— when asked to repeat the idea, his language breaks down into fractured insensibility, and his struggles to retrieve his thoughts before they are swallowed into the oblivion of his mind result in jumbled nonsensicality. Interestingly, Ollie often regards the mangled version of the concept as having equal validity as the first, coherent rendition and utilizes it as the springboard for their next enterprise — long after, we may infer, Stan, left to his own devices, would have forgotten the original idea entirely.

As strange as it might seem to apply such a term to a dim-witted buffoon, the Stan character in the films does have dignity, he does exert a certain amount of power even in his powerlessness. Within his ostensibly subordinate position he is capable of exhibiting a surprising strength and grace (as so many oppressed peoples have done). These attributes were bequeathed upon him by his creator perhaps as a way of embracing and forgiving his own frailties and fatal flaws, which are writ large in the character — in the same manner by which comedy as a whole allows us to laugh at our shortcomings, and by laughing accept them, to look more kindly on ourselves, and on others, and all of life.

If Stan is submissive to Ollie outwardly, we should not assume that it is Ollie alone who controls the relationship — throughout the films we see the evidence of the equality between them, of the intricate dance and balance of power, and hints of a deep, unspoken understanding between them. In "Going Bye-Bye!" (1934), a criminal's moll mistakenly locks him in a trunk while trying to hide him. She appeals to Stan and Ollie for help in getting him out, telling them that he'd fallen into the trunk while packing. Ollie looks doubtfully to Stan, who thinks for a moment and pronounces, "It could happen," at which point they agree to help her.

In "Dirty Work" (1933), a mad scientist cackles maniacally as he explains his new rejuvenation serum and ends with "Now to try it on a human specimen!" Ollie again looks to Stan, the pupils of whose eyes jerk to the side in an almost imperceptible yet unmistakable gesture, which precisely expresses, "Let's get out of here — now" and Ollie turns back to the scientist and says, "Well, we'll be going now!"

Every so often Stan takes charge. Once he actually understands that they've given the deed to the wrong woman in *Way Out West,* he becomes quite motivated, leading Ollie around, saying, "We'll get that deed or I'll eat your hat!" Ollie, suitably impressed, slaps him on the chest and says, "Now that's what I call determination!" Stan slaps him back on the chest, harder, causing Ollie to jump back in further surprise and awe at his friend's newfound determination and strength. In "Laughing Gravy" (1931), Stan shows a similar determination when the mean landlord throws his dog out into a snowstorm: "I'm going out to get my dog!"

In the physical altercations that arise when diplomacy has been exhausted, it is virtually always Stan who initiates the first blows, who commences to take everyone into the bizarre slow-motion round-robin of indignities. When the nurse, who laughs scornfully at them, turns and bends over her baby carriage in "The Music Box," it is Stan who delivers a savage kick to her posterior. After they've been forced by a brutish father to retrieve his bratty son's football in *Block-Heads,* the boy bends over to kick the ball and Stan neatly and forcefully kicks him in the backside. Stan begins the rice-throwing melee that ends "The Hoose-Gow" (1929), after the warden has shoved him facedown into the gooey stuff. Stan rises angrily, silently, and delivers a handful of rice splattering into the warden's face, as Ollie winces and makes halfhearted gestures for him to stop.

Ollie abhors the breaking of the thin membrane that separates daily "civilized" behavior from the expression of outright hostility. Once the deed is done, however (almost always by Stan), Ollie is only too happy to enter into the ritual of mutual retaliation, to enter even more wholeheartedly into the war.

It is clear that Ollie needs Stan for his fresh, instantaneous perception of the world; Stan in these cases acts swiftly yet cold-bloodedly: he sees an injustice, becomes angry, and retaliates immediately, without thought or consideration. Ollie is too socialized, or aspires to be, to initiate the violence against their common enemies. This is Stan's job, and Ollie soon proves himself equal to the task of following up on anything Stan lays down.

Much of the time Stan serves the purpose of acting out the antisocial, irresponsible, anarchic impulses that Ollie has — that we all have — but which society demands must be hidden, unacknowledged. As much as Ollie desires to become part of society, he is equally ambivalent about the cost of doing so, and this part of him is personalized in Stan. The exhilaration and release many of these scenes provoke come from the dismantling of the petty laws of "acceptability" and "seemliness" that govern our daily affairs and replacing it with the real law of honesty, spontaneity, an authentic, vigorous encounter with life that does not shy away from confrontation and hostility. This rearrangement of reality is almost always sparked by Stan and there is evidence in the films that Ollie highly values this ability of his partner.

After Stan kicks the child in *Block-Heads,* the brutish father returns and is informed by his son of what has occurred. The father kicks Ollie; Stan kicks the father (a familiar pattern in their contretemps, where Ollie always somehow ends up suffering the most, with Stan avenging his sufferings); the father kicks Ollie again, then turns to depart. Stan taps him on the shoulder, the father turns, Stan holds up a fist, then slams him in the chin with the other fist. The father stands board-straight, dazed for a moment, before Stan prods him lightly with his finger and the father falls crashing to the floor. The bratty son is stunned. Ollie, obviously overjoyed, skips over to the football and kicks it decisively back down the stairs in a perfect coda to the entire incident.

A similar moment occurs in "Busy Bodies" (1933), when Stan and Ollie enter into a fracas with a coworker. They stand, exchanging blows, until one of Stan's punches misses their opponent and hits Ollie by mistake. The coworker cheers this, laughing, saying to Stan: "I like you — you've got an honest face." "You do?" says Stan, and invites the man to sit down, offering him a cigar.

We see a close-up of Ollie's face, confusion changing to genuine hurt and jealousy, as what appears to be a new alliance is being formed between Stan and another. He looks on in pained puzzlement as Stan lights the cigar for the coworker — after which Stan promptly whistles for the foreman, indicating to him both the lit cigar and the "No Smoking" sign on the wall. As the foreman yanks the coworker out of frame, precipitating a horrendous cacophony of crashes, resulting from a punishment we can only shudderingly imagine, Stan briskly picks the cigar up from the floor, clipping off its end and replacing it in his pocket. Ollie joyously returns to work, humming a little tune. All is well in his world again.

What has been restored for Ollie is not just his friendship, but the meaning of that friendship — the solidarity between the two of them against the world, and Stan's place within that alliance as a dispenser of justice, of honesty and truth, of retaliation. It was all in doubt for a moment — but with the dispatch of the coworker, justice is done, his faith in Stan is restored, and their friendship, and their truth are reaffirmed.

Though the common perception of Laurel and Hardy is that, as Ollie says in "Towed in a Hole" (1932), they are adults acting like little children, they are in fact both children attempting to mimic the behavior of adults. Ollie seems perpetually on the verge of placing one foot in the world of responsibility and discipline. Stan will always remain too childlike to entertain any such aspirations— or, finally, to allow Ollie to— who in his heart, and at the end of every film, despite all devastations and abominations, will always choose Stan and irresponsibility over adulthood.

Stan is unable to conceptualize, to think abstractly or symbolically. Yet because of this, and in spite of his stupidity, he sees reality clearer than his partner who, like us, often only sees the human-created ideals and definitions that we superimpose over reality. When they bring a horse named Blue Boy to a rich man's mansion in "Wrong Again" (1929) to collect a reward, the rich man, thinking they've brought the famous painting by Thomas Gainsborough, asks them from upstairs to place it on the piano.

Ollie is puzzled by this instruction at first but quickly accepts it. He relates it to Stan, who expresses extreme doubt and skepticism. In a lengthy two-shot, Ollie devotes himself to explaining the strange mores of the rich to Stan, that they think "just the opposite of other people," thus the request to place a horse on a piano is only to be expected. For Ollie, the ludicrous demand is justified by the wealth and social position of its purveyor. It takes him some time to convince Stan of this.

In *Pack Up Your Troubles* (1932), as soldiers on KP duty, they ask the cook where they should put the garbage. "Aw, take it to the general!" he sarcastically retorts. Stan expresses some concern about this idea, but Ollie is resolute: "If the general wants it, he can have it!" There is a general tendency to submit to authority in Ollie that is made all the more disturbing when through misunderstanding he feels called upon to justify and carry out actions that are patently nonsensical. Though Stan in the end submits too, he at least is able to see when something contradicts basic common sense, and to make a show of resistance for a while. But it is too important to Ollie to fit in, to feel that he is a part of the important adult world.

In *A Chump at Oxford* (1940), as new students, they are cruelly misled by a gang of snobs who for their own amusement direct them on a wild goose chase through a labyrinthine maze. When Ollie asks one of them where the dean's office is, he is given a long, rambling stream of incomprehensible directions. Stan expresses his honest befuddlement, but Ollie says, "Don't worry, Stanley — I have it fixed firmly in my mind. Thank you, gentlemen!" It is desperately important for Ollie to appear to be in the know and in alignment with what he perceives to be the prevailing authority of the time, as well as to demonstrate the massive superiority of his intelligence over Stan's in the matter. Ollie can perceive dimly that there is a system, though he is as perplexed as Stan as to its purpose, meaning, or his role within it. His solution is to pretend as if he understands, to contrive to give the appearance of confidence, of all-knowing worldliness, evidently with the idea that if he keeps acting as though he understands and belongs, eventually the system will accept him and reward him. Stan is unable to conceive of a system, he only sees what is before him, and no abstract idea can change the nature of reality for him. He is incapable of being integrated into society.

This is perhaps most clearly displayed in "Oliver the Eighth" (1934), when Stan and Ollie arrive at the mansion of Ollie's newly betrothed to find that she and her butler are mad; they are presented with card tricks involving imaginary decks of cards, a meal of imaginary food. Stan looks to Ollie with a look that says, "But there's nothing there!" Ollie shushes him and encourages him to go along with the charade. Ollie desperately plays along with his host, as Stan fascinatingly alternates between outright rejection of this new surreal reality and complete acceptance and belief in it. Finally he shatters the spell by saying to the butler: "You're nuts!"

Stan is a fool, in the ancient sense of the word. His foolishness or stupidity often masks and is at the same time inseparable from the fact of the essential purity of his innocence, being devoid of all conceptual presumptions of reality, and who therefore from his unique perspective, and quite unbeknownst to himself, apprehends and speaks the truth. We see this in *Way Out West*, when they're bidding adieu to the woman who has just swindled them out of the deed to a gold mine — a fact the audience knows but that they do not yet know. Stan says, "Good-bye! I'll bet ya make a swell gold-digger!" Ollie shushes him and embarrassedly shoves him out of the room. Yet Stan in his seemingly dumb insensitivity speaks the truth of the woman and of the situation.

Because Stan is ignorant of the rules that govern acceptable human behavior, of the laws of reward and punishment by which society operates, when he contravenes these rules and laws it is not a rebellious, consciously anarchic act as it would be with the Marx Brothers, Chaplin, or W. C. Fields. He is simply reacting honestly and naturally to what he sees before him. He does not seek to create chaos and is quite bewildered that this should be the continual result of his humble attempts to merely exist in the world. He is not trying to inflame the situation when, after the criminal is sentenced to life imprisonment in "Going Bye-Bye!" he calls out, "Aren't you going to hang him?" There is no guile or meanness in his question. He is genuinely perplexed that the ultimate punishment was not brought to bear in the situation. When they are forced to beg for food in "One Good Turn"

(1931), and Ollie inquires whether a kindly old woman might be able to spare a piece of buttered toast, Stan follows up with: "And do ya think you could slap a piece of ham on it?" He isn't being a smart aleck, and there's no sense of him being conscious of his brashness or audacity. He's just being honest about what he would prefer to consume.

It is this honesty, this innocence, coupled with the stupidity with which it is intricately linked, that is responsible for the disasters that befall Laurel and Hardy. The honesty has the effect of being radical and anarchic simply because the people in the society around them are so divorced from the truth of their own emotions and impulses, from the truth of the very moment they exist in, that Stan and Ollie's foolish honesty enrages them. The very fact of its existence instantly commences to pull apart the elaborate structure they have built to keep their own honest emotions, their own inner reality, at bay.

We see this in the mass chaos scenes of their early films, when Laurel and Hardy innocently and inadvertently trigger a mass war of "reciprocal destruction" engulfing entire city blocks, which rages around them as the final frames unreel. There is the pants ripping of "You're Darn Tootin'" (1928), the big pie fight of "The Battle of the Century" (1927), the hat destroying of "Hats Off" (1927), the car destroying of "Two Tars" (1928), and the boating battle of "Men O' War" (1929). Stan and Ollie do not create these battles on their own, but their existence unmasks the hostility that is already there in the people around them, hidden behind the trite pleasantries of societal convention. This is proven by the number of participants who become involved in the melee quite oblivious of Stan and Ollie and its root causes. The populace wants to fight, it has always wanted to fight, and the trigger that the ignorantly asocial Laurel and Hardy provide is welcome and immediately seized upon.

The phenomenon at work here is no different from the one that manifests itself when Stan asks the old woman for ham on his buttered toast, when Stan kicks the nanny in the backside in "The Music Box," when Stan asks if he can take the Warden's order for a case of beer at the end of *Pardon Us*—there is the quick sense of liberation of being freed from societal expectations and societal roles, followed quickly by chaos and enmity. Stan is himself free of these expectations and roles, and thus everywhere he walks he precipitates disaster.

A key symbol of this strange freedom is one of Stan's most famous trademarks: his tears. The sight of a grown adult throwing off all sense of self-control and crying with confusion and fright in the manner of an infant, when one thinks about it, is really quite a bizarre one for millions to have thought it to be among the funniest they've seen. For Stan, there is no sense of self-control to throw aside. Stan cries openly, without shame, without self-consciousness; he is unafraid to be afraid, to appear weak, to lose control in a world where control, or the appearance of it, is everything. We laugh because he is so naked in his emotions, because it's part of that essential honesty of the character and thus at odds with the order of the world. Women cry and children cry, but men do not cry. We all rejoice inside because we secretly wish they could break down in this manner and return to the pure consciousness of the infant. Yet at the same time they are made a little uneasy as well, precisely because the crying is so emotionally naked and honest, which is probably one of the reasons Stan the actor disliked performing it.[6]

Notable Stan cries include his tears of guilt when he confesses that he drank the "half that was on the bottom" of the soda in "Men O' War," his shrieking as he does a frenzied dance with a discharging machine gun in *Pardon Us,* and his fearful sobs as he faces off with Walter Long in the boxing ring in "Any Old Port" (1932), his arms wrapped around his opponent's abdomen, hanging on for dear life as he's swung from side to side. Certainly one of his most memorable weepings comes at the climax of *Sons of the Desert.* But perhaps his most seminal cry comes in one of their very first films, "Putting Pants on Philip."

There is some disagreement among historians on where "Putting Pants on Philip" belongs in the Laurel and Hardy story. Laurel himself claimed that it was the first official "Laurel and Hardy film," though evidence suggests otherwise — the comics had appeared together in fifteen films before this, and in at least two of them they had portrayed characters closer — at least superficially — to the Stan and Ollie we know today than are seen in "Philip." Here Ollie is cast as J. Piedmont Mumblethunder, a respected man about town, and Stan is Philip, his nephew, fresh off the boat from Scotland and clad in kilts — hence the title.

The film consists of Mumblethunder meeting Philip at the docks and about his embarrassment and frustration at having to acknowledge Philip and accept him as family. Everywhere they go as they walk through the town — and the entire film is about them simply doing that — the townspeople pursue them in order to gawk and snicker at Philip's unseemly appearance. Stan is also given a trait here that is utterly foreign to the character he would soon develop: Philip, we are told, has one weakness — women. At the sight of a woman he leaps into the air and gives immediate chase. And so Mumblethunder is embarrassed on two counts by his new charge: Philip's strange "feminine" dress and his uncontrollable, antisocial mania for pursuing women.

On the face of it there would seem to be little here to unite this perfectly made little film with the later Laurel and Hardy comedies, but looking deeper we can see the dynamics of the partnership being set in motion, giving perhaps at least psychological credence to Laurel's denoting of it as their first film. The film is an exploration of Stan's "otherness," his incapability of being absorbed into society, of being accepted by it. This otherness is inseparable, again, from his infantility. Even what would seem to be the most jarring contradiction to this—Philip's skirt-chasing proclivity—is, as played by Stan, more related to the woman chasing of Harpo Marx than anything inherently sexual. Philip's pursuit, arms outstretched, is like that of a toddler chasing a brightly colored toy. As with Harpo, there is no sense here that Philip has an inkling as to what should occur if he succeeds in catching up with the female he pursues.

In the course of the film Mumblethunder goes from being simply embarrassed of Philip, insisting on making him walk behind him because he's an important man in the town (look ahead to one of their trademark routines, the "You after me through the doorway, Stanley!" business), to being protective of him, to becoming frustrated with him as an equal and interacting with him on that level. The focus of the comedy in the film changes from the relationship of the laughing crowd toward Laurel and Hardy to the relationship between Laurel and Hardy—about that time we notice that Mumblethunder's trouble arises as much from his own sense of self-importance and entitlement than anything his freakish new nephew does. We replace the laughing crowd, we become the laughing crowd, and from then on we will rush to laugh at them. The film is about their establishing a relationship with us as well.

Pivotal to all of this is the crying mentioned earlier. It comes when Mumblethunder takes Philip to the tailor's shop to have him measured for pants. As the tailor reaches up to measure Philip's leg, Philip leaps away, deeply offended. Philip conveys panic, an unmistakable sense of sexual violation. Mumblethunder and the tailor commiserate, then surround Philip, wrestling him to the floor and grappling with him. Philip escapes, and Mumblethunder chases him around, finally disappearing offscreen. Mumblethunder emerges, sweating, triumphantly intoning the measurements. Then Philip emerges, playing the broken, raped woman, bowing his head in shame. He sits in a chair, with Mumblethunder coming to stand behind him, resting his hand on his shoulder. Philip buries his face in his kilt and weeps.

This is the moment where the film becomes about the relationship of Laurel and Hardy, establishing the essential qualities of the interaction of the characters who would become Stan and Ollie. Obviously, the scene exists because some gag man (or Stan, or Leo McCarey, supervising his first film with them) thought it would be funny for Philip to react to being measured for a pair of pants as though it were a sexual attack. The playing of the scene makes it a parody of a melodrama cliché that the audience would have been quite familiar with: the humiliation of the newly deflowered maiden.

Beyond this, of course, are the homosexual implications of the scene, of which all the creators would have been quite aware. Stan is the "woman," or the submissively feminine partner in the "skirt," having been seduced by the more obviously male Hardy, who towers over him. This, in a film rife with risqué, sexual gags (the infantile women chasing, and Philip's kilt, which a street vent keeps blowing up, first exposing his underwear, then, after his undies are lost, exposing his genitals to a crowd of people offscreen, causing women to faint). Though meant as parody, Stan's tears seem real and tragic, uncomfortably so.

And of course, Stan's submissive, beaten-down posture in contrast to the rougher, aggressive and (momentarily) triumphant Hardy looks ahead to one level of the future Stan–Ollie relationship, where, in a superficial sense at least, the compliant, passive Stan is bullied and led around by his partner.

But to continue down this line of reasoning, we quickly see, is to miss the essential joke of the scene — something unforgivable when discussing comedy. And the joke is: Stan's character is so infantile that he reacts to being measured for pants ("I've never worn a pair of pants in my life!" he says via title card) with the same humiliated tears of one who is freshly sexually violated. His earlier determination not to be forced into complying was the same as his fight with the ship's doctor at the beginning of the film. When the doctor tried to inspect his hair for lice, Philip angrily ruffled the doctor's hair in retaliation. Though the film has played with the idea of giving Stan an uncontrollable libido, and now has opened up the question of his effeminacy and/or homosexuality, in the end we see established the basic premise of the Stan Laurel character: his asexuality. His tears are not of the broken woman or the deflowered submissive, but of the thwarted child.

You get the sense that this scene, created as it was just as Laurel and Hardy were realizing the inevitability of their becoming solidified as a team, had to be made. In the consciousness of their decision to create a series based on the intense relationship between two men, sooner or later that inevitable question of sexuality would have to be explored. Naturally, they do it comedically.

They both assume sexual roles here and play them out quite convincingly and with great panache. "Play" is the operative word — they are able to assume and play out these roles so well precisely because they are asexual, or presexual, children who have not yet been confined to sexual roles. They can play any role because they have no basic, essential sexuality that opposes any that they might assume. For Laurel and Hardy, sexuality becomes just another role they play, adopting their roles as husbands or suitors in the various films with the same gameness as they adopt roles as home builders in others, as policemen, chimney sweeps, or 18th-century bandits. They assume the outward trappings and behavior of these roles as children do when playing make-believe. Not being capable of understanding the complex realities at the base of the roles, they try them out for a while before being distracted by something else and going on to something new, as children do.

To say that they are children, however, is misleading, for children are by definition in a state of becoming. Stan and Ollie aren't in the process of becoming anything. They simply are — eternally innocent childlike spirits of the type that could not and do not exist in the world as we know it, or in any world that has ever been. They are simply clowns in the truest sense, ethereal visions of lunacy passing through and gently ridiculing a tense, gray, short-tempered world, gladdening our hearts.

In a film made later, after they established their characters, they explored the question again, and once again clarified the fluid, ever-changing nature of roles they play against each other in the relationship. In "Their First Mistake" (1932) Ollie is married and Stan is the bothersome friend his wife can't stand. The bleakly funny first scene ends with her becoming enraged by their friendship and beating them with a broom, chasing them out of the Hardy apartment. Stan asks, "What's the matter with her?" Ollie: "Oh, she thinks I think more of you than I do of her." Stan: "Well, you do, don't you?" Ollie: "We won't go into that."

Stan suggests they adopt a baby to keep the wife occupied and off they go. In the next scene, what was played upon in the first is made plainer. Ollie is served with papers of divorce, and Stan is charged with the "alienation of Mr. Hardy's affections." Stan tries to take off on Ollie, but Ollie stops him, opening up a dialogue beginning: "You're the one that wanted me to have this baby — and now that we've got it you want to leave me flat!" They enter into a scene that is another parody of a melodrama — Ollie is now the female lover and unwed mother about to be deserted by the callous father Stan, who has "sired" the baby. Ollie is disgraced by the situation: "I'll be ostracized!" Stan protests: "I have my future, my career to think of!" Stan tries to get away but Ollie runs ahead and blocks the door. The baby cries.

The ending scene is of them with the baby at night, trying to get it to sleep. Stan has now become the "woman," the mother, and Ollie, the father of the child. This is made explicit in a wild gag that has Stan taking the baby, who is screaming throughout this scene, and setting it on his lap. Shush-

ing the child, he reaches to unbutton his nightshirt. A shot of Ollie, looking with puzzled interest. Then Stan reaches into the nightshirt. Ollie looks
increasingly worried. Stan pulls a bottle out of his nightshirt (he had it in
there to keep it warm) and feeds the baby. Ollie turns to us in an expression of bewildered exasperation, throwing his arms into the air.

The disturbing image conjured in our minds of what Ollie half-
expected Stan to pull out of his nightshirt is surpassed by the climactic gag
of the film. Ollie, Stan and the baby are asleep in bed together. The baby
begins crying. Half asleep, Ollie reaches to the side table to get a bottle. He
holds it in the direction of the baby, still half-asleep. Sleeping, Stan gets the
nipple in his mouth and begins sucking. As he starts sucking, the baby happens to stop crying, so Ollie continues to hold the bottle there. Stan sucks
lustfully, turning away from the nipple at moments only to return in a frenzy
of feverish need.

As Stan finishes draining the entire bottle, some of the milk escaping
from the nipple and dribbling down his chin, the baby happens to start crying again. And so, of course, Ollie, still half-asleep, retrieves the bottle, fog-
gily notices that it's empty, reaches over and replaces it with a new, full one.
Stan continues sucking again, the baby happens to stop crying again, and
the bottle is quickly drained once more. At the end of this bottle, Stan succeeds in sucking the nipple right off the bottle and eating it as a midnight
snack, at which point the milk spills and the film ends, abruptly, with barely
a chance for Ollie to register his customary exasperation.

As others have noted, the film serves as a journey through all the possible roles Stan plays for Ollie: friend, lover, husband, wife, and finally,
infant. The underlying message here is the same as in "Phillip": it is all just
play, the determined conceits of a child mimicking what it has seen adults
do, taking on the external trappings and actions of a role and desperately
clinging to them, not even beginning to comprehend the core reality of the
role. Ollie and Stan both do this; because Ollie is the more socialized of the
pair it is he who ostensibly seems the more successful at playing the societally acceptable role — until Stan's very existence sabotages his masquerade and reveals Ollie to be the child he is. In the process, the latent
childishness of everyone in the near vicinity is often revealed as well.

Again, because Ollie is the more socialized of the two, it is he who is
most often married in the films. At first, it might seem that the humor of the
"married" films is the standard joke of the "Maggie and Jiggs" comic-strip
variety or of the later sitcom type: the shrewish, harridan wives, wielding
rolling pins and cracking down on the irresponsible, negligent husbands.
The real gag here, though, is that neither Laurel nor Hardy has any real
need to be married to anyone else. In the most meaningful sense of the

term, they are married to each other. The wives—especially Mae Busch in the film just cited—are furious from the first frames, perhaps for that very reason: they realize their superfluity. Then again, most of the side players in the films are short-tempered, on edge, surly, and/or in a constant state of irritation—that's simply the world that Laurel and Hardy inhabit.

Stan, here and in other films, peels Ollie away from the role of domestic responsibility. To look closely, however, is to see that Ollie goes quite willingly—Stan is merely the trigger, the "explosion" that breaks him out of the "jail" of his role. The "Well, we won't go into that..." is a declaration of his loyalty to Stan's vision rather than his wife's, who often represents society, and whose goals and aspirations of upper mobility and respectability are the officially acceptable ones of society.

This comes to an apotheosis in the final "married" film, *Block-Heads* (1938), where Ollie, who hasn't seen Stan in over 20 years, brings him home to meet his wife unexpectedly. Her manner immediately changes from the sing-song lovey-dovey cooings of the first scene—albeit clearly cold and cunning under that façade—to instant anger and hatred. He pleads for her to accept Stan throughout the film, she refuses, and when he finally rebels, declaring his intentions of leaving her, it is a rededication by Ollie of his loyalty to Stan and to what Laurel and Hardy is all about: that an honest relationship with someone, even if only chaos and destruction results from it, is better than a tightly controlled manipulated existence where unacknowledged emotions rage behind masks of phony politeness, in the passionless pursuit of control, security, in the name of a lifeless false peace. This is quite a leap of loyalty for Ollie to take for some one who's destroyed his car, his apartment, and made him carry him around for no good reason in the scant hours since he's been re-acquainted with him.

In several of the films Stan prevents Ollie from getting married in the first place. Or rather, in "Our Wife" (1931), Ollie—after two reels of Stan's bungling his elopement plans—does, in a perfect ending, get married to Stan (due to the cross-eyed justice of the peace). Ollie has another wedding day in "Me and My Pal" (1933), and Stan brings him his gift: a jigsaw puzzle. The entire rest of the film is about Ollie becoming so engrossed in Stan's puzzle that he misses his own wedding. In an excruciatingly drawn-out scene that is strangely moving yet hypnotic at the same time, we see Ollie being drawn in slow motion, away from urgency, away from responsibility and respectability, through curiosity and then to utter absorption in idle play: fun for fun's sake, into the world of Stan, embodied here, appropriately, in a child's toy.

For his part, Stan, free of the compulsion to even attempt to conform to these roles—most of the time—most often dresses in drag and "becomes" a woman. One of Stan's acts that he did in vaudeville with his common-law wife was one where he dressed in drag and played her mother. In perhaps the very first film in which Laurel and Hardy were paired up in a conscious manner, "Duck Soup" (1927), they play tramps who take refuge in a house. When a couple shows up intending to rent the house, the tramps are forced to take on the roles and play the master of the house and his maid. Interestingly, the plot of this first "team" film was bequeathed on them by the redoubtable A.J. Jefferson himself, Stan's father, who'd written it as a successful music-hall sketch 20 years before. Here, as in the later recycling of the same plot in "Another Fine Mess" (1930) three years later, there is little doubt as to who will play the maid.

The first film plays on the simple joke of the necessity of a man dressing as a woman. In the latter film, however, with the Stan character now developed, the gag is in how much Stan actually "becomes" Agnes the maid and how effortlessly this new female persona is borne out of him. In a classic scene, unlike anything else in the films, Agnes and the attractive, prospective new lady of the house (played by Thelma Todd) engage in a lengthy, giggly session of girl's talk. It's filled with double entendres, sexual innuendo, and outright silliness. Stan and Thelma Todd both have trouble keeping a straight face. The humor is in the character of Agnes rather than in the situation of a man desperately attempting to pass himself off as a woman, as it would be for just about any other comedian one can think of. The humor is in the very fluidity of the Stan character and its essential comic asexuality.

Stan wrestles with women in the course of the action in several of the films: in "Chickens Come Home" (1931) with Mae Busch and in *Way Out West* with Sharon Lawrence. The latter comes to a climax when the woman, trying to get a valuable deed from Stan, locks the door of her bedroom and sashays determinedly toward him. Stan scampers away, and for a moment he is Philip again, protecting his maidenly virtue from an aggressor. Then she wrestles him onto the bed and — completely appropriately — tickles him into submission. An attempt by a woman to "make whoopee" with Stan in "We Faw Down" (1928), culminates in a shoving match wherein Stan with great good humor repeatedly pushes her off her chair. We remember Stan and Ollie wrestling (playfully) with the woman on the bed in "Scram!" (1932) and their battle involving eggs with the glamorous Lupe Velez in "Hollywood Party" (1934). In all of the scenes they encounter the other sex as equals in a nonsexual way; there's no taint of vulgarity, no sense of the comics "on the make" as, again, there would be in the case of any other comedian one can think of. In some films, there is a giddy sense of the women being liberated from their roles by Stan and Ollie's accepting asexuality, as in the case of the judge's wife in "Scram!" and also in "Them Thar

Hills" (1934), where Stan and Ollie end up getting tipsy with Mae Busch while her husband Charlie Hall is off getting some gas. In both of these films, they inadvertently get another man's wife drunk and have an uproariously good time with them, in scenes of genuine elevation with no sexuality in them, then are swiftly punished for it by the mean, ugly-hearted husbands. The donnybrook that concludes "Them Thar Hills" is sparked by Ollie's objection to Charlie Hall: "Hey, you can't treat that lady that way!" Again, it's a recurring theme of the films: innocent liberation from socially defined roles and expectations, exaltation over that liberation, followed by disaster and chaos.

In some cases Stan himself is liberated by his assumption of a female persona, and he is able to perform heroic acts, as when he saves the day by 'becoming' Bo-Peep in her wedding ceremony to the evil Barnaby in *Babes in Toyland* (1934), in yet another bizarre depiction of marriage in their films (Ollie: "Well, I guess I'll be going now." Stan: "Aren't I comin' with ya?" Ollie: "You have to stay here with Barnaby now — you're married to him." Stan, weeping: "But I don't love him!"). Likewise, Stan foils the bad guys again by briefly becoming *The Bohemian Girl* (1936), substituting for her at the whipping post at the end of the film, grabbing the whip and chasing the torturers around the courtyard. Interestingly, the one film where both Laurel and Hardy appear in drag is "Twice Two" (1933), where they play, appropriately enough, each other's wives. This is often thought to be a pale reworking of "Brats" (1930), wherein they played their own sons. The difference here, however, is that where Ollie's female counterpart is, like his depiction of his son in the other film, simply a variation on his established character, Stan's female incarnation is as a shrill-voiced busybody, a gratingly unpleasant nuisance quite opposite in character to the usual Stan persona, though obviously no more intelligent.

The laughter and jubilation of the scenes in "Scram!" and "Them Thar Hills," like the other laughing scenes in "Leave 'Em Laughing" (1928), "Blotto" (1930), *Fra Diavolo* (1933), and *Way Out West*, are celebrations of existing outside of our roles, outside of our own and others' expectations. They show us that we can stand outside of life at times, outside of time, even, to put it in its proper perspective and laugh. In *Fra Diavolo* they even stand outside of the movie, when, as part of their laughing they recount and ridicule the entire plot we've just been watching for the last 80 minutes. And though Ollie's laughter is equally infectious and rewarding, it is that high-pitched manic cackle of his partner's that makes the strongest impression. In this laugh of utter abandon we can hear that Stan's ability to transcend reality and time is directly related to his essential lack of identity, the fluidity of his persona, which accounts for his otherworldly quality as well.

In his absolute innocence, Stan accepts reality, utterly, unlike his partner. He has no grandiose expectations, no ambitions—all he asks from life is food, comfort, and shelter. Though he is largely foiled in his attempts to attain even these modest goals by his incredible stupidity, still he is free of the shackles of obligation and duty, free of the roles society would have him play; he stands outside of the mental jail most of us live in. He interacts with life honestly, if dim-wittedly, rather than playing around with ideas about it. Because Stan would seem to have very little ability to think sequentially, and so therefore lives entirely in the moment, the eternal moment, one could say that he exists outside of time. Stan transcends social laws and roles largely through his sheer ignorance of them; so over the course of the films he is given as well a magical ability to transcend the laws of physical reality.

This quasi-magical aspect of Stan became more pronounced in the films as they went on. In "Men O' War," Ollie rather cruelly leaves Stan holding a bill in the soda shop, which he knows full well cannot be paid—the bill is for 30 cents and their sum total fortune is 15 cents. After a moment of fear, Stan deposits the money into a one-armed bandit and pulls the lever. Hardy and soda jerk Finlayson look on with disgusted exasperation, then with puzzlement, finally with outraged disbelief as the machine clicks to a stop, then disgorges a Niagara of coins.

This miraculous bit of luck on Stan's part serves the comic purpose of thwarting and triumphing over Ollie's cruelty, while the method by which it is accomplished—through another act of apparent stupidity (putting one's last cents into an amusement arcade machine)—exasperates Ollie even further while showing that Stan transcends his own most salient characteristic (his dumbness), turning it into a strength through his complete disengagement with what we call objective reality. The humor of this—that of someone apparently powerless and doomed to failure by his stupidity suddenly manifesting an unexpected feat of magic—fits the malleable, otherworldly aspect of Stan while balancing the intricate power structure within the Laurel–Hardy relationship. And, most important, it opens the door to a whole other level of Ollie being frustrated and astounded by Stan.

Stan fools Ollie with a game of hide-the-pebble in *Pardon Us*, then with other finger games and tricks in *Fra Diavolo;* he confounds Ollie with his proficiency with pee-wees in *Babes in Toyland* and his miraculous ability to steal in *The Bohemian Girl*. The gypsy background of this last film is ideal for the expression of the antisocial, "reality-sabotaging" aspect of the Stan character, who takes much more naturally to the role of con artist than Ollie. The operetta pictures in general were the perfect framework for the pixie-ish element in Stan to develop and blossom — the thatch wig he wore in them gave him a more androgynous appearance, in a setting that was itself magical and quite similar to the atmosphere of the British Christmas pantomimes that had enamoured the child Stan of play-acting in the first place. As the films became broader, less based in a recognizably "real" reality, these tricks of Stan's evolved into such feats as "lighting" his thumb, singing alternately in a woman's soprano and a man's deep bass voice (*Way Out West*), and "smoking" his clenched fist like a pipe, pulling down the shadow of a window shade and extracting a glass of water and ice from his trouser pocket (*Block-Heads*).

It is Stan's innocence that accounts for his magic and for his magical freedom from all roles, social, sexual or otherwise. He is the impossible eternal child, who has not yet been informed that these feats are impossible. So he attempts them with a pure heart — and succeeds. The surreal manipulations of reality seen in the later films are no more miraculous than the oblivious freedom Stan enjoys from temporal reality, and from the burdensome notions of identity, seen in all the films.

Over the course of the films Stan drifts further away from reality, and he pulls Ollie along with him. The utter unreality of the white magic Stan effects in the later films can be seen to be a logical progression — or evolution — from the more banal feat of Stan miraculously winning money from the one-armed bandit in "Men O' War." It should be noted that the Stan and Ollie characters, created in the early films through a gradual accretion of attributes and defined over time by a careful layering and shading of nuances, mannerisms, and subtleties, were not static creations. Rather, like portraits painted by their creators again and again, from different perspectives, at different times and in different emotional states, the characters — while remaining, at core, the same — were interpreted and 'played' with a subtly changing sensibility, a naturally forward-moving searchfulness as new possibilities, new resonances were found in their relationship.

The magical feats of the Stan of the later Roach films would have been unthinkable for the Stan character of 1928. The warmer, "cuddlier" Stan of the mid–30s is different from the more wiry, cunning Stan of the silent period, and both of them are different from the somewhat more ebullient Stan of 1939. The more extroverted, nonconformist aspects of the team's characters in the later Roach films have been noted by others, and the increasingly less docile, more aggressive Stan of those films comes to its climax in *A Chump at Oxford*, where he gives birth to an alter ego, Lord Paddington, the diametric opposite of the Stan character in every way. Throughout, the basic mechanism remains the same: the later Stan's actions, magical or otherwise, exist for the same reasons that the early Stan's did: to confound and bedevil Ollie. One realizes after a time the folly of speaking of either of the characters individually — neither can be fully understood except within the context of the other and within the understanding of their common purpose: to create laughter. And so Stan's magic here can only exist against the background of Ollie's supreme annoyance, his endless and almost overwhelming exasperation.

There is no lapse in consistent comedy characterization, but through the years the focus shifts to different aspects of the characters. As with everything in the films, the movement of the focus would seem to have been dictated by laughter — as Stan always said, their only goal was to create films with as many laughs in them as possible. If we can say that laughter is the shock of unexpected truth, and that the most enduring aspect of Laurel and Hardy's humor is based in the relationship between the two characters, we can also see that Stan and his writers never stood still in their examinations and explorations of the two characters from film to film and the uncovering of various unexpected truths locked in the personas of the two clowns.

All of this is what makes the films alive today. It is why Stan and Ollie are fully three-dimensional characters, not the glib caricatures so many other comedians are. They do not exist in a static hierarchy of straight man and stooge, or bully and victim, but rather they share power equally. When imbalances occur or when an unnatural order asserts itself, the entire structure is dismantled and rearranged, sometimes several times, until equilibrium is again restored (for a while). As in any enduring, successful relationship, theirs is a marriage of opposites finding unexpected correspondences, or connections, within each other. At the worst of times, one may get the sense that they do not want to be together, but at some integral level they realize they need to be together. Each is completed in the other, and though they might fight, and though their endeavors come to nothing, there is a deep certitude that they are necessarily joined together and always will be, however painful or embarrassing that joining might be.

One thinks of their repeated humiliations before the uncomprehending crowds as they attempt to exchange trousers in "Liberty" (1929), having gotten each others' on by mistake after their prison break. One thinks of them trudging off in the final frames of "You're Darn Tootin'," both wedged into one giant pair of pants, as if they've finally coagulated into one being. Each plays a multiplicity of roles for the other, a fact fittingly acknowledged in their very last short subject, "Thicker Than Water" (1935), when, thanks to a botched blood transfusion, they actually become each other.

If the standard perception of Laurel and Hardy is that they fail continually in every endeavor through their bungling stupidity, it should be noted that an equally important factor is their constant squabbling, the ongoing fight that continually bubbles up between them — in short, the very nature of their relationship. In a way, their relationship is entirely functional, for resentments are not allowed to simmer, grudges are not allowed to develop. If they have a problem with each other, no matter what they are in the middle of, the tools are laid down and they square off until it's resolved. In "Towed in a Hole" (1932), they take time off from repairing their boat to engage in a prolonged water fight, dumping pails of water on each other. Their work as chimney sweeps in "Dirty Work" (1933) is significantly impeded by the running battle between them, which culminates in their vow not to speak to each other anymore. In *Way Out West,* four years later, their attempt to break into a saloon to retrieve a mispresented deed is interrupted by a long squabble in which they jerk each other repeatedly to the earth on either end of a block and tackle.

One of the films that strongly illuminates this aspect of their relationship is "One Good Turn." It's generally considered one of their more average efforts, though enjoyable on that level. As with most of their films of this ilk, the main problem would seem to be a too intrusive, unnecessarily complex plot — Laurel and Hardy are at their best with little or no plot, with an inspiring selection of props and a vague premise on which they can improvise freely.

The most memorable aspect of this film for fans is the ending, where Stan flies into a rage and exacts a terrible revenge on Ollie, in a scene unlike any other in the films. Apparently, the sequence was inspired by Laurel's young daughter, who would often shy away from Hardy when he came to visit at the house. The scene was intended to show that though Stan is habitually bullied by Ollie, he could stand up for himself when the situation demanded.[7] Of course, anyone who carefully watches the subtleties in the Laurel–Hardy relationship knows that already. But the manner by which this truth is consciously displayed here, and carefully led up to, is revealing in itself.

They are hobos, depicted somewhat more realistically here than in other works. In one of the few topical references to be found in the films, Ollie describes himself and his friend as "victims of the Depression." Their only possessions are a tent, their battered trusty Model T, a pot of soup that Stan cooks over a campfire in the wild, and the clothes Ollie has just washed in a stream and hung up to dry on a wire between two trees. The fact that they have a car somehow makes their poverty seem even more seedy, more desperate, as if they've just recently and rapidly fallen into miserable insolvency — as, of course, so many had.

In the first five minutes of the film, Stan sets the tent on fire and tries to put it out by throwing the soup on it, and their clothes shrink to infant-size on the wire. Now they have no food, and no place to sleep. Ollie laments: "Now we'll have to humiliate ourselves by begging for food." Stan: "What — again?"

They chug their dilapidated auto into town and park before a promising home. It belongs to a kindly old white-haired lady — a character unique to their films, unless one counts Mother Hubbard in *Babes in Toyland*. Naturally, she responds to their expression of need by offering to prepare them a meal. Ollie grandiosely offers to work for her while the meal is being prepared, but she can't think of anything that needs to be done. However, Stan suggests that Ollie cut some wood. She admits as to how that might be helpful, so Ollie gallantly acquiesces.

Immediately as the woman is out of earshot, the gallantry disappears and Ollie is furious with Stan, shoving him: "What'd you have to go and suggest that for?" He is further enraged when Stan, in the course of chopping the wood, sends a sizable log banging down on the Hardy cranium. They engage in a scuffle, which is disrupted by the woman calling them in for their meal. Even in the course of partaking of the woman's charity, however, their squabble persists, as Ollie spitefully responds to Stan's pouring coffee on his lap by pouring coffee, cream and sugar on Stan's, who then spoons the mixture up and flicks it into Ollie's face.

This battle is interrupted by their overhearing of a scene going on in the next room: an evil landlord is threatening to put the old lady out of her home unless the mortgage is paid in full immediately. The woman crows that she has the money put aside, only to go to its hiding place and realize it's been stolen. She screams with agony as the villainous landlord exults in his foreclosure.

The boys are mortified to hear all this, and Ollie, typically, vows that "We've got to help that old lady" — with the same resolve he would later show in helping Mother Hubbard in a similar situation. They leave instantly, forgetting the meal and their squabble, and go off to auction their one remaining possession in the world — their car — to get money for the woman.

They do not know, as we do, that the woman, rather than being the completely unsophisticated granny she appears to be, is an aspiring amateur thespian, and that the scene they have heard was nothing more than a rehearsal for an upcoming community theater production.

They drive their car downtown and begin auctioning it off on their "errand of mercy." A drunk heartily bids for it, but he is inadvertently outbid by Stan, who, when a hard-of-hearing gentleman asks him the time, responds loudly, "1:15!" Unaware of the source of the bid, Ollie shouts "Sold!," and closes down the auction, the crowd disperses — leaving them alone with the depressing realization that they've just succeeded in selling their car to themselves.

The drunk, however, has misplaced his wallet in Stan's jacket pocket, unbeknownst to Stan (note the convolution here). Ollie now discovers it and is instantly convinced it contains the money that Stan has stolen from the old woman. He is outraged and furious over Stan's chicanery and will not accept his protestations of innocence. He is determined Stan will return the money to the old woman and make a complete confession. Stan has no idea what he's talking about and refuses to do so. Ollie grapples with him and they wrestle, completely destroying their car in the process. Now they have nothing.

Ollie half-carries, half-manhandles Stan all the way back to the old woman's house, where he informs her that his "one-time friend" has a confession to make. The woman, naturally, laughs and informs him of the reality of the situation.

Ollie, abashed, turns to Stan: "I've made a slight faux pas!" Ollie utilizes his gesture of placation and hopeful ingratiation — the tie twiddle — here for the first and only time on his partner rather than on the uncaring world at large. Stan, however, will have none of it.

His fury takes the form of a rapid staccato series of kicks and punches and eye-pokes, which dismay and horrify the old woman, until Ollie escapes and Stan follows in hot pursuit, out to the woodshed of their previous woodchopping endeavor. Ollie hides cringing in the shed, Stan shouts at him to come out. Ollie — the very picture of the cowardly bully now at the mercy of his victim — yelps "I won't!" Stan picks up the ax and chops the shed down, its roof crashing over Ollie so that only his head and shoulders protrude from the broken shingles.

Stan takes off his coat and proceeds to chop various logs in half, each one ricocheting into the air and plummeting down on Ollie's head — almost magically, as an act of earlier incompetence and stupidity becomes now a means of exacting retribution. Ollie, trapped as he is, cannot escape his punishment but only accept the logs bashing against his skull with a fascinatingly diverse series of agonizing howls of pain.

This ends when Stan picks up a ridiculously large log and prepares to chop it, vowing, "I'll show you." He chops, and the massive stump-sized log wafts into the air, then comes crashing down on his own head. He staggers about, stunned, returned to his dazed docility, picking up his jacket and moving from the scene as Ollie begins extricating himself from the shed's roof. The film fades out.

The ending is important because we see the beginning of the old order returning. Throughout the film, as they have moved in desperate straits, as they have traveled from one misunderstanding to another, as they have progressively lost more and more, as they have found new and unexpected ways by which to misapprehend reality, to embarrass themselves, to destroy what little they have, until in the end they have nothing, one thing remained constant: the unabated enthusiasm for battle at the heart of their relationship. Even in the direst circumstances, they are rarely distracted from the drama they carry about with them — the drama of their friendship. We get the sense that all that goes on around them is, yes, worrisome and deserving of attention, but that the real story for them is with each other. Disaster might be looming, but they still need to pour coffee on each others' laps if the situation demands it; Stan must still follow Ollie through the door, they still need to stop and sort out who has whose hat on whose head, sort it out several times, if need be, no matter what new cruel and brutal surprise reality has prepared for them.

Stan's rebellion here is inspired by Ollie's accusation of him and Ollie's sudden lack of trust in Stan and in their relationship. Though we have seen that Stan will stand for just about any amount of bullying by Ollie, this is one abuse of their relationship which he cannot abide — as in "Any Old Port," when he angrily takes a swing at Ollie after learning that Ollie has bet against him in the boxing match. For his part, Ollie has proceeded from one passionately wrongheaded misunderstanding — his immediate commitment to an "errand of mercy" after overhearing the rehearsal of a play — to another — his immediate assumption that Stan has stolen the woman's money after finding the drunk's wallet in his pocket. Ollie is driven to rush unthinkingly into any type of endeavor by his constant need to appear to be important, by his desperate attempt to seize onto some sort of comforting identity. Though his intentions are generally good — if rather grandiose — and display his warmth of heart, his lack of any substantial thought ensures that he will only succeed in embarrassing himself. Here, when the casualty of Ollie's presumption would seem to be the trust at the heart of the Laurel–Hardy friendship, Stan's role as deliverer of truth in their alliance comes to the forefront, and the punishment meted out on Ollie is swift and entirely commensurate with the severity of his offense.

Likewise, the end of Stan's reign of terror, coming about as a result of his own stupidity in chopping the huge log, is fitting as well, with him being instantly restored to his old role. As is the case each time, Stan assumes control, rebels, seizes the reins, but his mastery is short-lived — he is allowed to swing out only so far before he receives his comeuppance and is snapped back into his customary position. He is the eternal little man, always seemingly put upon, seemingly helpless and exploited, yet always, somehow, triumphant — and to underestimate him often proves a grave mistake. In his purity he exists beyond the corrupted world, beyond the role society would have him play in it. As the final frames fade and they depart the scene, they are together again, their delicate balance restored, moving into a seemingly empty future, Stan's anarchic powers retreating behind the veil of docility, of dim-witted subservience, until the next time.

2

OLLIE (1892–1957)

If there is anything we take from the performance of Oliver Hardy in any of the many films he made — he made over 200 before teaming up with Stan — beyond the laughter, we note the gracefulness, the comical daintiness as well as the true elegance and lightness with which he moves. In private life as well, his caddy at the club where he played his beloved golf noted: "He seemed to flow as he walked,"[1] and a woman patron noted, "We all wanted to dance with Babe Hardy ... simply because he was the best dancer at the club, bar none."[2]

What is unspoken here, but inferred, is the observation that Hardy moved gracefully — for a fat man. But the fact is that Ollie moves gracefully and elegantly for a human of any size. Too often when we see a heavy person, we consider him or her as a heavy person first, as a person, second. The real subtlety and beauty of Oliver Hardy's performances, and the incredible acting skill contained in them, are often lost to us in our prejudice, in our shuttered preconceptions of what constitutes beauty and normality. We know that Hardy disliked being fat all his life, and he rarely watched the films for that reason — he didn't like to be reminded of what he looked like.

As in so many cases, the central tragedy of his life gave birth to the gift he's given the world: to those majestic rhythms, the elegant, stately, emphatic music at the heart of the Laurel and Hardy relationship. "I always try to walk lightly," he told John McCabe. "I don't like to see heavy men lurching all over the place; there's no real need for it. I've always loved to dance and I suppose that's why I've learned how to walk easily."[3]

There is a supreme, unrestrained physicality to his work, that of one giving his all to each nuance, each reaction, while at the same time there is an all-pervasive sense of relaxation, of ease and comfort before the camera, which is shared by few other actors, comic or otherwise. How many, after all, have taken upon themselves the audacity of registering their commentary on the action to us directly through the camera, in lingering full-frontal close-up shots, as he does repeatedly? Even in medium shots, we may note that his eyes dart over to us from time to time, signaling to us his true awareness of what's happening, signaling his awareness of us. At the same time he remains utterly involved in the fracas that surrounds him.

His work contains the finely detailed subtleties of these nuances and ranges to the no-holds-barred reactions he avails himself of when the situation warrants it. "It was only natural when I started to do takes," he recounted later, "that I put everything I had into them."[4] Ollie's jerks of surprise or horror — his arms and legs flying out to every side, the frenzied slapping of his feet against the ground before he takes off running, the arms-leaping-high-into-the-air-then-slapping-down-against-his-sides gesture of utter exasperation — all show a comic whose entire body is fluent in the language of laughter. In *Sons of the Desert* (1933), the slamming of a slapstick against his posterior causes him to leap straight up into the air, his leg shooting out at a right angle to his body. In *Block-Heads* (1938), the gathering awareness that the soldier in the newspaper who stayed in a trench 20 years after the war ended is, in fact, his old pal Stan causes him to execute — impeccably — not a double take but a quadruple take, every part of his body working musically together in a tiny, perfect symphony of comedy.

He is a superb physical comedian, as seen in the falls he takes when repeatedly knocked to the floor by the passing board in "Busy Bodies" (1933). Each fall is not only spectacular but, more important, genuinely funny in the indescribable way that only physical humor is, worthy of any of the great comedians. And this from a man who didn't consider himself a comedian at all, merely a straight man for Stan. Yet Hardy is in every way as great a comedian as Stan is — something one realizes when one has watched the films for a while. Or perhaps a better term for him would be "comic," following the definition Stan subscribed to: that a comedian is one who does funny things, while a comic is one who does things funny. The smallest gestures of Oliver Hardy are finely calibrated to the task of "doing things funny."

Undoubtedly, much of the fluency of Hardy's movements flows from his natural athleticism. During the time the classic Laurel and Hardy movies were being made, his chief passion was golf. And if we are to take at face value the statement of his widow, who noted that Hardy considered his own outside interests more revelatory of the inner man than his career, we can see where his heart was much of the time these movies were filmed. It's never been a secret that, though he was the consummate pro before the camera, for a great deal of the time he spent on the set he was longing to be on the golf course. In contrast with his partner's almost total immersion in every aspect of the filmmaking, Hardy's approach seems outrageously cavalier, but it is precisely this superb sense of relaxation that Ollie contributes to the films, the bedrock around which the comedy flows.

The new, relaxed rhythm that Laurel and Hardy brought to film comedy — especially in their chef d'oeuvre routine, the reciprocal destruction festivals, where each party advances, takes turns laying down an indignity, then calmly retreats — is the same leisurely, civilized, orderly pace of the golf game.

He was tall (6'2") as well as heavy, or, as he liked to say, big-boned. Like other famous overweight funnymen, such as Roscoe "Fatty" Arbuckle, Jackie Gleason, and John Candy, Hardy came from a broken, fatherless family (Arbuckle's father abandoned him after his mother died when Arbuckle was 12. Gleason's father abandoned him and his mother when Gleason was eight, Candy's father suddenly died when Candy was five). It was generally understood among his family that young Norvell Hardy — as he was known — had begun eating so much as a child because he missed his father, whom he had never known, and so we might say that his chief physical attribute is a manifestation of his father's absence. Little Norvell Hardy's father died 11 months after he was born. Norvell's dad's first name was Oliver, and Norvell took that name for himself when he later broke into movies, as a tribute to the father he'd only heard about.

The information on his name is notable because of the importance of names in the Laurel and Hardy story, and the importance of identity in the films, particularly to the Ollie character. As we all know, the comedians used their own names in the movies, never shying away from identifying themselves with two whose names are synonymous with incompetence and disaster. In particular, Ollie is emphatic about proclaiming his full identity to the world: "I'm Oliver Hardy. Oliver Norvell Hardy. And this is my friend, Mr. Laurel...." Apparently, Hardy was rarely addressed as Oliver in real life and was known to all as Babe (a nickname he in fact disliked, finding it somewhat demeaning — no doubt because it was a comment on his cherubic, portly appearance). And so it is mostly his screen character who bears the name of the father he never knew.

Interestingly, one of the major roles Ollie plays for Stan is as a father; at any rate, a great deal of his behavior toward Stan could be categorized as fatherly. In the films, Oliver Hardy, who never had children of his own in real life, seems to regard it as his duty to instruct Stan on the proper, "right" way of doing things, and to correct him. Whether it be ringing a doorbell, doffing one's hat, or signing a hotel register, there is a right and a wrong way to achieve these ends; to be able to discern the difference is of the utmost importance to Ollie, and he is at pains to instruct Stan on the finer details of these matters.

Usually, of course, when he is upbraiding Stan about the transgression of the all-important law, he himself is simultaneously guilty of an equal or greater offense, as in "Below Zero" (1930) when he berates Stan for committing the faux pas of peeling olives on the end of his fork at the restaurant, then laments "Such ignorance!" as he dips a stalk of celery in the sugar bowl and chomps on it noisily. And there are the times when Ollie corrects Stan on the incorrect use of a word, only to display his equal ignorance by substituting another that is just as ineptly used (Stan: "We heard the ocean is infatuated with sharks." Ollie: "Not infatuated! He means infuriated!"— in "The Live Ghost" [1934]). Ollie is no more intelligent than Stan but he is driven by the need to teach and correct Stan, chiefly in order to appear superior. It is a need to behave in a fatherly manner and is reflected in Ollie's idea that he in fact shelters and "takes care" of Stan.

We see this in *Flying Deuces* (1939) when Ollie, attempting to convince Stan to commit suicide with him, paints a picture of a future with himself deceased and Stan left alone in the world: "People would stare at you and wonder what you are, and I wouldn't be there to tell them!" Ollie feels responsible for Stan, that he has to explain him to the world and to explain the world to him, that Stan would be lost without him. Stan concurs with this idea utterly. In *Sons of the Desert*, the Exalted Ruler of their lodge exhorts his charges that in their mission to attend the upcoming convention "the weak must be helped by the strong!" Ollie casts a solicitous glance on Stan that bespeaks full consciousness of the responsibility he feels for his "weaker" partner. Stan returns the glance gratefully.

Needless to say, there is little evidence to show that Stan has a corresponding sense of responsibility for his partner — such sentiments are generally beyond his scope. In their last film, *Utopia* (1951), Ollie says to Stan: "Haven't I always looked out for you? You're always the first one I think of." That this isn't entirely true is mostly immaterial to Ollie and it should be for us — his intentions have always outreached his grasp, and if his self-image as the perfect, ever-loyal friend is in many ways a false identity, we forgive him, because we are compelled to in order to forgive ourselves.

Ollie needs to take charge of Stan so that he can feel superior to somebody. Unshakably fixed in his mind is the idea that he is the adult and Stan is the child. It is, like most of his ideas, a false idea — as is demonstrated time and time again, he is just as helpless as Stan, if not more — but he cannot abandon it, because for him to do so would mean the loss of his (false) identity. It is this insistence on being the father, his insistence on a strict adherence to the right way of doing things, that leads him into disaster. But even then he will not bow — he will drink the disaster to its last dregs, turning even it into an extension of his vision. He will sit patiently until the chimney has discharged its last brick on his head ("Dirty Work") or placidly recline in his easy chair and remove a piece of lint as the rain falls on him in his ruined house ("Helpmates" [1932])—but he will not relinquish his ideal.

Ollie seems to be of the viewpoint that it is better to preside over and experience the complete obliteration of his ideal rather than to give in to reality, to allow it to be corrupted, to turn his back on it and pretend it didn't matter that much, to abandon it—as any sensible person would do—and try a new tack. The only way he can be loyal to his vision is to go down with it, accepting the pain and the humiliation as the price of being someone as principled as he believes himself to be. This is seen in his loyalty to Stan, despite the destruction the friendship rains on him. If Stan is thoroughly ignorant of the existence of ideals, Ollie is obsessed by them, but he isn't quite aware of all the fine details involved. He is a man in search of an identity, aping the outward manifestations of the ideal—the mannerisms, the way of speaking—and turning them into self-created rituals, while not understanding the reality they represent and point toward. He repeats the rituals fervently, but they never reveal the code of success for him, they never provide him with the identity he seeks, and they never provide his entrance into society. However, society, as portrayed in Laurel and Hardy films, doesn't seem that pleasant a place to enter anyway.

We know that his namesake, Oliver Hardy, Sr., who died at age 48, had been a soldier in the Confederate Army in the American Civil War. In the notice published at the time of his death, we read that he passed on "having survived the War for twenty years"[5]—and we are left with the sense that it's possible his war wounds contributed to his death. In any case he had fought in a war on the losing side, a war that signaled the end of a culture, which, whatever its virtues, was irrevocably tainted by the obscenity of slavery. His son came to consciousness at a time when that culture and his father existed only in the memories of the adults around him, like figures that had vanished into the past yet still cast long shadows over his life. No small wonder that he made his life's work the creation of a character obsessed with identity.

If Stan's primary character trait is the fluidity of his identity, and the oblivious freedom he enjoys from the very concept of identity and of societal roles, Ollie is driven by his need to assume an acceptable, impressive identity—at all costs—no matter how much it is at variance from the objective reality before him.

Ollie's chief concerns are aesthetic in nature. All of his aspirations— his romantic yearnings, his business plans, his desire to ingratiate himself with people (his societal ambitions)—in fact, his entire being seem to be motivated by the need to impose his sense of aesthetic order on the world. His gestures, his mannerisms, the elaborate curlicues his hands and fingers perform when he rings a doorbell, signs his name or doffs his hat — all are rituals created by him to express this sense of aesthetic exuberance that lives inside him. The most notable of these — the tie twiddle — is the apex of these creations, taking the basic desire behind all the "civilized, polite" behavior Ollie seeks most to imitate, and refines it, compresses it and focuses it so precisely that it gives birth to an entirely new and unheard-of gesture in the annals of human behavior. In the purity of his earnestness, he uses it to express shyness, embarrassment, or friendliness. Sometimes it is a plea for forgiveness, but always it is a plea for acceptance.

The gesture reveals itself to be more of a nervous tic, or an uncontrollable expression of his character, when he twiddles his tie to someone he's talking to on the phone, as he does in several films. Ollie takes great delight in graceful, audacious, symmetrical movements, and he carries them out even when no one else is around to observe — simply for his own ample enjoyment and pleasure.

The excessive graciousness and courtesy Ollie extends to just about anyone in the films who isn't Stan is, as has been documented, only an exaggeration of the Southern manners practiced by the real Oliver Hardy. "Yes, I guess you could call it Southern manners," he said. "That's the way I was brought up. I was taught to be courteous at whatever cost to myself and so in the pictures, I always am very mannerly with people because I think that's the way one should be all the time."[6] In "Thicker Than Water" (1935), Ollie states to the woman who asks him to bid for her in the auction: "Madame, being a true Southerner, courtesy is my middle name, to say nothing of the chivalry!" Legend has it that someone on the set of an early movie noted Hardy's natural courtliness and suggested he broaden it and use it as comic mannerism in the movies. Again, there is the undeniable link to his father and to the Old South his father fought vainly to preserve, which was still celebrated well into the twentieth century as a place infinitely more soulful and civilized (in song, in popular culture) than the Yankee forces it was routed by.

Is it too much of a leap to suggest that in depicting the Southern virtues of gallantry and hospitality, albeit comically, through the sheer innocence of his character, Hardy seeks to detach them from the atrocity with which they are forever tainted, resurrecting them in their glory for the purpose of joy and laughter?

When Hardy noted, "Of course, I exaggerate for comic effect, but I still mean it. It's basically the way I feel,"[7] he revealed himself to be the opposite of his screen character in one of many ways: he was able to hold a cherished ideal and still see what was humorous about it, to spend his life kidding it. Through humor, he was able to keep himself and his ideal in perspective.

Likewise, in the use of his full name in the films, he said, "One thing I want to emphasize: I never use my name to make fun of it. I'm proud of my name — all of it."[8] He was able to take pride in his name and in his heritage, to serve them sincerely while portraying them in his art for humorous effect — and by so doing, allowing them to live again, now cleansed and renewed by the healing perspective of laughter. In contrast, the Ollie character is able to keep nothing in perspective, is possessed by delusions of greatness, and rushes headlong without thought into any new enterprise.

Many have remarked on the way the Ollie character was opposite to Hardy the actor. Naturally shy, displaying no evidence of the presumption, pretension or pomposity of his screen character, Hardy's unassuming modesty is seen in his conviction that his role in the films was simply to make Stan funnier. There is the oft-quoted Hardy reply to anyone asking of the team's future projects: "Ask Stan."[9] Throughout their career, Laurel was paid twice Hardy's salary, simply in recognition of the fact that he did quantitatively twice Hardy's work, staying at the studio for another full day's work (editing, story sessions) after the shooting stopped. "For all that Stan does for us," Hardy stated, "he deserves what he gets, and more."[10] Well aware of what worked in their relationship, and of what had propelled the team to its great success, Hardy, with unfeigned humility as well as a canny pragmatism, was quite happy to take a back seat to Stan offscreen, handing the reins of artistic control entirely over to his diminutive partner. He was made even happier by the fact that this arrangement allowed him unimpeded access to the golf course when not in front of the camera.

The marked contrast between Hardy and the character he created displays the keen eye for human fault and frailty the comedian had. In many ways, the Ollie character is the most human of all the great clowns, the one most like us. He is eternally frustrated yet eternally hopeful; he holds high ideals yet at the same time he can be duplicitous, deceptive. All that he asks from the world is respect, and all he is searching for is dignity, identity — yet providence steadfastly denies him these. He is pompous and kindhearted, arrogant and gentle, hypocritical and cowardly, yet all in all he is well-meaning. We forgive him his faults because they are our own, and because he is so swiftly and mercilessly punished for them in our place. In his finely observed depiction of the human capacity for self-delusion and deceit, Hardy proves himself worthy of the term Carl Reiner used when he described Hardy and his partner as "satirists of human nature."[11] As Hal Roach stated: "No-one had to tell Babe Hardy what to do — he just did it.

All those gestures and mannerisms he invented were his own. I never saw anybody, including Laurel, direct him. He was a hell of a good actor."[12]

Unlike Stan, whose beginnings were steeped in show business, Hardy came from a completely nontheatrical background. After the death of his father, his mother was pressed to make ends meet, and she ran a hotel in Madison, Georgia. The young Norvell avidly observed the comings and goings of the disparate types who patronized the hotel — undoubtedly as an escape from the pain of being the town's "fat boy." He came of age entertaining hopes of becoming a professional singer.

Also unlike Stan, and unlike all the other great clowns — Chaplin, Keaton, Langdon, The Marx Brothers, W. C. Fields — who learned their craft over many years of performing comedy on the stage in vaudeville, Oliver Hardy was entirely a child of the cinema. The development of his art came to fruition in front of the camera, a mechanism he came to know so well that he attained an intimacy with it unheard of elsewhere in the movies.

Oliver Hardy's career in film began on the other side of the screen. At 18, he operated a movie theater in Milledgeville, Georgia, and saw hundreds of films. Told of a movie company then shooting 200 miles to the south in Jacksonville, Florida, he quit the theater and headed down to see what life was like on the opposite end of the lens. In those days, the infancy of movies, films were shot entirely outdoors in natural light and were often based around whatever was happening in the area at the time. Hardy simply followed the crew around by day and watched, lugging film and props, helping the carpenters and painters. By night he pursued his career as a singer in the Florida nightclubs. One day a "fat boy" was needed for a comedy sequence. Hardy was there, and so he stepped before the camera for the first time.

One of the hallmarks of the Laurel and Hardy style is the conscious, deliberate manner of comic performance. Viewers today are not generally aware that the type of comedy the team did was basically an anachronism at the time they performed it — their form of physical humor was widely regarded as passé even as they achieved their greatest success with it. The great days of slapstick were over as Laurel and Hardy came to prominence. The public's taste was moving more toward romantic, "sophisticated" comedy, clever banter, screwball farces. Audiences felt they had pretty much seen it all in the area of madcap physical hijinks.

The manner by which the team's broad clowning retained relevancy — and was, in its own way, revolutionary — was by admitting that, yes, the public had seen it all, and to derive much of their humor out of that very fact. If comedy before them was fast-paced and hectic, defined by the amount of gags that could be crowded in, and how those gags kept the observer ever in a state of surprised laughter, the Laurel and Hardy response was to slow down the pace to an almost funereal rhythm, cut down the gags by three-quarters, and remove almost entirely the element of surprise from the gags. They took great delight in "planting" the gag, happily showing you where it is, allowing you to anticipate it for a few moments, then actually doing the gag. There are no double-crosses here — they don't play the trick of showing you the gag and then blindsiding you with another one. The gag, the old one we all know, is telegraphed — we laugh in anticipation. Then it is executed with expertise and precision — we laugh again, because of the skill in execution, but also from a sense of completion, of satiation: what we thought would happen, knew would happen, has happened. In the aftermath, we derive extra amusement from the lingering reaction of the two characters to the gag. All of this achieved, they then tip their hats and move leisurely onto the next gag.

In an early film, "From Soup to Nuts" (1928), Stan and Ollie are butlers at a fancy party. While serving a cake, Ollie slips on a banana peel and falls face first into an immense cake he's carrying. For another comedian this would be a slight gag — it really isn't a gag at all — within a multiplicity of laugh-inducing events so that a moment later it would be forgotten. Here, however, the gag is carefully led up to, and deliberately, emphatically executed. First, we see a dog carrying a banana in its mouth, moving between the legs of one of the diners beneath the table (discomfiting her to some extent), eating the banana beneath the table, then scampering out onto the floor and depositing the peel.

Here comes Ollie, holding the massive cake proudly before him on the platter, his head tilted back magisterially, advancing like a majestic ship through the dining room. His total conveyance of faux dignity, of smug self-importance, of his sense of invincibility, is wonderful. He slips on the peel and falls face first into the cake. He does not rise up in panic, embarrassment, or anger like any other comedian would — or as would any person in real life. He merely lies there for several seconds, completely motionless, half-submerged in the cake. Then, slowly, he lifts his head to stare at us with morose exasperation through the cake.

It becomes not a case of how numerous or inventive the gags are, but how they are handled, how inventively and beautifully they are executed. We know that if in any film Stan is holding a lit candle, it will sooner or later be applied to Ollie's posterior ("The Laurel-Hardy Murder Case," [1930]; *Way Out West,* [1937]). They know that we know this. This awareness becomes part of the gag. We laugh, because we know the only question is when and how it will happen, and how long Ollie will puzzle at the growing discomfort in his nether regions before he cries aloud with pain.

The telegraphing technique of gag deployment is writ large in "Brats" (1930), wherein Stan and Ollie's sons leave the taps on in the bathroom about halfway through the film. Throughout the rest of the comedy we are given cutaway shots of the bathroom slowly filling with water, until in the film's final moments the two fathers are dispatched to procure a glass of water for their sons. Ollie imperiously brushes Stan aside, as he advances toward the door: "You might spill it!" He opens the door and a tidal wave bursts forth, which washes the two men to the other side of the room.

This credo of their comedy is expressed almost as a manifesto in one of their even earlier comedies, "The Battle of the Century" (1927), one of their first big hits. Here, the banana peel and the other old hoary slapstick cliché, the pie fight, are brazenly, audaciously resurrected and lit up again with a new electricity. But precisely because they've been seen before, they are all the more hilarious, because they are brought back with such infinite care and panache. This is why the team often recycled gags and storylines in their films; it is really never a matter of what Laurel and Hardy do, but rather how they do it — their facial expressions and movements, their careful lead-up to the gag and their lingering reactions after it has occurred.

In "Battle of the Century," the man who slips on the peel is a delivery man for the L.A. Pie Factory, who ends up covered in his wares, thus sparking the pie Armageddon that ends the film. It is often noted of the film how it was consciously constructed around a cliché, with Stan at a story session saying that if you were going to use pies in a film at this date, the only way you could do it was to have more pies than anyone had ever thrown in the history of the movies. An entire day's output of real pies from a factory was purchased and put into use.[13] Yet less noted is Stan's later statement that the key to the film's success was that each pie was deployed "psychologically."[14] That is, each one that struck contained an inventive gag, and showed how, quite believably, such a ridiculous spectacle as hundreds of people striking each other with pastries could logically, reasonably come to pass. Great care is taken in the depiction of the escalation of hostilities so that what is to come is artfully foreshadowed, and all promises made are thoroughly, generously delivered on in the end.

This mechanism, this sense of invention out of all that had come before, would serve the team all of their career. It was a consciousness, a form that could have only come about through their coming together at the very moment they did, acknowledging and referencing all the comedy forms that had come before them, and in that acknowledgment finding their own form.

It achieves its most refined, early expression in their first masterpiece,

"Big Business" (1929). They are door-to-door sellers of Christmas trees and become involved in a fracas with homeowner James Finlayson. It steadily gains momentum over the course of the film until at the end Finlayson has destroyed their car and the trees they're selling and they have nearly wiped his house from the face of the earth. It is one of their most violent comedies, yet nothing happens in it that is not carefully planned. It is slapstick deployed consciously, deliberately, with all participants emotionally invested in their roles as though they were performing *Henry VIII*.

Also notable is the pace with which the violence occurs, and the fact that most of the violence is done not onto the personages of those involved, but rather perpetrated against their respective senses of dignity. That is, Finlayson emerges from his house with garden shears and cuts one of their trees in half. Stan and Ollie then remove the address numbers from his house with their pocketknife, and take it upon themselves to carve off a piece of his doorframe. After a brief physical skirmish, Finlayson takes Ollie's pocket watch, inspects it leisurely, then smashes it against the wall. Ollie then pulls the entire mechanism of Finlayson's doorbell out of its socket....

Again, little physical pain is inflicted. The hostility is not allowed to degenerate into a gross wrestling match; noone strikes the other, then falls to the ground in a fight to the finish as they would anywhere else. Instead, decorum and ceremony must be observed. Unlike real war, where only might and power win the day, the goal is to wound the other's dignity and honor with as much ingenuity and style as can be mustered. Nothing so low and base as mere physical violence is respected. One merely stands and suffers the injury done unto one, observing it with interest, as if it were happening to someone else. One does not completely react to it until one is sure his adversary is utterly finished. Then, action stops for a moment as the full implications of the indignity are comprehended and savored. Then, one begins the retaliation, the adversary looking on to see how the style and invention of his atrocity will be bested.

It is this insistence on order, on the appreciation of the aesthetic qualities of the violence, on the code which decrees that all energies shall be focused on the ingenious perpetration of indignity, which would seem to unite this form chiefly to the Ollie character. Its rhythms are his: the preoccupation with order, with grace, with dignity — all speak from the heart of his primary concerns. Ollie dislikes conflict — his entire being beams with placatory goodwill; he really would like to become a functioning member of society. But he can only be pushed so far. And once that earnest goodwill is gone, it is gone completely. Even in hostility, however, he clings to a concept of reality that is well ordered, symmetrical, and — as his habitually flowery gestures make even the most mundane task an occasion of deportment and rarefied splendor — strangely beautiful.

As in his stoic sufferance of the rainstorm in "Helpmates" (1932), ruination may come, but he will not descend to its level. He will maintain his dignity and grace, displaying that they are so vast they can envelop and contain even these disasters.

In the mammoth car-wrecking war that is "Two Tars" (1928) — an earlier run at the idea for "Big Business," but less focused because of the diffusion of hostility over a greater number of people — Stan and Ollie amble down the length of the chaos they have created. A motorist opens the door of his car, striking Ollie in the chest. The team look at each other, nod decisively, each grabs a front fender of the car, and they bend it back genteelly into a C-shape, then turn and stride leisurely on. The vandalism is done precisely and symmetrically. We remember Ollie's precise, symmetrical gestures as he clears water, and/or, pie, mud, rice from his eyes. When, in "Big Business," Stan and Ollie commence their wholesale demolition of Finlayson's house, they enter into a little game wherein Ollie stands on the lawn swinging a shovel at vases pitched through the house's broken window by Stan. Destruction becomes a sport, a dance, an expression of creative artistry.

It is the same artistry Ollie displays in all of his gestures, embellishing reality with a spontaneous beauty that he obviously feels is sorely lacking. When he finds himself on Mae Busch's windowsill in "Tit for Tat" (1935) and must embarrassedly ask to use her stairs to get down to ground level, it is not enough for him to merely ask the question. His fingers have to mime the action of his feet descending the staircase. Whenever he signs his name to something in the films, no matter how insignificant the document, it is with the same grave, imperious flourish as might have befitted Napoleon registering one of his edicts. A doorbell cannot be pushed without the forefinger circling the button several times in a slowly shrinking orbit till it is suddenly drawn back and then connected with its target, decisively and emphatically.

Likewise, the slow, measured pace itself is something one instinctively associates with Ollie more than Stan. Many have pontificated whether it was the influence of Hardy that created the new slow, rhythm the team practiced, and which slowed Stan Laurel down from the every-which-way frenetic comic of the early films to the master of relaxed timing who can create 30 seconds of hilarious comedy merely by sitting and eating a hard-boiled egg ("County Hospital" [1932]). Such questions are perhaps unanswerable, but certainly Hardy's great ability to convey warmth and relaxation on the screen, and through it, is a large aspect of what the team communicates through their work, the steadfast canvas on which all the comedy is painted.

Undoubtedly, the development in the early films of the two characters by Laurel, Hardy and director Leo McCarey made the slower pace an increasing inevitability—it was McCarey's point of view, which Stan concurred with, that film comedy up to that point had been too fast, too hectic. As he would display throughout his career, McCarey's preference in comedy was for that which was based on strong characterization; his work is a celebration of the nuances and vitality found in the untrammeled expression of human personality. Stan's early conception of the team's characters—that of them possessing a heretofore unknown and monumental, even transcendent, dumbness—perfectly dovetailed with McCarey's ideal. The desired slower pace was functional, practical, a case of form matching content exactly—characters with the glacial thought processes of Stan and Ollie couldn't move quickly, and so the films took on a tempo that mirrored their meandering intellects.

In keeping with this, the films began to be shot at 15 frames per second rather than the customary 12 used for silent comedy—and so they take place in "natural time" rather than at the sped-up tempo we often associate with silent comedy. Parenthetically, this was a great boon when they needed to adapt to sound—they were already performing in "sound time." This slightly more naturalistic world allows Hardy in particular the space and time to express and develop his character. As an actor utterly at ease before the camera, who learned and refined his craft completely within its sights and confines, Hardy understood that the actor's relationship with the camera was paramount. He knew the exact amount to "feel" so that it would be registered by the camera. He had attained the "unconscious consciousness" of the camera's distance, its position, its "reality." He was already a master of what was then a very new medium, having developed his art entirely within its confines.

Stan, like all the other great comedians of the time, came to his artistic maturity on the stage. And, like all the other great comedians of the time, he had to learn to adapt his clowning to the camera—to "scale down," to interpret his art into the language of the mechanical eye rather than to a theater full of people. Hardy had no old performing habits he had to unlearn, and his naturalistic manner was perfect for the new naturalism of the films.

If Ollie was the nominal leader of the team onscreen, and he moved with the unhurried grace of someone not too far removed from the world we live in, it means that Stan in following him must move even slower. We see Stan's clowning, following Hardy's lead, growing slower and slower as the films progress, until he attains the mesmerizingly blank, fumbling tempo we most associate with him, within which his unique brilliance as a clown is allowed to fully bloom: the hard-boiled egg episode noted before, his confused reactions to the statue in "Wrong Again" (1929), his "play" with the saw in the ship's hold in "Towed in a Hole" (1932), his gradual intoxication in the wine-bottling scene in *The Bohemian Girl* (1936). These show quite a change from the hurried pace of his earlier, solo work, with its vaudevillian desperation to keep things moving toward the next gag.

Now the gag is of secondary importance. More important is the reaction to the gag. And so, along with the slow tempo we have the unique Laurel and Hardy timing, most visible in the reciprocal destruction jaunts, but woven through the heart of all their work. This timing is that an indignity is inflicted, causing a laugh — then all action stops as the victim is given a generous amount of time to assess and lament the damage. When the victim has wrung every last drop of discomfort, outrage, pain, frustration, anger, disgust, rage, desperation over the indignity inflicted upon him, then — and only then — does the action pick up again. It's as if there is an unspoken agreement in the films that all characters must be allowed a pause to feel their emotions in all their complexity down to the last pang and throb before they can avail themselves of physical action. In most cases the clowns' reactions are more humorous than what they are reacting to.

We see this particularly with Ollie. Time and time again, he will suffer stoically — patiently waiting until he's absolutely sure fate has done its worst — before he rejoins the parade of human activity. When Stan planes the backside of Ollie's trousers off in "Busy Bodies" (1933), Ollie turns and watches and waits patiently while Stan attempts to glue the piece of cloth back on, presumably affixing it to his underwear. When he falls down the chimney in "Dirty Work" (1933), and several bricks come tumbling down on his head, he does not yelp with pain and leap out of the fireplace to avoid more pain; rather he sits there waiting for more bricks to fall, and when they do he suffers them patiently, and he does not stir until the very last brick has fallen (this is repeated with the tumbling cheeses falling from the shelf in *Swiss Miss* [1938]). It all takes place as if in adherence to an obscure spiritual discipline by which one transcends the indignities inflicted on one by maintaining one's own dignity in the face of the absolute worst of what fate has to offer — no matter how impossible or absurd this task becomes.

As everyone knows, the person afflicted with the most indignities in any of the films is Ollie, and his reactions to them, interwoven with his essential need to maintain his dignity in the face of them, create his most identifiable characteristic: his camera look. It is the classic sequence found throughout their films, going right to the essence of their relationship: Stan commits a misdeed or an act of stupidity. All action ceases: we are given an extended close-up of Ollie looking directly at us, fuming with barely controlled rage. Other comedians have used the camera look in these films, fleetingly, appealing to us for sympathy, or for collusion in a crime. But no other performer commits himself to a relationship with us as Hardy does through his camera look; in his hands it becomes so far removed from the camera look of any other performer that it becomes something else entirely — a language unto itself.

Plainly, Ollie has a real need to communicate his pain to us in the most direct, unashamed manner — it evidently serves as some form of expiation or catharsis for him. Without it, how could he go on, plagued by misfortune — and by Stan — as he always is? It serves as a catharsis for us as well, for we become frustrated with Stan, too, yet at the same time we can't help loving him as Ollie does. The human touchstone Ollie provides allows Stan's clowning to ascend to the abstract, the ephemeral, the otherworldly.

The laughter takes on a different dimension, when in the next millisecond Ollie performs an act of equal or greater stupidity than that which he had previously lamented. Now we are in a position of laughing at someone who'd just taken us into his confidence. Our relationship with Ollie is more complicated than our relationship with Stan. Since he is more like us than Stan, he is able to form this deeper bond with us, through which he communicates his emotions directly to us through the screen. We feel this bond being formed but are somewhat uncomfortable with it, because through it we must relate as well to Ollie's pomposity and hypocrisy, his selfishness and his pride. When he is punished so rapidly for it all — ludicrously, absurdly — it serves as kind of comic justice, a clownish exorcism for all our own failures and frailties.

The camera look is not a gimmick nor an ironic commentary on the action contained within the story, as in the relationship of George Burns with the audience on "The Burns and Allen Show." It is undeniable that Hardy is breaking the fourth wall in addressing us so directly, but he never breaks character. In fact, the look is an integral aspect of the character. It is not like Groucho telling the audience they can step out into the lobby before Chico plays his piano selection, nor is it like the comments Hope and Crosby made in their movies about the fact they were in a movie (and like so many have done since). Rather than alienating us from the world depicted in their films, Hardy's camera look brings us into it. It is a daring innovation and an audacious leap of artistry for Hardy the actor, a natural progression from the unique intimacy of his relationship with the camera, as well as an expression of one of the main tenets of Laurel and Hardy's comedy noted before — that there's nothing new under the sun, so why stand on ceremony? Why not simply turn and face the camera and communicate your emotion directly into the lens? Unhurriedly, deliberately, completely, with not a drop or nuance of it left unexpressed when the shot ends.

Hardy's fellow naturalistic actor Marlon Brando rightly identified the camera look as the centerpiece of the team's humor: "Hardy's exasperation with Laurel," he cited, when asked what he found funny about the team: "Doing dead takes into the camera, shaking his head."[15] It is essential to their art: because virtually all their greatest scenes consist of just the two of them, there is no one else for Ollie to register his disapproval or disgust or anger with Stan but us. Take away this mechanism and one has taken away much of the essence of Laurel and Hardy.

And, as with so many of the other weapons in their arsenal, the camera look is fully functional and utilitarian not just artistically but technically — as has been documented elsewhere, the looks were often lengthened or shortened after premieres of the films so that they would match perfectly the laughter that accompanied the gag Hardy's "look" was reacting to.[16] They performed the function of pauses so that the laughter would not override the set-up for the next gag — though, of course, the look was a source of laughter in itself.

Beyond being funny or functional, the look fully communicates the essence of the Ollie character in a way that nothing else could. In addressing us directly, Ollie becomes one of us while at the same time he is imprisoned in a world that is plainly not ours but is close enough to make us laugh with recognition — in much the same way that Ollie could not exist in our world, yet his pomposity, his vanities, do exist with us everywhere. The look acknowledges the fact that we are watching a film and makes us aware of the limitations of the medium while at the same time it transcends that acknowledgment and its limitations. It transforms the camera from its role as documenter of a comic performance to being a vessel through which comedic emotion and sensibility — the painful admission of how very painful it is to be human — is directly and unstintingly communicated, through all time and for all time.

If the Stan character's defining moment in "Putting Pants On Philip" is his bursting into tears in the tailor shop, Ollie becomes uniquely himself in his final lingering camera look of disgust and resignation from the mud hole before the end title asserts itself. In a sense, this moment can be said to represent the birth of Laurel and Hardy as we know them. As always, the manner by which it is led up to is equally important.

In the film the Hardy character is the uncle having to suffer the existence of his freakish nephew, shepherding him through "his" (Hardy's) town, fearful of the loss of dignity that this familial aberration will visit upon him. Throughout the film, Stan has been pursuing — uncharacteristically — a woman through the streets. Near the end, she passes by, and Hardy forestalls Stan's pursuit with his typical gesture of "you stand back, wait here, let me approach her — I'll show you how it's done." He approaches the woman with beaming smile and florid gestures. She flicks him in the nose with her forefinger and departs.

There is a camera look here, one of burning annoyance and eviscerated pride. But then Stan pursues the woman to where she's worriedly engaged with the problem of attempting to cross a massive mud puddle. Stan gallantly takes off his kilt and lays it over the puddle. The woman scampishly leaps over the kilt and the puddle, skipping off in a lighthearted rebuke. Hardy, recovering from his own ego bruising of before, seizes upon this and laughs heartily at Stan's comeuppance. Stan moves to pick up his kilt from the mud puddle but Ollie stops him, pointing importantly to himself and insisting the kilt remain where it is for his safe deportment across the mud. He steps out onto it and, of course, the entire length of his body is swallowed by the unsuspected depths of the mud hole. His head bobs to the surface and he glares at us with despair, frustration, exasperation, resignation. End.

The ending is perfect because throughout the film Hardy is motivated by the fear that Stan will destroy his standing in the community, his identity, his dignity. There is no doubt in the mind of Hardy's character (not yet Ollie) that he is more important, more respectable, more dignified, that he is simply and inherently better than Stan, and all of his activity is an attempt to contain Stan's "otherness," his freakishness, so that it won't wreck Hardy's self-image. Yet in the end it is displayed that Hardy's greatest danger lies in himself: his presumption, his arrogance, his hypocrisy. Far from Stan, these are what inevitably lead to his downfall. In the film, as noted before, Hardy moves from being a sort of reluctant guardian for Stan to interacting with him as an equal, and in the last shot he is shown to be literally and figuratively "below" Stan, thoroughly stripped of all dignity and all the pretensions to dignity he had fought so stealthily to preserve — as now all his fellow townspeople gather to laugh at him. It happens entirely through his own misplaced pride, his sense of entitlement and privilege. He stares at us, utterly thwarted, resignedly admitting his failure, in a mute appeal for the empathy he will receive nowhere else. And Laurel and Hardy are born.

The film illustrates and sets in motion the basic dynamic of the team's relationship: Ollie fears that Stan's stupidity and 'otherness' will divest him of the dignity he so desperately clings to, yet it is Ollie's own stupidity and cunning that bring him low — unmasking him of all his pretensions so that he stares at us completely naked in forlorn resignation as the comedy ends.

Hardy utilizes the camera look to express the emotions Ollie cannot express in the world he's living in. Without the release of his expressions to us Ollie would not be able to keep going on. As much as they are expressions of disgust or impatience with Stan, they are admissions of failure, or of deceit, admissions he cannot make in his "real" world. In most of the time he's onscreen, Mr. Hardy lives a very harried and troublestrewn existence. If he wants to stop a moment and rest his bones and simply stare at us for a while before the onset of his next disaster, surely we shouldn't deny him this.

Yet even as he appeals to us for sympathy he evinces the characteristic that leads him stumbling into his next catastrophe. It is his inability to admit that he falls short of the perfection he so fervently pursues, which is reflected in his need to blame Stan for all his failures— as seen in the famous Hardy catchphrase "Here's another nice mess you've gotten me into!" So devoted to his ideals of order and perfection, Ollie can't face his own reality, can't bear the pain of failing to embody them — so he blames his failures on Stan, his dependable scapegoat.

A part of Ollie realizes the dishonesty of his position, and the camera looks convey the pain of his awareness that he is not who he would like to be. We see this in the above cited "look" from "Philip" and it is the classic one, recurring throughout their work, from the stoic resignation of his gaze in "Helpmates" to the frustrated resignation of his glare in the climactic scene of Sons of the Desert. And, of course, there are other innumerable examples of this in the scenes of disaster that form the endings of almost all their shorts.

Hardy also allows the camera look to convey other types of self-realization as well, as when he shares his discomfort with us after berating the maid for hiding his hat in "Hog Wild" (1930), when all the while (he now sees), it was perched securely on his head. When he tries to put Stan up to asking the sociopathically irate Toy Maker for money in Babes in Toyland (1934), telling him, "Go ahead — he told me you and him were just like that," he shoots us a telling look that lets us know what a whopper he's telling, and that he's well aware of what he's letting Stan in for. When he lies to his wife in "Their First Mistake" (1932) and later in Block-Heads (1938), he shares with us a look in which he confides to us that he's lying, along with his trepidation in doing so, and also his tremulous disbelief that she's actually swallowing the lie, mixed with his tenuous relief that she has. Quite a lot to express in one swiftly darting look, yet such is the fluency and virtuosity of this new language Hardy has created.

There is also the look of utter exasperation, when he turns to us in speechless offense at a blunder Stan has made. His eyes widen with chagrined disbelief that anyone could be so stupid, and his arms fly up at his sides, his hands disappearing out of frame, as if his ghastly astonishment were so great that he seeks to break out of the film into another dimension in order to fully express it.

Then there is the coy look, when Ollie shares his embarrassment in the film with us, or rather, he behaves toward us as he does with other characters in the movie — he is embarrassed before us and seeks to ingratiate himself into our good graces. This is seen when a shovelful of manure flies out a stable door and hits two men in "Wrong Again" (1929) and the culprit is revealed to be Ollie; he stands shyly, mincing with effacing contrition, alternating his fey glances between the two men and us. Later, in *Babes in Toyland*, he plays little finger games along the edge of a box when he is discovered trying to break into the villain's house, looking with meek, babyish embarrassment between the scowling face of the villain and us.

By far the most common camera looks, and perhaps the most amusing, are the subtle ones Ollie delivers to us within a scene, which come and go so quickly that they are often missed upon the first viewing of a given film. These are the ones, so numerous that one would be hard-pressed to find a scene in which they do not occur, where Hardy merely darts his eyes toward us to indicate his disgust with an idiotic action or statement of Stan's. One that springs to mind is in the opening minutes of *Flying Deuces* (1939), when they are inspecting the caricature a Parisian artist has just done of them, and Stan remarks that it "sure is good photography" — Ollie's quick, silent expression of painful exasperation to us tells that we are definitely back with our old friends again.

Special mention in any discussion of Hardy camera looks must go to the incredibly expressive glances tendered in the closing scene of *A Chump at Oxford* (1940), wherein Ollie, forced to be the manservant of Stan in his new persona as the cerebral Lord Paddington, communicates his agonized disbelief at his situation to us time and time again. We are again reminded of how integral these looks are to their comedy: with Stan now off in the austere realms of his cold, cruel alter ego, Ollie's covenant with us is our only remaining bond of familiarity with the world inside the screen — and, obviously, the covenant performs the same function for him.

In his unnatural subjugation to Stan, in a forbidding environment, in a foreign country, Ollie can express his discomfort and rage only to us— until, as sometimes happens, he is pushed too far. Here he is given a humiliating lesson in deportment by Lord Paddington, which culminates with Hardy tripping over a footstool and crashing to the ground. After a last, quick glance of outrage to us, he turns and explodes, reclaiming his dignity, restoring the balance of their relationship as he shouts out a torrent of angry recrimination. It is after this that Stan is magically restored to his old self, and it is notable that once Ollie ascertains this, his anger disappears entirely and he welcomes Stan back with love and comradeship, embracing him and laughing loudly. For a moment he remembers a jibe of Lord Paddington's about the Hardy double chin, and he looks at us doubtfully for an instant, tenderly fingering said chin ... then the thought is gone as quickly as it came, and he is back to laughing, ushering his bewildered old friend out of the room.

Ollie's camera looks are a barometer of his well-being. When things are going well, Ollie is borne along on his good fortune and has no need to share his emotions directly with us. As we know, such occasions for Mr. Hardy are extremely rare. It is when he becomes estranged from his more often than not abrasive reality that he seeks communion and understanding through the camera lens. In the scene above, only we can share in his indignation at the Lord Paddington situation, because only we, along with him, can know how stupid Stan was in his previous ("true") incarnation.

It is evident, with the ease that he used them, that the camera looks became second nature to Hardy the actor. He knew instinctively when and how to use the looks; he never let them become a self-conscious gimmick, never allowed them to shatter the tenuous approximation of reality depicted in the films. As often as they are utilized with what seems to be unconscious ease, they are always deployed judiciously, with strict adherence to the unspoken rules that govern their existence. For instance, none of the other characters seem aware of Ollie's communion with another world or feel the need to comment on it, and the looks are always silent — Ollie feels no need to communicate with us verbally.

An exception to this last rule seems to appear at the beginning of their sound short "Helpmates (1932)," one of their masterpieces. The film opens with Ollie staring directly into the camera, intoning a mournful rebuke, a lecture of disappointed remonstration to someone who has clearly let him down:

> Now aren't you ashamed of yourself? A man of your supposed intelligence acting like an emptyheaded idiot! What did you do? I'll tell you what you did — you took advantage of your wife's absence and pulled a wild party! And that's not all — you lost all of your ready money in a poker game!

At this point, the camera draws back and we see that we have not been looking into Ollie's face at all, but into the reflection of his face in the mirror before which he stands, continuing to lament his fall from grace: "Could anything be more crass? More disgusting? There were times when I held high hopes for you — but that time has passed. I'll tell you what's wrong with you in two words: im-possible!"

Tellingly, in this one seeming contradiction to the camera look law, we see that Ollie is addressing no one but himself. Yet the emotion is the same as that which he expresses in the standard ritual — his concept of himself as an extraordinary person, and his disappointment when reality and his own actions refuse to validify that concept. Ollie is self-aware enough to issue a morning-after mea culpa into a mirror, but he is not aware enough to tone down his sense of self-importance even in the throes of self-admitted disgrace — it's merely an extension of the pomposity that is soon to lead him into another catastrophe.

Shortly thereafter, Ollie contacts Stan in order to marshal him into help cleaning the party-devastated house before Ollie's wife arrives from her trip. In stark contrast to Ollie's tortured self-examination, Stan is found to be asleep, submerged so deeply in the realms of the subconscious that it takes three attempts for him to be able to communicate with Ollie over the phone. Once cognizant of the fact that Ollie needs his help, however, Stan is able to appear fully dressed and ready for work on Ollie's doorstep within a split second of hanging up the phone.

The rest of the film is the archetypal depiction of the result of Stan "helping" Ollie and all that entails, which in this case is the ruination of three successive suits of clothes, assorted pratfalls, explosions, foothills of shattered crockery, and much spilling of water, flour and soot — ending in the penultimate Laurel and Hardy moment already referenced several times here, the complete reduction of Ollie's home into a charred, smoking shell.

Running parallel to all of this slapstick destruction is an articulation of many of the cornerstone truths of the Stan and Ollie relationship: though Stan's efforts visit nothing but devastation on him, Ollie remains determined that Stan will help clean his house. Or rather, based on the evidence of the film, Ollie remains determined that Stan will in fact clean his house for him as he, Ollie, prepares himself for the trip to meet his wife. There is no question in Ollie's mind, and there is little in Stan's, that it is right and proper for Ollie to expect this of Stan, and that it is right and proper that Stan will uncomplainingly accede to doing whatever work Ollie assigns to him.

This logic at the heart of their relationship is also evidenced in "Men O' War" (1929), one of their earliest sound comedies. In one of their finest sequences, they adjourn to a soda fountain to treat two young women they've just met to some refreshment. Because of their limited finances, they are only able to afford three sodas — as Ollie informs Stan, it will be necessary for one of them to forego a beverage, so when he is offered, Stan is instructed to politely refuse. Naturally, Stan is too stupid to be able to remember to do this, even when cued to do so several times as Ollie repeats the orders and asks: "And what will you have, Stanley?" Ollie's frustration mounts until it almost becomes a murderous rage, and though on the surface of it the humor is mostly resultant of Stan's witless stupidity and Ollie's exasperation, on a deeper level we see how revealing it is that it is never questioned that it is Stan who must sacrifice, that Ollie could save himself a great deal of annoyance and embarrassment if he would only consider sacrificing himself. That this never occurs to Ollie displays that his self-importance and pomposity are inseparable from his own stupidity, which is obviously at least as intensive as Stan's. That the basic unjustness of the situation, quite aside from Stan's inability to grasp it, never occurs to either of them, and is never drawn attention to in the film, is testament to the subtlety of their comedy, as well as to the depth of their characterizations even in this early film.

The unjustness of the situation does occur briefly to Stan, however, in "Helpmates," when, understandably, he bristles at some particularly authoritarian bullying of Ollie's. "Say, what do ya think I am, Cinderella?" Stan asks, and in what was no doubt intended as a wry comment on the team's relationship, notes: "If I had any sense I'd walk out on you!" "Well it's a good thing you haven't any sense!" Ollie rejoinders as he leaves the room, to which Stan agrees: "It certainly is!" Fittingly, Stan's momentary rebellion fizzles out (as it always does) as he spends the next several moments fruitlessly attempting to piece together exactly what it was he just agreed to in a series of gorgeously drawn-out close-ups of abject puzzlement.

Here and throughout the films, Ollie repeatedly brings disaster upon himself through his insistence on his importance over Stan's. Though virtually every move Stan makes in "Helpmates" results in catastrophe, Ollie's reaction is generally along the lines of "Get this mess cleaned up!"—as though he genuinely expects Stan to be suddenly capable of competence, all prior evidence to the contrary notwithstanding. It's as though he hopes through the sheer strength of determination and force he can force reality into his vision of what it should be. In "Helpmates," this folly is taken to its apotheosis when his insistence that Stan is capable of cleaning his home results inevitably in the removal of that home from the earth. In the final moments of the film Ollie sits stoically in the roofless wreckage as the clouds rumble above, and the universe rains down its parting shot of judgment on him.

Along with his misplaced, and ever disappointed, faith in Stan, Ollie's intractability unfailingly causes him suffering as well. He is unable to change course or to re-think when things are going badly—as when Stan has wrecked his second suit of clothes in "Helpmates" for instance, or in his determination to get the radio aerial up at all costs, despite the fact that even his wife wants him to forget about it in "Hog Wild" (1930), in his determination that Stan shall have his steak dinner in *Block-Heads*, despite his destroyed car, his destroyed marriage, and his soon-to-be-destroyed home, all courtesy of Stan's presence. This intractability is seen in many of his smallest gestures, as when he continues to pour hot water on the floor after Stan moves the tub away in "Laughing Gravy" (1931), or when he submits himself to be doused with water by Stan twice while teaching him a lesson in "Helpmates." One can see it in an image from "The Music Box" (1932), when, after chasing the piano as it escapes jangling down the massive length of stairs, he grabs hold of it and allows it to drag him down with it, evidently not considering the option of letting go of it until it reaches the street. Once Ollie has committed himself to a plan, or even a small physical movement, he will not diverge, he will not be distracted, and he will not compromise, no matter what disorder rages about him. If misfortune should dog my every step, he seems to be saying, bring it on! Each disaster only inspires him to a loftier goal. He will stay the course.

To a certain degree, determination is laudable and without Ollie's ambition there wouldn't be much to move the plots of the movies forward. As noted, Stan would be perfectly happy simply to exist. Conjoined with Ollie's determination is his vision, the vision he is ever trying to impose on reality — one of grace, fluidity, elegance, a deep enjoyment of life's simple pleasures. We see it in "Them Thar Hills" (1934), when he's happily preparing for the meal in the trailer. We see it when he's dancing a little dance of jubilation on the morning of his wedding in "Our Wife" (1931). We see it in his soulful singing of "You Are the Ideal of My Dreams" at the beginning of "Beau Hunks" (1931). He has a vision of the way life should be, and no matter how many times his vision is turned asunder, eviscerated, burned to a crisp by reality and handed back to him, he keeps coming back to the table: he remains loyal to his ideal. Though he is often to be viewed in a state of defeat we get the idea that fortune only has to smile at him slightly and he'll be up again, reinvigorated, ready for the next enterprise.

Certainly we see his dedication to the ideal of friendship in his instantaneous acceptance and forgiveness of Stan at the end of *A Chump at Oxford* when his old friend is restored to his usual dumb self. We see it at other times when Ollie shows a moving loyalty and concern for Stan, who is pretty much incapable of returning these sentiments. In a way, Ollie's relationship with Stan mirrors his relationship with reality, with life and with his ideal. From Ollie's perspective, Stan causes him nothing but trouble, yet

Ollie remains firmly committed to their relationship, no matter what disasters it brings crashing down on their heads.

We get a good idea just what this commitment means to Ollie, and how much he feels he suffers for it, in every film. In "Any Old Port" (1932), an old friend hails Ollie and asks: "How's things?" "Oh," Ollie replies, casting a frustrated glance at Stan, "just as usual!" When, in "The Fixer-Uppers" (1935), Ollie is in the position of having to fight in a duel in which he'll almost certainly be killed he says: "I can't say but that I'll be glad when this is finally over." Stan: "Why?" Ollie: "At last I'll be rid of you!"

Yet at the same time Ollie is genuinely solicitous toward his partner. We see this in "Below Zero" (1930), in the oft-cited sequence where they are beaten by some toughs for their inability to pay their restaurant bill, then tossed out into a frigid alleyway — Stan is dropped into a rainbarrel, Ollie merely thrown into the snowy street. When Ollie comes to, he looks around for Stan with rising panic, finally grabbing a stick and resolutely running to bang at the door, shouting: "Stan! Stan!" In *Pardon Us* (1931), they are separated when one of the guards at the prison where they're being held orders Stan to see the dentist about his "buzzing tooth." Stan sits weeping with fright in the waiting room as he sees several results of the dentist's handiwork wheeled groaningly past him — then Ollie appears smiling at the door and Stan's fears are allayed. As his pal comes to comfort him, Stan clutches his arm happily.

When Ollie meets Stan again after 20 years in *Block-Heads*, Ollie is genuinely downcast when he thinks he sees that Stan has lost a leg. He braces up and approaches Stan, coming to stand over him, beaming, with his arms folded behind his back, grinning with the anticipation of surprising him with his presence. Stan looks up from his paper dumbly, then returns to his reading impassively, and for a moment we fear that Ollie's grand expectation will only be met by Stan's dull indifference — we have an uneasy sense that the disparity of their emotional commitment to the relationship will be all too clearly displayed. But then Stan double takes, half-rises from his chair: "Ollie—!"

And when Stan says: "Gee, it's been a long time. Have ya missed me?" and Ollie replies: "I certainly have!" he imbues that familiar cadence within the team's vocabulary with a deep, sincere warmth and tenderness. As others have noted, it is mostly Ollie who evinces concern and empathy for other characters within the films, reaching out with assistance when he sees it is needed—for the old woman in "One Good Turn," for the drunk in "Scram!" (1932).

At the same time, Ollie shows little compunction about betraying Stan, about taking advantage of Stan when the opportunity presents itself. In

"Oliver the Eighth" (1934) when they both answer a wealthy widow's personal ad, Ollie thinks little of disposing of Stan's letter as he mails his own. In a typical gesture in "The Hoose-gow" (1929), Ollie carefully weighs the respective picks they've been given to work with on the road crew and makes sure that Stan gets the larger, heavier one while he takes the lightweight model. One of Ollie's favorite maneuvers is to get Stan to do the dirty work by accusing him of the very fault he himself is guilty of — as in "The Live Ghost" when he tells Stan to go investigate a noise on the haunted ship and Stan tries to take the candle with him: Ollie: "What? And leave me here in the dark? Selfish!" And there is the general bullying Ollie subjects Stan to, all resultant of the imperishable conviction he holds that he is empirically, objectively, self-evidently more important than Stan, better than Stan, and deserves to be treated as such.

The fact is that Ollie does have a sincere, heartfelt vision of his friendship with Stan and of friendship in general. The humor of the Ollie character is that he has these lofty ideals and continually fails to meet them on any level. The honesty of the Stan character is what unmasks Ollie of his unrealistic pretensions time and time again. They are like two parts of one mind: the socialized one that tenuously believes in the structure of civilization and clings to all the "necessary lies" that makes it work, and the pure unprinted-upon part of the mind, whose terrain is empty, for whom the only truth is the moment, who will always remain unassimilated by society, whose very existence exposes all its "necessary lies" to ridicule time and time again.

The structures of their films are rituals in which the pretensions of socialized homo sapiens are stripped away, showing that much of our behavior is merely a façade behind which we stand naked and afraid. There rituals illustrate the thin line that separates us at all times from outright chaos, from utter disaster, and by depicting these things farcically again and again they allow us to bear the consciousness of them, as well as to, in a way, celebrate our constant proximity to danger, to abject and irrevocable failure. By laughing, we can triumph over "the worst"; when we have experienced the stark truths and cruel inequalities of life as absurd, we can gain freedom from them and we can gain faith and strength to live, if only for the moment we're laughing.

The sense of a chasm between Ollie's ideals and his reality, and the duplicitousness and self-deception on his part as a result of that chasm, forms the basis of one of their most celebrated features, *Sons of the Desert* (1933). It is certainly their most carefully crafted and constructed feature, and it is crafted around the basic dishonesty of the Oliver Hardy character.

In the film, Stan and Ollie are members of a fraternal lodge to which they must make a sacred oath, guaranteeing their attendance at the upcoming convention in Chicago. Stan is hesitant to commit himself to the oath until he is prodded to tearfully do so by Ollie, and later he confesses his fear that his wife may not let him go. Ollie: "Do you have to ask your wife everything?" Stan: "Well, if I didn't ask her I wouldn't know what she wanted me to do." Ollie: "I never realized that such a deplorable condition existed in your household. Why can't you be more like me ... I go places and do things and then ask my wife!"

Immediately as we arrive at the Hardy home, however, we see that quite a different situation exists than Ollie would have us believe. The mere mention of the upcoming convention by Stan in Mrs. Hardy's presence has Ollie cringing and shushing him, and within minutes an earsplitting tirade courtesy of Ollie's better half has overwhelmed them, punctuated by various pieces of crockery being shattered over the Hardy cranium.

True to his code, Ollie is not long dissuaded by this. After all, he has made a sacred oath to attend the convention, and besides, the lodge is a metaphor for the larger society Ollie desires so much to be a part of: the world of adulthood he needs so badly to be accepted by, which can confer upon him the identity he intensely feels the lack of. Here, as in other "married films," "Their Purple Moment" (1928), "We Faw Down" (1928), "Blotto" (1930), "Be Big" (1931), — all of which inform and lead up to *Sons of the Desert*— the rite of passage to the world of adulthood for Laurel and Hardy is through lying to their wives. It is in successfully deceiving his wife that Ollie feels he reclaims— or, perhaps it is more accurate to say, establishes— his manhood. It is the way by which he continually attempts to gain membership into that callous, casually immoral brotherhood of worldly men, which he feels is the essence of true maturity, here symbolized by the Sons of the Desert.

And so in the next scene we find that Ollie has cooked up an elaborate scheme whereby he pretends to be deathly ill, and a fake doctor is paid off to prescribe an ocean voyage to Honolulu. It is Honolulu because Ollie knows his wife can't stand the ocean, so therefore Stan will have to accompany him. Ollie puts every bit of himself into his simulation of sickness, he shamelessly milks his wife for sympathy, and the profusion of confiding camera looks in this sequence attest to his consciousness of the enormity of the sham he's trying to pull.

But it works, and he and Stan duly make off to the convention. On their return, however, wearing leis and singing a song about a Honolulu Baby, they discover that the ship they were supposed to be returning from Hawaii on has sunk, and that the boat with the survivors isn't due until the following day. They are in the house reading this in the newspaper when they hear the wives coming in, so they hurriedly scamper up into the attic. Ollie notes that they need simply to camp out in the attic for the night, then present themselves to the wives the next day.

Complications with a thunderstorm and an errant lightning bolt interfere, propelling them out of the attic through a trapdoor onto the roof, where they stand in their nightshirts beneath sheets of driving rain. By this time, Stan is all for going down and confessing to the wives, but Ollie typically refuses to do this and keeps Stan from doing so by blackmailing him. "If you spill the beans, I'll tell Betty [Stan's wife] that I caught you smoking a cigarette!" he vows, interestingly threatening Stan with the exposure of behavior symbolic of the very adulthood Ollie so desperately seeks to attain.

Stan, appalled, caves in, and they slide down a drainpipe to the street, where a cop intercepts them. When he asks the curious-looking pair where they live, Ollie naturally stonewalls him, and Stan naturally tells the cop exactly where they live, and so in short order the cop presents them to their wives.

It is worth noting that through all of this, as Ollie has progressed from one increasingly complicated deception to another in his attempt to fit into the sophisticated adult world, Stan has remained pretty much untouched in his innocence. He has been towed along in Ollie's wake and participated in the subterfuges, but there isn't a lot of evidence he fully comprehends the implications of the chicanery — mostly he seems to be going along with the flow and living in the moment in his usual manner. In the "Doctor" scene when Ollie moans that Stan will have to come with him to Honolulu, Stan says no—for he asked his wife, and she said he could go to the convention, so he'll presently be leaving for Chicago. Likewise, when Ollie reads aloud from the paper about the sinking of the ocean liner, Stan's reaction is to simply observe that it certainly was a good thing they didn't go to Honolulu. Stan is simply unable to maintain deception, not through any moral stance, but because his very nature, which lives only in the present and comprehends little beyond that, isn't capable of entertaining any one particular concept of reality for very long, whether it's a deliberate mistruth or not. And so his mere presence will always unmask the deception and the pretensions of the ones around him or, it should be said, the one around him.

It was Stan who revealed the truth behind Ollie's initial lie of the film that he was the king of the castle, and it is Stan's stupidity that continued throughout the film to undermine the cunning, elaborate deceptions Ollie devised to somehow maintain that first lie: deceptions and schemes he has full confidence in counting on Stan's expert assistance to pull off. And now as Stan's guileless honesty causes them to be turned over to their wives, we come to the climactic scene in which Stan completely divests Ollie of the last shred of his pretense to becoming the bizarre stereotype of an adult, which Ollie in his innocence believes is the ideal, and confines him forever — again — to the world of the child.

The scene is set up as a trial and the wives are the judges. They have seen a newsreel of Stan and Ollie clowning at the convention, and so they know the extent of the deception. They do not tell this to their husbands, but rather, having a bet between themselves as to which husband is the more honest, play dumb and attempt to extract the truth from their spouses.

Stan and Ollie enter, concocting a completely ridiculous story to account for their whereabouts. This is quickly dispensed with by the wives who ask them point-blank for the truth, appealing to their higher natures.

Predictably, Ollie clings to his lie, calmly, smugly, blandly. And just as predictably, Stan bursts into tears and weepingly confesses. And, in one of the highest points in all of Laurel and Hardy's films, this climactic weeping is counterpointed by the ultimate frozen, impossibly static shot of Oliver Hardy glaring into the camera with smoldering frustration and rage, somehow mixed with disgruntled resignation. In many ways it's a beautifully comic inversion of the standard sensibility we see around us, in which men are men who tough it out, who lie to their wives, who stick to their guns. Ollie here, however, seems more pathetic and sad the more he sticks to his absurd lie. It is Stan who becomes heroic by bursting into tears, something which is generally regarded as the most humiliating thing an adult male can do in public.

It is Stan's cry, the signature characteristic of the Laurel persona, triggering Ollie's camera look, the signature characteristic of the Hardy persona, that brings the harsh light of reality on the pretensions of Ollie and the rest of us, showing us with a child's whimper that we are all of us children, acting with the same motivations we had as children, only now using elaborate language and intellectual creations to justify and conceal them.

As if in a morality tale, or a parable, they each receive their just deserts at the end of the trial: Stan being rewarded by his wife for telling the truth, Ollie being punished — devastatingly — for clinging to his lie. It is entirely commensurate with the intractable, stubborn quality of the Ollie character that, even when given the opportunity to confess and to honor the truth, he remains steadfast in his dedication to his scheme, to his false vision of reality. It is also commensurate with his nature that this dedication should pave the way for him into disaster: the apparent destruction of his marriage.

There is a symmetry to the ending that is almost too neat for a Laurel and Hardy film, and we are relieved that the film ends with Stan being beaned on the head with a saucepan by Ollie, then stumbling around witlessly as the end title asserts itself. Like the exploding cigar that sabotages the false "reconciliation" ending of "Big Business" (1929), this image of Stan's vacuity reminds us that though Stan seems to be rewarded here for his superior morality, Stan is, above all else, stupid. He is a fool. The real issue at the heart of their "trial" is not that Stan is better simply because his inability to sustain deception makes him more "honorable" than Ollie, but rather that Ollie causes himself so much trouble by pretending to be someone that he is not, by pretending that reality is something different than what it is.

Superficially, it can be observed that Ollie is in some ways more intelligent than Stan—certainly he seems better able to function in society, is probably marginally more competent than Stan is at completing certain tasks. But whereas Stan is on some level cognizant of the fact that his minute intelligence causes him to be overwhelmed by reality, Ollie operates under the idea that he is capable of mastering reality, shaping it to fit his rather grandiose ends. And so in this, larger, sense, Ollie is considerably less intelligent than Stan, for it is his presumption, his lack of humility, which unerringly leads him to great suffering—suffering that never leads to wisdom but rather to a camera look of withering disgust, before he picks himself up and readies himself for the next ill-conceived venture.

Throughout *Sons of the Desert*, Ollie's camera looks provide running commentary on the journey through his web of deception, from his standard looks of frustration with Stan at the outset, to his conspiratorial looks as he misleads his wife; from the looks of annoyance in the raucous convention scenes, which cease as he gradually becomes subsumed in the convivial atmosphere; to the joyous looks he and Stan both give the newsreel camera in the parade footage, which sets the wives straight about their husbands; to the final, ultimate camera look, already noted, where in the end he is finally stripped of all pretension, facing reality in all its ghastly horror. Again, it is Stan who performs the duty that is his function within their relationship; piercing through Ollie's false ideas and his pretensions to sophistication and worldliness, Stan reveals Ollie to be the child he is.

According to his biographer, Oliver Hardy was acutely aware of living a paradox, in that he was a heavy man who hated being heavy, yet attained fame as one whose name has become virtually synonymous with fatness. Hardy's ambivalence about his predicament would seem to be mirrored in his screen character, who in any given film is dissatisfied with the discrepancy between his current reality and his ideal and is driven to take action, however wrongheaded, in order to bring reality in line with his vision of what it should be. In this, Ollie reflects the ambitions of the rest of our species, who have the requisite intelligence to see that life can be better but who lack the intelligence to achieve that "better life," who somewhere along the way become misled, confused, corrupted, and finally dumped into that inevitable mud hole. If, as has been documented, Hardy the actor found the identity he craved through his art and through his final acceptance of himself, Ollie still stands on the sidelines of society awaiting its acceptance, hungering for the identity he feels only it can give him, fingering his tie with the rest of us, who also "once expected great things of ourselves."

Though it is the Stan character who is initially the more obvious clown and attracts us with his otherworldly charm, the character of Ollie reveals its depths and charms more evenly over time; his innate self-deception coupled with his unrealistic, headstrong idealism resonate with greater strength as one becomes more aware of how widespread and endemic these attributes are to all of humanity.

3

THE FILMS

Success, though fulfilling, isn't very amusing. Failure often is — as long as it is not we who are the failures. A graceful pirouette executed by an accomplished ballet dancer may be breathtaking, but it can never be funny. A half-somersault pratfall — or a "108," as it was known on the Roach lot — can be side splitting. To splash mud on a rag-clothed beggar is appalling — the opposite of funny. But to splash mud on a pompous, overweening authoritarian symbol of power and wealth, who obviously values his own dignity more than anything else on earth, to splash mud on his carefully groomed clothing, his impeccably imperious face, and by so doing to divest him of that dignity — that's very funny.

There's no doubt that the 97 films Laurel and Hardy made mostly at the Roach studios between 1927 and 1940 were made with one objective only — to be as funny as possible, to contain as many laughs as their creators were humanly capable of fitting into them. Stan Laurel stated quite clearly that this was their goal, their only reason for being.[1] Their great success was, and is, entirely due to the fact that they have aroused pure, sincere laughter — a momentary vacation from the woes which plague humankind — for millions of people on the planet, those who have existed and have passed, those who are, and, one supposes, many millions who have not yet been born.

If the potency of the comedy has been proven beyond all doubt through time, we might wonder what it is that constitutes this potency. Their humor, which is that of deflated dignity, of misguided aspirations, of disappointed expectations, failure, effort and exertion without result, and outright expressions of hostility sabotaging civilization, is one which reflects the truth of our existence. It causes us to pause and laugh at the absurdity of our condition in a cathartic release and allows us to gain perspective on it. That is why the laughter aroused by great comedy is so deeply satisfying and remains with us long after the cheap laughter aroused by merely clever mediocre comedy has been forgotten. Cleverness eventually exhausts itself, and its audience too, but great comedy drinks from a deeper well: the well of human suffering.

None of the creators of these films was driven to create cinematic essays on the frailties and heartaches of humankind. They were simply trying to create the biggest laughs possible, a desire that was inseparable for them from their economic survival — they were paid to be funny, so they tried to stay at the top of their game for as long as they could. They were just trying to amuse themselves and amuse others. They had faith that what they found funny others would as well, and their faith was vindicated.

The creators of these films were led by instinct to what was funny, and their successes were due to the fact that they trusted and followed these instincts. There was no reasoning out how certain gags would touch upon eternal truths of the human condition, or how a certain plotline would make a striking commentary on this or that political question. Laurel himself denied there was ever an ostensible aim to his comedy beyond just getting laughs, and he was critical of any comedy — even Chaplin's — that did have a goal beyond that.

The fact that the films are so unswervingly dedicated to pure laughter, however, means that they do inevitably shed light on eternal truths, that they do comment on our common predicament, for this laughter, so necessary for maintaining our sanity, erupts as we acknowledge the shocking truth about our predicament. Our laughter results from the giddiness of embracing and accepting this truth completely, if only for a moment.

There is a worldview expressed through the films that seems at first to reflect our world like a circus fun-house mirror would. As we laugh, there is a creeping sense in the heart of our laughter that the mirror, which at first seemed to distort things so grotesquely, is actually a more accurate instrument of reflection than we had previously thought.

There are themes and images in the films that occur again and again, attesting to what many of the co-stars, editors, directors, and even the producer of these films stated: over the course of 13 years, the team had many different writers and directors, but the man in effective creative control was Stan Laurel. The uniformity of intention and execution of these films, no matter who the nominal director at the time happened to be, likewise attests to the fact that the world depicted in them sprang largely from the mind of one man.

The comedy touches on tragedy in the way that the comedy of Chaplin, Keaton, and W. C. Fields does, and in the way the comedy of Bob Hope, Abbott and Costello, and Danny Kaye does not. It's important to note that Laurel and Hardy had their greatest success during the Depression, a time before America became an empire, when it felt as though it was in a state of collapse; there was much despair, and people weren't really all that confident about the prevailing social order. In concurrent "highbrow" comedy films there is a decided empathy for the unsophisticated, even cockeyed, eccentric and a scornful attitude toward the selfish, highfalutin rich — as seen in *You Can't Take it with You* (1938), and *My Man Godfrey* (1936). There was a sense of the innate dignity, even superiority, of the common person over the phony, the celebrated, the well connected.

Charlie Chaplin expressed this sentiment through the empathy for the common worker he displays in *Modern Times* (1936). Yet Laurel and Hardy are the true workers in the factory in a way that Charlie can never be. Stan and Ollie are losers, and they answered a great need at a time when many suspected that they themselves were losers in a very big way.

We note that Laurel and Hardy's star faded quickly with the onset of the 1940s and World War II, and while this is undoubtedly due in part to the inferior films they were forced to make by the larger, uncaring studios, it's undeniable that tastes in comedy were changing, opening the door for Bob Hope, Abbott and Costello and the rest. The comedies from these performers were about winners, being on the side of the winner, as everyone fervently — and understandably — desires to be during wartime. The new brash, conformist outlook left little room for empathizing with two trusting souls who, through their inability to achieve even the simplest tasks, exist as a permanent question to the worth of all human activity. There was too much work to be done to be indulging that line of thought, and the veneration of the eccentric and the misfit was jettisoned in favor of the worshipping of the status quo and the middle American taxpayer ever-advancing up the corporate ladder, mouthing patriotic pieties about "our boys over there."

Stan and Ollie are losers, yet there is something so grandiose and dignified about their losing, that it becomes more alive and beautiful than anything else in the miserable, short-tempered world they inhabit. This is a world where wives routinely settle arguments with blazing shotguns. Where you can spend an entire day carrying a piano up an endless flight of stairs, only to have someone chop it to pieces with an ax when you finally get it to the top. Where sometimes in the course of an argument it becomes necessary to insert your opponent's proboscis into the socket of a lamp, turn the lamp on, and thereby char the tip of your opponent's said proboscis. Where entire city blocks dissolve into a vast battlefield of people throwing dessert foods at one another.

The most pervasive attitude of the films is a wry bemusement at the various institutions humans have created. As we've seen, marriage is always presented as a sort of horrific travesty: a roiling, agitated whirlpool of violence and hostility. Weddings themselves are farces, almost always ending in some sort of bizarre configuration of confusion. Generally the police are glib bullies—a recurring gag where a policeman complains "You almost blew my brains out!" then turns to display the burned-off, smoking seat of his pants, would seem to bespeak a certain ambivalence toward authority. Doctors are either insane cranks or compassionless bureaucrats. Even nurses and nannies are sour and cruel, and the person you rescue from suicide can make your life a living hell. Everybody's sarcastic, flip, arrogant, mean, and most of all, they have absolutely no mercy. They are ruthless. Automobiles fly into pieces at the slightest provocation. Or they're sliced in half, bent like an accordion, or compressed paper-thin. Mud puddles are eight to twelve feet in depth.

There is a basic bemusement at human endeavors in general. Failure is the common theme. Several of the films end in death, and one with a suicide, one with the homicide of its stars. Several of the films end with grotesque mutilations of the human body. Few of their films have happy endings.

As far as observations on human nature go, the pleasantries and niceties of the civilized social interactions people engage in are seen to be façades, which, when they are (quite easily) torn away, reveal bottomless, unsuspected depths of anger and an insatiable appetite for vengeance, for warfare.

Naturally this world has been created to act as a foil for Laurel and Hardy, trusting innocents wandering through a treacherous landscape who are only trying to do their best but always meet up with hostility. How much of the potency of their humor is due to the truth we sense within these broadly drawn caricatures?

Obviously, the creators of "Big Business" (1929), wherein Stan and Ollie, in the course of selling Christmas trees door to door in sunny California, enter into a fracas with a potential customer wherein his house and their car are utterly destroyed, were not intending a film that illustrates, as a recent (2003) film society program stated, "the manner by which capitalism inevitably leads to war."[2] The only thing on their minds was the invention of a story on which they could hang as many gags as possible. They were creating a situation that would also give birth to new gags on the set as well, for like all of the films, this one was largely improvised once they got there.

But isn't the horrible destructive fury unleashed for the better part of the film directly resultant of Stan and Ollie's misguided entrepreneurship, and doesn't the very title, acidic to the extreme, wryly comment on the economic aspects of the conflict as well? And the facts that it's Christmas and that Stan and Ollie are selling Christmas trees, those very honored symbols of a most sacred day, of love and peace and "goodwill to all," and that this unleashes the tidal wave of violence, cannot that be taken as a comment, too? The opening title reads, "The story of a man who turned the other cheek — and got punched in the nose" — the burlesque version, or the Laurel and Hardy version, of the commandment of the man whose birth the trees are symbols of.

This most disturbing depiction of commerce leading to outright savagery is observed by a gathering crowd of onlookers who are quite mortified by this breakdown of civilization yet at the same time curiously passive, watching the events unfold like spectators at a soccer game — along with the policeman who arrives, not to bring all the violence to a stop, but to sit in his car and calmly notate the atrocities committed, apparently waiting for the conflict to come to its climax, whereupon he moves in to dispense judgment and punishment. Is this situation not a phenomenon we have experienced countless times as a species, now given back to us as farce, in a compelling dream that moves in a stream of grand inevitability as a dream does? And the fact that the climax of the battle comes as one man viciously attacks a piano with an ax, while another blows up a car, then manically attacks all the pieces of the car with a hammer, trying to "kill" it, are these insane attempts by humans to wrestle and defeat machines relevant to the commentary as well? And then there is also the fact that all of these events were filmed a scant nine months before the complete breakdown of the worldwide economic system.

Again, all the artists involved were only trying to think up some "business" to pack two reels of film with as much hilarity as possible. Yet in the purity of this intention, in their instinctive, intuitive pursuit of laughter, the stark truths of the world and the existence they burlesque are inevitably evoked and depicted with a piercing, if unconscious, clarity.

In a later, equally essential, film, "The Music Box" (1932), Stan and Ollie are given the seemingly impossible task of toting a piano (again the piano — that stolidly middle-class symbol of respectability and pretensions to "culture") up an absurdly long length of stairs. They are bedeviled in their work by the piano itself, which evidently is not incredibly enthusiastic about reaching its intended destination, as well as a scornful, contemptuously mocking nanny out walking her infant charge; a bullying, abusive policeman; and an arrogant, blustery — and somewhat unhinged — intellectual with a massive sense of entitlement and privilege. As the two humble workers persist in their backbreaking toil, trying simply to fulfill by the sweat of their brow the almost mythologically daunting duty that has been assigned them, they are assailed by the demonic recalcitrance of the machine; by the scorn of a woman entrusted with that most sacred of trusts—the care of an infant; by the smug bullying of a man entrusted with the discharge of law and order; by the unreasonable demands of an elitist, societally celebrated "wise man" with a string of impressive degrees affixed to his name.

The two workers in the end determinedly achieve their goal, in spite of all these afflictions. The film is in many ways a meditation on work, that perhaps most sacred activity known to Western society, and the manner by which, after all, most humans on the planet spend the greater part of their time here. Up to a point, the film is about persistence and toil against insurmountable odds, the faithful fulfillment of the task given to one, no matter how seemingly impossible. As in "Big Business," however, events reach their climax with the piano being hacked viciously to pieces with an ax—showing all of the labor and dedication to have been in vain.

One could note that as the player piano is being slaughtered by the ax, it begins burbling "The Star-Spangled Banner," at which point all involved solemnly stand to attention with their hands over their hearts until the professor hurriedly switches it off and returns to the task of destroying the piano.

The same sort of analysis could be applied to any of their films and be equally valid. Slapstick comedy by its nature is ultimately subversive, as the absurd violence it contains is amusing and cathartic (and amusing for that reason) only insofar as it is leveled at that which is regarded as sacred, or is celebrated and revered as such by society—it is the banishment of all our false gods by ridicule. The slapstick violence of the Laurel and Hardy films is never an end in itself, as it was in the Keystone Kops and other lesser early silent comedies, or as it would be for The Three Stooges and the "shock" comedies of today—with their endless kicks delivered to various groins—where crudity and pain in themselves are seen to be the ultimate cause for laughter. With Laurel and Hardy, the violence is less painful than absurd, a manner by which the pretensions and aspirations of humanity are leveled, and we are reunited with our true, childish selves, behind the masks and behind the learned rituals of society.

The team was quite aware of the fact that the comedy they did was lowbrow and, as such, out of fashion according to the contemporary mores of their time. They reveled in the form that had given them birth—the two-reeler—and both resisted for as long as they could the pressure to go into feature-length films. This attitude, one imagines, would be directly opposite of most artists of the time, who would look upon going into features as a "graduation" into a form that carried with it a great deal more prestige. This is of one piece with the outlook of the films themselves, where pretension, and aspirations to "upward mobility" are roundly ridiculed.

One of Stan Laurel's biographers accused him of "reverse snobbery" in that if given the choice, he would rather have spent time with the grips and cameramen more than with those in loftier, more respectable positions.[3] All evidence suggests that both men were genuinely humble, uninterested in entertaining aspirations beyond their station. Laurel and Hardy remained dedicated to slapstick, with physical humor as their metier throughout their career.

Because that career was largely guided artistically by Stan Laurel, it's instructive to note the music hall act Stan created in 1910, which his biographer cites as "the first act in which ... (he) creates a comic entity essentially his own."[4] Titled "Rum'Uns from Rome," it was 15 minutes (just under the length of the standard two-reeler) of knockabout set in ancient Rome. In one of the gags, an ax fight takes place between Stan and his foil in the act, in which, through stage trickery, it appears as though Stan buries his ax in his opponent's head (the fellow disappears into a trap door in a Roman column, proffering a fake head into which the ax is imbedded— then he reappears with his head bloodied and apparently bisected by a duplicate ax). Stan, taking pity on his victim, then removes the ax and swaths the cranium in reams of bandages, which he then secures by hammering in a nail.

The violence here is as ridiculous as it is savage—and, in the case of pounding the nail in, resultant of a dim-wittedness we have not seen the last of. We are invited to laugh at the absurdity and the grotesque aspects of the violence: traits that resurface again and again through Laurel's work. Though pain is depicted, sometimes quite graphically, its ultimate value is that it makes human beings look silly, that it robs them of their dignity— care is taken so that it isn't repellent or vulgar. Audiences watching the sketch live before them were likely laughing as much at the device by which the unfortunate's head appeared to be gored by the ax as at the savagery of the action.

This presages the mechanism employed in the Laurel and Hardy films by which violence is abstracted into a sort of ephemeral shorthand. We see this in the brilliant use of sound in their first talkie, "Unaccustomed As We Are" (1929). Stan stumbles at the top of a staircase, then falls from view, while Ollie looks on aghast. A horrendous cacophony of crashes follows as Ollie reacts to what we can only imagine.

Likewise, in "The Music Box," we see the piano crate and we see Stan entering from the left, carrying a ladder. The end of the ladder disappears behind the crate; we hear a "thunk." Stan stumbles back, reacting to having struck something mighty solid with the end of that ladder. Ollie leaps up from behind the box, nursing his eye and howling with pain.

Both these segments depict violence only slightly less painful than that described in the Roman sketch, yet both use the idea of distancing the audience from the violence by the cleverness through which it is portrayed. At the same time, the audience is forced to become complicit in the violence by virtue of the fact that they are now compelled to imagine it.

This same sort of shorthand is seen in the sequences where the team falls from a height into a body of water in "The Music Box," and in "Hog Wild" (1930) and the resultant splash entering the frame from below is obviously caused by two buckets of water thrown from offscreen in opposite directions.

The element of the grotesque is another main element of Laurel's approach to humor. The use of the fake head embedded with the ax above is kin to Stan's massive swollen stomach after drinking the rainbarrel full of water at the end of "Below Zero" (1930); the sight of Stan and Ollie sitting with their legs wrapped around their necks at the end of "Going Bye-Bye!" (1934); with their heads twisted back to front 180 degrees in "The Live Ghost" (1934); or Ollie's elongated neck in Way Out West (1937). We are invited to laugh at the sheer outrageousness of the malformations we are shown, and the "freak endings" to many of the films that Laurel was so fond of also gain power from their preposterousness in contrast to the more customary homely, prosaic nature of the films—we laugh at the shock of suddenly seeing something so patently outlandish before us. Both comedians prided themselves on the methodically "real" nature of the films, and presumably both derived no little joy from throwing in a completely impossible gag right at the end of one of their faultlessly crafted pieces where humans move from catastrophe to catastrophe with irrefutable logic.

Of course, according to the worldview expressed in the films, life itself is grotesque. If Stan and Ollie are doomed to fail in every enterprise, their unsuccess isn't entirely due to their lack of intelligence. As we've seen, the world they inhabit is mean, cruel, short-tempered; the people they encounter are venal, cynical, and possessed by an unfathomable bitterness. If Stan and Ollie are dumber than everyone else — and even that's debatable — they are also different from the rest of the population depicted in the films in that they are not bitter, they are not cynical. They are magically immune from the sour world weariness that afflicts the rest of humanity. They are sincere in their mission, whatever it happens to be, however misguided it is, and Ollie in particular remains dedicated to his ideals, no matter how often he falls short of them. No one in the world around them seems to have any ideals at all. Figures of authority grimly impose control from above, while the common mass are industriously engaged in gypping each other, scavenging their subsistence from the backs of their fellow humans.

In any consideration of Laurel and Hardy, we are unavoidably obliged to encounter the disaster they bring on themselves and others. But from the perspective of any sane person, the world they inhabit in the films is already a disaster — the two clowns merely tear the mask off of it. The world is already a disaster because everybody's so tense and miserable with each other all the time. Likewise, in the failure of virtually every enterprise the team attempts, we are reminded that whatever the successes of our own enterprises, we are ultimately losers, we ultimately are made failures by death, which takes life itself from us. Through their images and situations the films parody the starkest truths about our world and our existence in it, they are made grotesque and absurd for our amusement because if they weren't embodied in beautifully executed comedy routines they'd scarcely be digestible at all. If disaster can be made to look grotesque we can then laugh at it and attain a sort of victory over it.

It makes perfect sense comedically because Stan and Ollie, in their innocence and undying optimism, need a cynical, uncaring world around them to act as their foil. Though Stan and Ollie are dumb, we see time after time that what the rest of the world does with its supposedly superior intelligence isn't all that commendable either. The people Stan and Ollie encounter may be more intelligent than the clowns, but they are invariably colder and crueler than Stan and Ollie could ever be. They also seem to be more miserable than the team, who, after all, have each other.

But the word "foil" can't be brought up without immediately following with the man who is the epitome of that term, as well as the embodiment of all the attributes listed above: Mr. James Finlayson.

This perpetually angry man, who can never encounter Laurel and Hardy without becoming utterly outraged and then embroiled in a terrible row with them, was the only supporting performer who came close to being featured as an equally prominent comedian with the team. In early films, in fact, he is given equal billing with the two comedians. The mere presence of Stan and Ollie is enough to send this doughty, pop-eyed Scotsman into paroxysms of disdain and disbelieving disgust — the vehemence of his reaction to them starts there and generally grows exponentially larger. One of comedy's most enthusiastic proponents of the gospel of "over the top," Finlayson was a scenery-chewer of the first order, whose dreams of being a star comic in his own right never came to be, likely because the "pull-out-all-stops" vigor of his performances was too taxing for audiences. This very quality, however, made him perfect as the walking exclamation point of the Laurel and Hardy films, his frenzied disapproval — and the absurd prop moustache he invariably wore — giving him both the look of an agitated insect as well as suggesting the harried Keystone Kop comedy stylings of which he was a dedicated throwback — exactly contrasted the gentleness and relaxed inanity of Stan and Ollie.

Whether he is seen as the complacent homeowner of middle-class leisure in his signature performance in "Big Business," a cantankerous authority figure in *Bonnie Scotland* (1935), or a pseudo-villain who tries to chisel and cheat the team in *Our Relations* (1936) and *Way Out West*, Finlayson is a man striving furiously to retain his dignity before being thoroughly divested of it by Stan and Ollie. Do what he will, they will always succeed in dragging him down to their level, however he insists that he does not belong there. He has nothing but contempt for them, but he can never escape them. He's simply trying to maintain his modest place in the world, but the presence of Stan and Ollie always tears him from it. Undoubtedly he hates them on sight because he realizes that they are the conduit through which he will unfailingly disgrace himself; he knows he will be made to confess that he is more akin to them than to the rest of the competent, businesslike world within which he's found his tenuous perch — hence the passionate sorrow mixed with the outrage of his "Doh!"

Another adversary is the diminutive Charlie Hall, another angry man but without the grand astonishment of Finlayson. Hall was an all-purpose performer who, unlike Finlayson, appeared in countless unfeatured roles in the films — such as waiters, cabbies — and who every so often was given a position of more prominence. He conveyed a painful sense of grievance, obviously in place long before the beginning of any given film, which was only aggravated by his encounters with the team. His battles with them in "Busy Bodies" (1933), "Them Thar Hills" (1934) and "Tit for Tat" (1935) display a man whose permanent disgruntlement is made ridiculous by his expression of it: Stan and Ollie always succeed in making him look thoroughly absurd. In "Tit for Tat," Ollie's offer to forgive and forget is met with icy refusal by Hall — he has nothing but cold-blooded hatred and spite in him.

Granted, his displeasure with the team isn't completely groundless. But there seems to be a general displeasure about life in Hall of which his anger at them is only a part. His treatment of his wife, for instance, before meeting Stan and Ollie in "Them Thar Hills" doesn't reveal him to be a very nice guy. In "Laughing Gravy" (1931) he is their landlord and is so driven to distraction by their antics that he seems near tears as he pleadingly begs them to leave: there's something almost childlike in his weeping. Even in his smaller roles, as the postman who says "That's it up there — on top of the stoop" in "The Music Box," or the desk clerk who tells Stan that the basement is downstairs in *Saps at Sea* (1940), he is glib and vaguely malevolent.

At equal prominence is Mae Busch, who shares much of Hall's brassy, sarcastic aspect. Always remembered as Ollie's wife, she also essayed other roles, such as a blackmailing tramp in "Chickens Come Home" (1931), a crazy attempted suicide in "Come Clean" (1931), a gangster's moll in "Going Bye-Bye!" a lovelorn artist's wife in "The Fixer-Uppers" (1935), and a mad serial killer in "Oliver the Eighth" (1934). That she was equally believable as a character upholding respectable middle-class values as she was in a role as someone thoroughly on the borders of society is due to her great gift as an actress, of course, but it's also due to the one quality all of these characters have in common as played by her: a sustained hysteria

Mae Busch is unhappy and she's going to let everyone know about it. To listen as she's going into one of her tirades is to feel as though one is being clouted repeatedly about the head. Many a time she is a tragic figure, as in "Their First Mistake" (1932), or as the suicide in "Come Clean." She is the source of dark passion in the films, as she commits adultery openly in *The Bohemian Girl* (1936) or reminds Ollie of his indiscreet past in "Chickens Come Home." She stretches a bit to show some concern for Ollie as his wife in *Sons of the Desert* and she's actually quite pleasant in "Them Thar Hills" and its sequel. But generally, Stan and the writers used Mae Busch's ability to convey hysteria in giving her roles as someone who lived on the last precipice of anger and despair before plunging into irretrievable insanity.

There are other great performers, such as Anita Garvin and Billy Gilbert and Edgar Kennedy, who were great artists in their own right. The snarling, bruiser tough guy was usually played by Walter Long, and if an inebriated lush was needed, Arthur Housman was the man for the job. And there are also the performers who play countless small roles in the films, such as Sam Lufkin and Harry Bernard, who float through the background of the comedies like distant, barely familiar relatives, playing a bellhop here, a truck driver there.

Often the other actors follow Laurel and Hardy in their practice of keeping their real names, or a variation thereof, onscreen. Thus, Finlayson is known as Finn in *Our Relations*, or as Mickey Finn in *Way Out West*, or just plain James Finlayson in "One Good Turn" (1931). When Charlie Hall opens a store in "Tit for Tat" it is known as Hall's Grocery; and after Charlie, suspecting Ollie of carrying on an affair with his wife played by Mae Busch, observes "There's no beating around the bush with me!" we have perhaps something in the nature of a triple entendre. Even actors on the screen for a split second are referred to by their real names, such as when the porter in *Block-Heads* played by James C. Morton is greeted with "Good morning, James!" or when Ollie's old friend in "Any Old Port" (1932), played by Harry Bernard is greeted with "Hello, Harry!"

This is all part of the larger naturalness and informality that runs through the films, a sort of relaxed unpretentiousness seen, as we've noted, in Hardy's use of the camera look, in their use of slapstick clichés now reinvigorated by their deliberate yet casual approach to them.

Contributing to this is the fact that all the films were shot in sequence — rather than the standard economically more efficient practice of filming all the scenes on one set, then moving to the next, finishing the scenes on that one, then moving on, regardless of the order the scenes would be appearing in the finished film. The Laurel and Hardy films were shot sequentially for the very good reason that quite often they did not know what the next scene would be until they got on the set. Improvisations and improvements were made to the script there, which was often just an outline that they treated as a "suggestion" at any rate. Many times they changed the direction of the entire film. Several of their classic films, such as "Big Business" and "Perfect Day" (1929), were originally envisioned as more elaborate pieces, but they found the first scenes so rich in comic possibilities once they began playing them that they became the whole movie — they found no difficulty in spinning 20 minutes of comedy out of the initial situation and were happy to call it a day.

This method not only allowed them to compose the action of the films freely, like music — rather than assembling them in the standard practice like a mosaic — but it contributed to the inner logic of the films, their practical "reality." One situation logically gives birth to the next, just like in real life, and so the accelerating chaos created in the films unfolds in an orderly, entirely logical manner before our eyes. This "logic" is crucially important to their comedy (as it isn't for Chaplin or the Marx Brothers), for it, along with Hardy's camera look, is the bedrock of the audience's identification with Stan and Ollie's plight. The films plod along methodically, in strict adherence to the laws of gravity and probability — aside from the occasional explosions of freakishness noted above — and make their homely way into the quagmire of defeat. Everything that happens is logical, but nothing makes much sense or seems particularly grounded in sanity.

Accompanying this stately procession is the sprightly, ever-optimistic music (in the sound films), which bubbles along with gay bemusement even as someone's having a handful of hair cut from his head and pasted to his chin with molasses. At times, it is true, the music can be poignant, or somewhat menacing, but generally it is joyful, ebullient, sunny, even when accompanying images that are gray and foreboding. In many ways the music is like Stan and Ollie themselves, upbeat in a downbeat world, open to life, and persistent — oft times it merrily ambles along through an entire film, sometimes at the forefront, often faintly but insistently warbling away in the background, at the periphery of the soundtrack's domain, framing the crashes and howls.

Le Roy Shield and particularly T. Marvin Hatley were the primary composers of these melodies. Hatley also composed the fractured hurdy-gurdy tune that opens the Laurel and Hardy films and is their theme song, "The Dance of the Cuckoos."

The particular care taken in the making of the films, and the dedication to quality seen in filming them in sequence despite the cost of doing so, is also seen in the extensive previews given to the films at the time of their making. As noted before, many a time the Hardy camera look would be lengthened or shortened after a preview, based on how long the laugh was—the object was to create a perfectly timed comedy on film, where the actors, as if onstage, wait out the laugh before going on to the next business at hand. So the comedies were refined scientifically in a way, tailored to the highest point of efficiency in fulfilling their ultimate purpose of eliciting as much laughter as possible.

This dedication and care could have been manifested nowhere else but at the Hal Roach Studios, where Laurel and Hardy made all their best films. The studio was one that was completely dedicated to comedy and nothing else, and there was a personal dedication by Hal Roach himself to the quality of that comedy. He made possible the expense involved in taking so much care with these nuances of craft that elevate the films from being forgettable transient diversions of their day, to being utterly unique cinematic experiences— and, of course, some of the funniest films ever made. It was a small studio, for the most part producing two-reel comedies. It was the only studio in Hollywood where characters of such subtlety and depth as Stan and Ollie could have been created over a series of films and allowed to grow and function.

This was something the team themselves found out when they left the studio and went to the larger studios, expecting gamely that they could take the same method, the same working practices, the same care and attention to detail, in short, the entire entity known as Laurel and Hardy, along with them. They were in for a rude awakening. The approach toward the art exemplified by Hal Roach as compared to the approach taken by the faceless, bureaucratic executives of the larger studios is like comparing a dedicated, painstaking crafter of shoes to the management of a shoe factory. Roach was a visionary, like Sam Phillips of Sun Records. He created a completely singular environment: the only place in the universe these films could have been conceived and created.

And of course the films couldn't have been conceived or created if not for the meeting of two middle-aged comedians of middling success, from vastly disparate backgrounds—from different countries— who found themselves at that place in the universe in 1926.

4

SILENCE

The silent films of Laurel and Hardy can be divided into three stages. There are the early films where they seem for the most part to be coincidentally thrown together in the same film — in some of these entries they don't even share any scenes. They are simply working actors playing parts in comedies produced by Hal Roach, who was casting around trying to find a comedy star who would replace Harold Lloyd. Lloyd had achieved success with Roach, then left for greener pastures. Roach had a stock company of versatile comedic actors he kept working in a succession of comedies called the All Star series. Laurel and Hardy were two of these actors and their respective talents ensured that they would be featured in various roles in the series with increasing prominence.

The second stage of their silent film career consists of the films in which they are consciously teamed, put together purposely with the objective of creating a new entity. This was done at the inspiration and largely through the guidance of director and supervisor Leo McCarey. In these films we see the genesis of the characters and the relationship between them, the evolution of their comedic style and aesthetic.

This dovetails into the third stage, wherein their modus operandi is firmly established, and they achieve mastery over their form — turning out their first masterpiece ("Big Business," [1929]) shortly before the introduction of sound.

Sound would flesh out the characters in many ways and shift the emphasis of their comedy to some degree, but the essence of their work — all that they would become, and all that they would elaborate on in their future efforts—can be found in their silent films. To many audiences, now familiar mostly with the team's sound comedies, the silent films may seem austere, less welcoming. At the same time, there is a purity to these works, as with all of silent cinema, in that they are more faithful to the all-encompassing world of dreams, of the subconscious. Laurel and Hardy were born in this silent world of image and gesture — they were not confined to it, but they took the part of this dream land that was themselves into the more realistic, raucous territories where their disasters smashed and crashed with real smashes and crashes.

The freer qualities of silent filmmaking — the less technical concerns than what sound films ushered in, the ability to shoot anywhere (on location, out of doors) with relative ease — possibly allowed the characters the space to grow in ways that perhaps they couldn't have in the sound films that the silents laid the foundation for. Laurel himself preferred the silents and later described as the most pleasurable part of his career the days when they were working to make themselves known as a team.[1]

When Stan Laurel began work for Hal Roach in 1926, it wasn't for the first time. He had been contracted to make comedy shorts for the producer twice before, once in 1918 and again in 1923. These series of shorts were both part of his continual attempts to escape the hectic strain of constant vaudeville touring by establishing himself in movies. His biographer notes that a great part of this determination was also fueled by Laurel's desire to escape the tempestuous relationship he shared with his common-law wife and performing partner, which grew considerably more heated and abusive while on the road. Laurel needed to find his place in film or — seemingly — be confined to the endless cycle of travel and strain forever.

After the second failed attempt with Roach in 1923, Laurel was approached by independent producer Joe Rock to make a series of two-reelers. Rock astutely recognized that Laurel's problem, personally as well as artistically, was his common-law wife. Laurel was known at this time throughout the industry as a drinker, who often let his personal problems impair his work. It was well known that his wife insisted she be in the films, often cast inappropriately as an ingenue.

After several unpleasant encounters with Mae Laurel, the producer worked out a plan by which she would be dispatched back to her native Australia at his expense. In this manner, Rock guaranteed his investment in Stan, and the series of two-reelers were completed smoothly and without disruption.

News of Mae Laurel's departure and of Stan's subsequent rehabilitation and full-fledged rededication to creating comedy spread through the industry, and new offers began coming through for Stan. Hal Roach was ready to welcome him back into the fold. Whether Stan left Rock because he genuinely feared he would never receive the percentages promised him, or simply because Roach offered him more money, the comedian returned to the Roach lot in 1925 — but not as a comedian.

Since Rock still had Laurel two-reelers to release, he rightfully insisted Stan refrain from appearing as a comedian in the Roach films. And so

Laurel, who had always been involved in all the creative aspects of his solo films, returned to Roach as a writer and director. In the latter function he was trained by Richard Jones, a man Stan revered and who taught him much about the mechanics of film comedy — an education that would serve Stan well in the coming years.

Stan began directing one- and two-reelers. In several of them he used Oliver Hardy, who had been working on the lot since 1924, as a character actor, foil, and heavy (that is, a villain, so-called because of the heavy makeup such roles generally required). Stan had been aware of Hardy for years — they had worked together in the Stan Laurel comedy "Lucky Dog" in 1919, and they had both subsequently supported the comedian Larry Semon at different times in his comedies. When Stan had worked as a comedian for Joe Rock, Hardy had been suggested as a foil for him, but Stan steadfastly refused, for the same reason he would later rejoice in him — he knew that Hardy was explosively funny. At that time he felt he didn't need the competition.

In one of those strange twists of fate, it was because of an accident of Hardy's that Stan was propelled from his director's chair into clowning again. Hardy was to play the role of a butler in a two-reeler entitled "Get 'Em Young." The weekend before shooting was to begin, Hardy, an enthusiastic gourmet, burned his arm while cooking. Stan was pressed by Richard Jones to fill the role at the last minute. When he demurred, being perfectly satisfied with writing and directing and apparently having no desire to return to acting again, he was offered a raise. He played the part.

Jones saw an added quality in Stan's clowning that convinced him Laurel had a future in performing. Stan was not so convinced, or at least that was his position until another raise was forthcoming — predicated on his continued taking of parts in the comedies they were making.

It is sobering to think that one of the greatest clowns of all time needed to be so persuaded to step reluctantly before the cameras once more. Was it because of the agreement with Joe Rock in which he had promised not to perform at Roach's? Or was it because he'd finally found security in writing and directing gags rather than in performing them, a security he didn't care to risk by returning to the rather more precarious occupation of clowning? If it was true that he felt completely fulfilled in his writing and directorial tasks, he was undoubtedly aware that in his past clowning he'd never found a suitable form for his talents, that, as he later said, he never made up his mind about what kind of comic he was going to be. Was it this artistic crisis he was seeking to avoid, and the lack of success and the pain connected with it?

The answers to these questions are mostly unknowable, but what is known is that the next film Stan was obligated to appear in also featured the hefty fellow who'd propelled him back into films to begin with, now sufficiently recovered from the nasty grease burn on his arm.

"45 Minutes from Hollywood" features both Laurel and Hardy, but like several other of these early films that do so, they do not share any scenes. In many of the early films, there seems to have been no attempt to team them — because Stan had returned to acting they were both featured in many of the same films simply because they were two of the best comics on the lot. In time, it became clear that they were the two best comics on the lot, their parts grew increasingly larger, and their teaming became inevitable.

In hindsight, their teaming would seem inevitable in the next film they appeared together in: "Duck Soup." Long considered a lost film, it was recovered in the 1970s and rewrote the accepted history of the team, which stated that the Stan and Ollie characters grew gradually over a period of time in a series of films. In "Duck Soup," they seem, by some strange fluke, to be already a crude version of the characters that would define them.

As noted before, the film was based on a sketch by Stan's father, Arthur Jefferson. The idea — of two hobos on the run from the law hiding in a house, then forced to impersonate the master and his maid when people come by to inquire about renting the estate — would also be used three years later in "Another Fine Mess" (1930), when their characters had fully matured.

Yet here in the first film where they share pretty much equal screen time, we see Stan in his derby hat already, alternately diffident, mildly resentful, or weeping with confusion — a rather more canny fellow than the blessed simpleton who would evolve later, but still put upon, still emanating a curious vulnerability. Hardy affects a top hat and a heavy five o'clock shadow, but already he has the officious air, and a stubborn insistence on dignity and decorum. He also sports a monocle in the early scenes, as another manner to grasp onto an illusionary aristocratic identity. He bullies Stan, shoves him around, knocks him on the head once. When hiding from danger, he jumps behind a curtain, and when Stan comes to join him, he callously kicks Stan out. When Stan finds a card on a door and begins to read it, Hardy takes the card from him and points to himself self-importantly in the familiar "I'll handle this, if you don't mind" gesture.

For all of his pretension to high society and dignity, the Hardy character — who is a hobo forced to impersonate a millionaire — is notably coarser than the Ollie we come to know later. The Laurel character is likewise coarser, more prosaic, than the Stan to come. They are clowns in the familiar guise of the tramp, but they don't have the shining innocence of the later characters, the methodical dumbness.

What these characters do have in common with the later teaming is the fact of their relationship — they are together as a self-evident duo from the first to the last — and, also the pretension to dignity, particularly on Hardy's part, no matter what straits one finds oneself in.

At the time the film was just made as one in a succession of films, each one trying for as many laughs as possible. Stan, in casting about for a story for a film, brought from his past the premise of a sketch of his father's. The film is only mildly amusing, so likely attained little more than moderate success— perhaps if it had been funnier, the partnership would have been established then and there. But one wonders if, as more conscious effort was applied to the teaming of the two comics months in the future, this film was referenced, for its sense of what their relationship should be, and the thwarted desire for dignity, which is the mainspring of their endeavors.

A faint memory of "Duck Soup" must have persisted, and so it could be said that many of the important ingredients of the comic creation that is Laurel and Hardy were bequeathed on the team by that grand old man of the theater: the gag creator of the previous generation, A. J. Jefferson.

Since no great fanfare attended the release of "Duck Soup," the two comedians were placed haphazardly in a succession of films over the next six months. In "Slipping Wives," they share brief, antagonizing scenes as a delivery man and a butler. In "Love 'Em and Weep," Stan has a predominant role, Hardy a bit part. Laurel is also featured in "Why Girls Love Sailors," with Hardy in the supporting cast — they share one scene together. In "With Love and Hisses," they are featured more equally, but in adversarial roles— Laurel is the dim-witted recruit, Hardy as the sergeant is his foil. In "Sailors, Beware!" Laurel is a cabdriver and Hardy is the purser of a ship — they share a few scenes together.

The next film that would return to the idea of specifically teaming them together from the opening frames is "Do Detectives Think?" Finlayson here is a judge who, at the beginning of the film, sentences a killer to hang, and the killer vows revenge. Naturally the killer escapes, and just as naturally — according to what's natural in silent short subjects made in 1927 — gets a job as a butler at Finlayson's mansion. A detective agency is phoned to secure protection of Finlayson; the manager vows to send over two of its strongest men.

The door opens, and — incredibly — Laurel and Hardy walk in, replete in derbies (Hardy has followed Laurel's lead regarding headwear since their last teamed film) and clothed in their familiar rumpled business suits and respective bow ties and neckties. Hardy sports a dapper, small mustache, which seems to hover in the very center of his exactly round face though it needs to be trimmed back a bit here, so its absurd pointlessness can evoke the grandiose and trivial vanity of its possessor. Laurel is still in the mode of glib dumbness, rather than helpless imbecility, and his normal, slicked-down hairstyle contributes to this. He is dumb, but he is not as likable in his innocence as the later Stan is—he's not "out of this world" yet. It's striking how much this is emphasized by his hair lying shiny and flat on his head rather than standing straight up in gravity-defying shoots. Even his derby is a normal, mundane one rather than the more appropriate child's derby he wears in later films.

In the first few seconds after they enter, they perform the first true Laurel and Hardy gag. Stan goes to sit on the manager's desk, moving aside the mail spike. Ollie stops him with his "not you, but me" gesture, and officiously lowers himself to sit on the desk instead. The mail spike punctures his posterior and he leaps up in pain. Hardy is beginning to dominate Laurel with his sense of self-importance. Laurel is beginning to cause Hardy pain. The dynamic is beginning to get set in motion.

The derbies and suits are undoubtedly their approximation of what seedy detectives were thought to wear in 1927. This apparel would become essential to the Stan and Ollie perception of themselves and their relation to the world. Their aspiration to attain success, or at least to imitate the trappings of that success, at all times, is signified by the unprosperous small business men's suits they wear, always trying to get out of the red, always pursuing respect and acceptance yet always being three steps behind, watching helplessly as it slips from their fingers. Their shabby formality displays the distressing sense of being like children, playing dress-up in clothes that they mistakenly believe (and hope) will cause them to be regarded like adults. They ritually appear in them time and time again with the idiotic confidence that they confer upon them some sort of instant dignity, completely unaware that their threadbare attempt at gentility renders them more absurd than if they had made no attempt at all — yet this practice also reflects their optimism. As beaten down and down-at-the-heel as they become in most of their films, they never relax their sartorial insistence on their jackets and neckties. No matter how bedraggled they are, they insist on meeting fate in at least their own modest attempt at effecting dignity. After all, they must always be ready for that grand opportunity they fully expect to arise at any time.

Here, though, the suits are only the guise of two dubious detectives, as are the derbies, which will become even more important accoutrements of the Laurel and Hardy personas. The derbies are, quite literally, the crowning glory of Stan and Ollie's obsession with trying to fit into the world, of attempting to serve some vision of dignity and refinement that exists entirely in their own minds. Their insistence on wearing identical headgear at all times is as bizarre an aesthetic pretension to respectability as Ollie's quarter-inch-sized moustache. The commonality of their hats is something that joins and unites them against the world, from which they derive identity and strength.

We are reminded of that other rather famous derby-wearing comedian: Stan's former roommate, Charlie Chaplin. Laurel was probably correct when asserting to his biographer that, rather than following Chaplin in his use of the derby, the team were following in the same tradition as Chaplin was adhering to—using the hat generally accepted as the one that identified comedians in the British music hall tradition.[2] There, as in the case of Chaplin, Laurel, and Hardy, the derby was the chosen headwear of the clowns because it bespoke a reaching for dignity that the wearer was completely incapable of ever attaining. The derby signifies the clown's occupation—in his aspirations and failures he satirizes our own aspirations and failures, and when these artists are at their best, not far from the surface are evoked the biggest failures of all—tragedy, death—and in the pure laughter they provoke we obtain freedom from even these.

Chaplin's use of the derby was quite different, for though he wore it to confer dignity upon himself, there was no doubt in the Tramp's mind that he was considerably more dignified than any of the people he encountered. Chaplin was entirely convinced of his own dignity, and, though the perpetual outsider, he often seems rather ambivalent about entering society at all. The Tramp has his own code and morals and aesthetic and doesn't really care about the judgment of the world he's living in—his derby is like a crown, and his cane is his scepter, for he certainly is king of his own chosen domain. His tragedy—his pathos—is due to the fact that he is always, and always will be, alone in that kingdom.

For Stan and Ollie, the hats are the hopeful pretensions toward the dignity Charlie is convinced he already possesses. Their ambitions are more modest than his, their pathos less pronounced—for they are not alone, they have each other. The source of humor in Laurel and Hardy is due to their failures in attaining dignity; for Chaplin, it is in his agile, absurd attempts to maintain that dignity in a harsh, unjust world. But all the clowns ultimately obtain a much larger dignity than that which they aspire to: the Tramp in his singular dedication to his strange ideal and in how he triumphs in his uniqueness over the stale, drab society around him; Stan and Ollie for their dedication to their vision of how wonderful they imagine it is to belong to that society and to be important. They are on the periphery of society looking in, and are looking fondly at all of us, with no malice or bitterness—they only ask to be accepted. There is something poignant and pure about their faith in a better tomorrow, in their devotion to their vision of how sweet life can be. But they are never accepted, and for all their good intentions, everywhere they go they wreak violence and disaster.

They are more recognizably children than Charlie is—whose spirit is ageless in that it encapsulates all ages and all sexes. There is a sense, again, that they are merely children playing dress-up, and in their clumsy attempts to fit into "the world of adults" and in their physical clumsiness in general—it's evident why children often become their instant fans. They are grown men whose traumas are children's traumas, whose problems are children's problems. And along with the disasters they get themselves into trying to fit into the adult world, on another scale we have Stan as child and Ollie as adult, with Ollie instructing, correcting and "disciplining" Stan. Though Stan continually fails in his ineptitude, Ollie ultimately always accepts Stan on some base level, and he takes care of him no matter what misery his "mistakes" may bring. This is a comforting message indeed to children, whose lives are the series of fumbling mistakes they make as they attempt to adhere to the rituals of the strange world they've been born into. As with Stan and Ollie, the sober world of adults is largely a mystery to them and one they can only imagine and aspire to.

This childlike aspect is sounded strongly in the second scene of "Do Detectives Think?" The two detectives are on their way to Finlayson's mansion, which happens to be right next to a graveyard. Their hats are blown off by a sudden wind into the graveyard, and Hardy sends Laurel in to fetch them. This initiates a lengthy scene in which the two become petrified by open graves and shadows on the wall. The segment, which contributes nothing to the plot of the film of the whole, attests to the existence of the intention on someone's part to bring the two comedians together—the scene seems to exist simply to establish and explore the sense of their being frightened children in a world beyond their comprehension.

Also established here is the prime ritual connected to their headwear—the endless hat-switching routine. Their hats having been retrieved, Laurel hands Hardy a derby as he dons the one he believes to be his own. Upon putting the derbies on, they find they have the wrong ones, so Laurel repossesses them, hands Hardy what he believes to be the proper derby once more—only to find they have somehow reversed themselves again. Hardy grows steadily more annoyed as Laurel regains the derbies, and through some perverse sleight of hand, renders the incorrect headwear once again.

It is obvious that it is utterly beyond Laurel's power to provide the two men with their proper hats. It is evident that they will never ascertain they have the wrong hats until they've placed them on their heads. And Hardy, his fury growing with each new confused indignity, will nonetheless trust Laurel to furnish him with the correct hat the next time, and the greater his anguished frustration will be as Laurel again helplessly hands him the wrong hat.

It is our first glimpse into their dumb helplessness before intransigent material reality. They simply can't cope with the simplest of tasks, and they never learn in the least from experience. This accounts for the slowness and the repetition of their comedy: two major complaints of their detractors. The humor lies in the accelerating cycle of confused frustration and the various levels of psychological nuance portrayed therein. In one sense, their routines of this type, of which the hat switch is the premiere example, express a view of the nature of reality. Who knows what it is that continually drives Laurel to give Hardy the wrong hat? It seems as much a mystery to Laurel as it is to any of us. Why does Hardy leave himself open to becoming progressively enraged when he could easily examine his hat before he puts it on — or take charge of handing out the hats himself, since it apparently means so much to him? The two men never think of asking themselves such questions. They merely keep passing the hats frustratedly back and forth. And if left to themselves, they will steadfastly continue doing so for all eternity. In "Do Detectives Think?" they get the wrong hats a full five times. The routine defines the characters and their relationship to each other and to the world.

After this, the film returns to its rather typical All Stars series plot. They arrive at Finlayson's mansion, and a lot of getting scared and running around transpires. They realize Finlayson's butler is his would-be murderer. At the end, Laurel captures the murderer and puts him in the closet. It happens to be the closet where Hardy is hiding. Hardy emerges with two black eyes— and shortly thereafter administers two black eyes to Laurel. They depart the scene after one more hat switch.

Certainly we can see here at least a crude rendering of the characters that are to be. Just by their appearance alone, they would seem to be very near to Laurel and Hardy in their final incarnation. However, perhaps it's understandable that this fact didn't seem so inevitable in 1927 because they were placed in several more films in which they played radically different characters in different costumes.

"Flying Elephants" (1928) is a prehistoric jaunt featuring the two comedians as cavemen in animal skins. They are cast as adversaries and do not share a scene together until the end. "Sugar Daddies" features Finlayson in trouble again, trying to avoid a forced marriage. Hardy is his butler and Laurel is his lawyer. It is one of the films in which all three comedians are given equal prominence and screen time. All that anticipates the future here is Hardy's insistence on Laurel removing his hat when he enters the mansion — prefiguring the many times in the future when Ollie will be at great pains to remind Stan to remove his headwear when entering a domicile.

The next film in which they seem consciously teamed is "The Second Hundred Years," (1927), wherein they are two prisoners sharing a cell. They wear the requisite horizontally striped uniforms and, most notably, both comedians shaved their heads for their roles in this two-reeler comedy. The sight of their bald heads is an occasion for unwaning wonderment, a vision of unending oddness, an oddness that unites and defines them in contrast to the world around them. In their baldness they have been symbolically— and, as events were to prove, literally—shorn of their past, in order to freshly grow into their new life, and their new partnership.

Their names in the film are Big Goofy and Little Goofy. They try to escape by tunneling out—and end up digging straight into the warden's office. They are returned to their cell, as a water main they've punctured while digging their tunnel floods the warden's office. They escape by turning their uniforms inside out, seizing some painter's supplies and "painting" their way out of prison. They leap into the back of a limousine, eject its passengers, and don their clothing. The identities they've assumed just happen to be those of two French penologists who've come to study American prisons—and so they are handily dispatched right back into the prison, where, after attending a dinner given in "their" honour by the governor, they are led on a tour of the cell block and are recognized and swiftly reincarcerated.

With its succession of inventive and clever gags, "The Second Hundred Years" is by far the best of the films they have been teamed in to date. In his role as Little Goofy, Laurel is given a little more prominence than Hardy here. Laurel is still moving quicker and more energetically than the Stan we will soon come to know. For his part, Hardy is still the large, gruff, rough-hewn fellow. From the opening frames, however, there is the sense that they are together and belong together—the first sighting of them, their physical contrast made more evident by their matching uniforms, seems "right" in some indefinable yet undeniable way. There is also the growing sense that Hardy is Laurel's "protector"—a sort of big brother and father rolled into one. An expression of this is in a bit of business used several times here, but rarely, if ever, after—confronted by fearsome circumstances, Little Goofy repeatedly leaps up into Big Goofy's comforting arms.

It is also here that they share their first great scene. As they saunter from the prison in disguise as painters, under the watchful eye of a suspicious cop, they assiduously whitewash all in their path—though not without a certain aesthetic flair into the bargain. Starting with the touching up of a curbstone at the prison gates—done with keen appraisal and meticulous exactitude, they progress to the street, where storefronts, lampposts, fire hydrants, and automobiles all get a freshening up. They enter into this "job" with full dedication and enjoyment and the message is clear: they are children, easily distracted and as easily engrossed in new and spirited play — they are mutable in their attentions, open to all possibilities. There is a palpable sense of freedom, of copacetic music between the two comedians as they perform the routine. Their chemistry is obvious.

The scene, like so much else in the film, was the brainchild of Leo McCarey, who had been watching the two men performing, both separately and together, for some time. McCarey, now hailed as one of the great American directors for later work such as *Going My Way* and *The Awful Truth*, was at the time a writer and occasional director for the All Star series. He had been pushing for a while for Laurel and Hardy to work together more often — likely, he'd been responsible for their growing prominence in their last several films. He recognized that they were the two best comedians at the studio and was the first to see the complement they provided for each other artistically. Further, he saw that what they had in common, more than all the other comedians on the lot, was a deep integrity and sincerity at the heart of their performances — that they were great actors, able to invest their characters with real warmth and humanity, with solid psychological truth.

McCarey had been working with Roach comedian Charley Chase and had constructed with him a modus operandi for the making of their comedies, whereby slapstick was no longer completely madcap and slapdash, but underpinned with psychological reality and logic. This approach insisted upon convincing characterizations, and the solid motivations for the actions of those characters, however absurd or violent they may be. The nuances and subtleties flowing from that sense of the inner reality of the characters give more weight to and make more memorable the slapstick antics.

The nature of McCarey's genius was in this area of characterization, and this is what made his films distinctive for his entire career. There was nothing McCarey liked to do better than to flesh out some memorable characters onscreen and then to play with them and watch them interact, fight, love — all for the audience to simply visit and partake of their common humanity for the duration of the movie. *Going My Way* (1941) features a young priest, Bing Crosby, interacting with an older one, Barry Fitzgerald, for the entire film. The film is about their relationship, and in a larger sense about youth replacing age, about the generational march of time, and about the relationship we have with the aged, even as we are becoming the aged. The film is alive with the love McCarey has for the two characters — his films in general express a love for humanity in all its frailties and failures. At the same time, they are sharply observed psychologically — his characters are so vivid precisely because they are alive with complexity. So true is he in devotion to humanity that he accepts it in its untidiness, its contradictions, its complications.

In *Going My Way* Bing Crosby humors old Barry Fitzgerald over the course of most of the film, letting win him a golf game by letting the old man think he's scored a hole in one. There is a scene about three quarters of the way though the film when the two men are playing checkers. It has a leisurely, improvised feel, a strong atmosphere of warmth and humor. It's completely enjoyable, but it serves no purpose to the plot — except for the fact that Bing Crosby wins. It is important for McCarey, in his allegiance to the reality of the characters, to show that the old man is not without dignity, that Bing Crosby has not been robbing him of his dignity through his kindnesses, that their relationship contains enough honesty for the younger man to let the older man lose. So much does McCarey believe in the integrity of his characters, in their reality, that he includes a scene specifically to address any potential imbalance in their relationship, and to affirm their humanity.

It is this humanity, and the warm expression of it, that McCarey saw in the performances of Laurel and Hardy separately, and perhaps he saw that in tandem each was able to draw even more of these qualities from the other. He saw two actors with the capability to actualize his ideal of comedy, which unfolded leisurely and elegantly and was rich with psychological logic. If it was he that was responsible for their increasing prominence, for their "showcase" segment in the graveyard in the middle of "Do Detectives Think?", "The Second Hundred Years" is his most aggressive effort at teaming them. As well, it is a swiftly moving and very funny comedy.

In his efforts to move Laurel and Hardy together and promote them as a team, McCarey faced considerable opposition — from Stan Laurel. Not only was Laurel not interested in teaming with Hardy, he really wasn't interested in being a film comedian at all. He felt he had found his identity as a writer and a director, which he longed to return to doing. If "Duck Soup," their first film, featured them playing their eventual screen characters in embryo, and each successive "consciously teamed" film shows them further refining those characters that they seem to slip so easily and naturally into — as though preordained — surely Laurel was beginning to feel the inevitability of the new creation. Yet he resisted that inevitability, having derived incredible artistic satisfaction from actualizing his comedic ideas from offscreen.

Hardy, for his part, as the veteran of over 200 supporting roles at various studios, was intensely desirous of the solidification of the new partnership and of the steady work and increased income it would mean for him.

Somewhere around this area, through the making of this and their next few films, Laurel was able to make the transition, was able to realize that the creativity he'd found such fulfillment in backstage, rather than being terminated, could be funneled into this new entity that was coming to be — that the excitement and pleasure could be transferred undiminished to this new end. As each great film followed another, with a thrilling sense of discovery and exploration, he saw that all his ideas could be expressed through this new entity — fully, gloriously — and that this expression would be his life's work. At the same time, he must have felt relief at finally accepting himself as a comedian again and ceasing to deny his genius in the sphere of performance.

Along with this, Laurel shared many of McCarey's convictions about comedy — Hal Roach later stated that Stan "adored" Leo McCarey.[3] Laurel, too, felt that comedy was better at a slower pace, so that one could savor its many subtleties. He was also an adherent of the philosophy of strong characterizations and action that was firmly rooted in logic of the personalities of all involved. Contiguous with the slowness was Laurel's growing recognition that the two characters should be dumb — not somewhat dumb, but vastly, unimaginably, beyond all prior observation or experience dumb. This was beginning to be foreshadowed in the hat-switch routine. His conviction that the two clowns should be monumentally stupid dovetailed perfectly with McCarey's and his own preference for the leisurely, natural pace — two dull-witted cottonbrains unable to think quickly certainly wouldn't be able to act quickly.

Stan and Ollie in their stupidity are rarely loud or brash or reckless and unthoughtful, as so many stupid people are. Part of their slowness, their grace, is a result of their extreme gentleness, their pure aspiration at being gentlemen, in every sense of that word, however stupid they are. Such is their gentleness that it is that much more lamentable when their endeavors end in violence and destruction — as most of them are wont to do. However, they remain committed to their ideal of being "gentlemen" with a purity of purpose and innocence that is inseparable from their stupidity. Though the characters can never become the societal gentlemen they aspire to be, their dignity is in the fact that they are that rarity: two truly gentle men. They possess genuine gentleness, and it's likely that McCarey saw that that was the one thing the two seemingly disparate men — disparate in every sense of the word — shared both onscreen and offscreen.

By all accounts, all of these ideas, qualities, and artistic excitement came to fruition in their very next film, "Hats Off," (1927), which was something of a sensation at its release. One contemporary reviewer stated, "It is no exaggeration to say that the entire audience bordered on hysteria at the climax of this two-reeler," after stating that he himself laughed so hard he wept.[4] Stan Laurel later recalled: "I never heard laughs— so many laughs— in so short a time before."[5]

"Hats Off" featured the return of the derbies and the rumpled suits. It also featured James Finlayson, less as an equally featured comic than as a frustrated foil of the inept twosome. As a result of his brushcut in his last film, Laurel's hair was beginning to grow upward in tangled, unkempt spikes. The film is the tale of two washing-machine salesmen, sweating as they transport that massive appliance up and down a seemingly endless flight of stairs— the same business, and evidently the same stairs, as would be used for the premise of their later sound masterpiece "The Music Box."

The return of the derbies also signaled the return of the routine inseparable from the identical headwear: the endless hat mix-up. If its introduction in "Do Detectives Think?" was the first inkling that these characters might be fighting a losing battle with material reality, its dominance in "Hats Off"— in many ways it forms the essence of the latter comedy — verifies this most important truth about the new entity being formed. For as harried, frustrated, and confused as the two aspiring salesmen are by their task — and by their endless staircase — as much so are they undone by their constant inability to place the correct hats on their heads each time they lose them.

It happens repeatedly, and in the end culminates in the establishment of another Laurel and Hardy trademark: the "reciprocal destruction" routine. Leo McCarey had recently attended a dinner in New York at which the impish snapping loose of a few bow ties among friends spread throughout the entire function until it was virtually tieless.[6] This sudden acceleration to swift retaliation, this reversion to childish spite, to vengeful anarchy, McCarey observed, was really closer to the surface of civilized behavior than anyone dares to realize. The exhilarating drive to fight, the will to power, is only one step away at any time. In our admission of this— and of the fact that society, civilization, are really only façades constructed to conceal and give superficial order, give a presentable face to this dread pursuance of superiority — we laugh with relief at the portrayal of that which we know inwardly yet don't dare to acknowledge: that society is the thinnest of membranes protecting us from the complete chaos that is ourselves and that civilized behavior is simply a shield behind which lurks a tireless appetite for violence and destruction.

Having endured various business frustrations and physical indignities over the course of the day, the two clowns become enraged over their inability — once again — to place their derbies on the correct heads. They begin to attack each other's derbies. Passersby become involved in the fray. The fight spreads like a contagion until the entire street is filled with men ripping off each other's hats and destroying them. The fury between the two men infects the populace at large — which is only too ready to lay aside their simulation of responsible conduct and act our their part in the savagery. The two clowns, trying to get in step with society, ultimately destroy it. Their steadily building and repetitive ritual of incompetent frustration finds catharsis by dispersing itself through the general populace.

It was this final segment that inspired much of the great acclaim with which "Hats Off" was received. The film introduces so many factors that are integral to Laurel and Hardy — and its popularity ensured that they would all become part of their standard repertoire. By all accounts "Hats Off" was the chrysalis of their career, binding them, showing the potency of their magic together to be undeniable.

The term "by all accounts" is used because no copies of this apparently seminal film are known to presently exist. As many have observed, because of the flammable quality of nitrate film, and considering the cavalier attitude taken toward these films by their creators, we are fortunate that any of these ancient comedies survive at all. All that we have left of "Hats Off" are still photographs, its continuity script, and the praise of its reviewers. It is the only Laurel and Hardy short to be lost in its entirety and, as the years pass and the chances grow more and more remote that it will ever be found, it becomes more and more likely that this foundational film that elicited so much laughter in its time will remain forever the stuff of myth, a film known only by its legend. As these words are written, time is presumably taking the last minds with the faintest fading memories of having seen "Hats Off" from us forever.

After this triumphant breakthrough, their next film would seem, superficially, to backtrack. In "Putting Pants on Philip," they are not in their accustomed derbies and suits, and their partnership is not a self-evident fact from the beginning frames. The film is the tale of the honorable Piedmont Mumblethunder (Hardy) claiming his nephew, Philip (Laurel), fresh off the boat from Scotland. Embarrassed by Philip's kilts, and his general weirdness, Mumblethunder tries to get him into some pants. The film is a variation on one of the oldest comic situations known: that of the culture clash, or fish-out-of-water device.

The idea for the film originated with Stan Laurel, who had spent a considerable part of his childhood growing up in Scotland. He had several close Scottish friends and often wondered how they would fare if they chanced to visit him in California. The idea is fully and inventively developed here, and the result, like the two films before it, is an excellent comedy that undoubtedly did much to advance the team. Even if "the team" as we know it doesn't seem, at first glance, to be particularly present in this effort.

Looking closer, we might see that Hardy's character — pompous and smug, and so concerned with his own dignity and social standing — anticipates Ollie's obsessions and aspirations. Likewise, in Laurel's character, the "other," who comes to knock Hardy from his perch in society, who embarrasses and torments him simply through the fact of his existence, who turns Hardy's character into a figure of ridicule before the eyes of his community — (in the end, Hardy is humbled and lowered beneath ground level, up to his ears in mud in one of those handy colossal mud puddles) — in all of this we see the Stan of the future, sabotaging Ollie's presumptuous attempts to make his way in the world. Though the two familiar characters that are Laurel and Hardy are not here, the basic situation of "Philip" is the essential dynamic of Stan and Ollie writ large: the struggle toward absorption in society and the conflicting anarchic drive away from society, or the adult and the child.

Part of the film's greatness is in its pacing, in the way Hardy is continually thwarted in keeping Laurel's weirdness — his distinctly un-Stan — like proclivity for chasing women in a Harpo-esque manner — under wraps, out of the attention of the town's populace who seem endlessly fascinated by this bizarre new foreigner. Continually, Hardy thinks he has Laurel under control, only to see a mob of people running along the street to see the latest spectacle his nephew has made of himself — he's constantly trying to keep this alien anarchism tamped down, out of sight of the running mobs. The recurrent scenes of spectators rushing to and fro across the screen give a dreamlike tempo to the film. The large-scale societal disruption, incited by the anarchic conflict within, straining against confining roles and rules civilization thrusts on us, is an emerging theme of these early, "new" comedies.

Philip's oddness here isn't just that he's a Scot and wears a kilt, but from the very first time he's seen and Hardy remarks "Imagine — someone has to meet that!," it's obvious he's some strange sort of manchild, biting the ship doctor's thermometer, ruffling the doctor's hair in response to being inspected for lice. He manically pursues women, yet later in the tailor scene, with its "deflowered maiden" parody, he takes on the role of "woman" (or passive homosexual) himself. His identity is that he has no identity; his otherworldly quicksilver nature confounds all societal and sexual roles, so that he brings mayhem upon society at large and disaster on Hardy, who is so concerned with identity and with his place in society.

In all of this — but particularly in the delineation of the pomposity and pretentiousness of the Hardy character — we may see at least a partial rationale for Stan Laurel and others later calling "Putting Pants on Philip" the "first Laurel and Hardy film." All concerned at the time must have been quite exhilarated with the creation of such an excellently crafted comedy. Hal Roach would later pick it as being one of his favorite films among the literally thousands of movies he produced.[7]

Their next film is another classic, "Battle of the Century," which author Henry Miller would later call "the greatest comic film ever made."[8] The battle of the title refers to a landmark boxing match of the time (Tunney vs. Dempsey), as well as its parody within the film — Stan here is a boxer and Ollie is his manager — as well as to the vast cataclysmic, apocalyptic orgy of reciprocal destruction that concludes the film. The latter device, so successful in "Hats Off," comes back with a vengeance to bring down the curtain on the "Battle of the Century."

The film opens with the first battle, in the boxing ring, with Laurel doing his best to face down a swarthy opponent and Hardy egging him on from the sidelines. Stressed here, more powerfully than ever before, is Stan's hopeless obtuseness, his almost paralytic dumbness. When through a fluke he succeeds in felling his opponent, he's told to retreat to his corner as the referee counts the unconscious pugilist out. Stan continues to walk over to look over the ref's shoulder to see how the guy's doing. The ref then stops to order him back to his corner, then returns to counting the guy out from the top. Each time, the guy is given more time within which to revive, and each time the referee and Ollie yell at Stan to return to his corner. At one point Stan becomes involved in a tussle with the referee. Ollie grasps the ropes, boiling over with anger, with enraged frustration at the denseness of his partner — a shade of things to come.

The opponent finally does revive and knocks Stan out. The next day — the two comedians again wearing their derbies — they meet a salesman on the street and Ollie takes out an accident insurance policy on Stan. Ollie then sets himself to the task of arranging accidents for Stan. A banana peel he's thrown before Stan's feet is slipped upon by a delivery man for the L.A. Pie Company. The man gets up, covered with pie, and heaves a pie at Ollie. Ollie heaves a pie at the man. In short order, bystanders are pied, and dispatch swiftly to the pie delivery man's truck to slake their thirst for revenge. Soon, the whole town — it seems like the whole world — is caught up in this mad drive to sling pies. There are pies going into stores, into dentists' offices, causing mess and mayhem everywhere. The town has whipped itself into a frenzy of pie throwing that is beyond arrest, beyond recall — and which apparently has no end, as it continues unabated as the final credits roll.

The greatness of The "Battle of the Century" lies in its audacity. As the originator of this deliberate audacity, Laurel went to Hal Roach to authorize the purchase of an entire day's output of the L.A. Pie Company for their new two-reeler. Among the many blessings to be conferred upon him by the gods of comedy, surely an especially big one is in order to be given to Hal Roach for consenting to this purchase of over 3,000 real pies. The majestic dolly shot of the street on which uncountable numbers of people passionately pelt each other with pastries is truly monumental, remarkable and unforgettable.

It might be noted that with these four films, which brought so much attention to the team, in which they made such massive strides forward in their art, toward defining their new partnership, the concentration is not so much on the partnership but on the situation surrounding it. The widespread societal disorder they end their comedies on is becoming a signature, a ritual, as the chase was for the old Keystone Kops films. The films are not yet entirely about the characters of Stan and Ollie, as they will become later on. These characters are beginning to get shaded in, but their richness is yet to come, the richness that would easily form the basis for all their works in the future. In these earlier films, they are more part of the greater human disaster rather than the engineers of their own personal, particularized one. They have layers to grow before the films narrow to specifically focus on their own intimate crises.

They grow several layers closer in "Leave 'Em Laughing," the film that presents them closer than ever to their final incarnation. It is another work that ends in social disorder, but it opens with them in one of the iconic settings in which they shall be pictured in humanity's mind's eye for all eternity: in bed together. The common fact behind all of their films henceforth will be that Stan and Ollie sleep together in the same bed and that they unfailingly wear long white nightshirts while doing so. It is perfectly normal and natural for them to do so, they say through their manner and their actions, and it would be quite lost on them that anyone could ever conceive of it being not normal and not natural. They are brothers—the love they have for each other is truly brotherly, in the ideal sense. They have, at base, absolute regard for each other; to share a bed is merely an extension, and an expression, of this intimate and considerate regard each has for the other.

And what could be more intimate than the gag where Stan's hot water bottle opens, as they're snuggled under the covers together, and Ollie looks into the camera with looks of quizzical concern — and growing alarm — as he wonders about the source of the moisture? Ollie's anxiety over the mysterious fluid is familiar to any preadolescent sibling — the intimacy it presumes is part and parcel of all the dread realities and anxieties common to the child's emotional landscape. The gag effectively answers all speculations as to the nature of Stan and Ollie's habitual bed-sharing.

Ollie has given Stan the hot water bottle because the latter is suffering from an aching tooth. Ollie's solicitousness in this further outlines the cozy domesticity of their relationship — he is impatient and clumsy, yet grudgingly attendant to Stan's ailment, and Stan is weeping and helpless. The characters and the relationship between them are beginning to be defined. The predictable gags ensue in their tiny apartment, replete with tying the offending tooth to the doorknob in an attempt to extract it. In the end, a visit to the dentist is required.

Several gags playing on the concept of the dentist's office as a chamber of horrors are trotted out, and the somewhat unpleasant joke of having Ollie's tooth mistakenly extracted instead of Stan's is seen here, but this is all prelude to the final scene, which is one of their greatest. Both overdosed on laughing gas, they stumble out into the bright midday sun, overcome with hysterics. It is their first, and possibly the best, use of their "laughing jag" routine.

They are completely undone, far beyond the call of sobriety. They stumble to their Model T — another iconic accoutrement of their characters, seen here for the first time. It is nearly beyond their capabilities to get into the car, for Stan to crank it into action. They try to pull out and bash into the car behind them. They find this incomparably amusing. They pull ahead and crash into the car ahead of them. This just adds to the convivial atmosphere. They do this several more times, then angle their car out onto the street, where it sideswipes another car. This just about does them in, and when the angry motorist leaps out to confront them, he is greeted by their exuberant cackling.

But this is nothing compared to their encounter with traffic cop Edgar Kennedy, seen here with them for the first time. They pull up to his intersection and cause an immediate traffic jam. Angrily, he tells them to pull back. They do so, but Ollie keeps mischievously inching forward again, giggling with delight. There are incredibly evocative juxtapositions of their carefree, mocking hilarity and the officer's grim, scowling, increasingly furious face of authority. They are helplessly convulsed in their spasms of merriment, while he simply glares with disapproving, uncomprehending rage.

After his road is cleared, he gestures for them to come forward. Ollie tells Stan: "Go see what he wants," so Stan gets out of the car and staggers to the cop, at one point stopping to bend over and clutch his abdomen with the pain of his laughter. He comes practically sprawling at the cop's feet, who attempts to indicate to him that he meant that the automobile should come forward. Stan gestures to Ollie, who gets out of the car and stumbles over, amused to no end, finally falling into the cop's arms.

In short order the cop tries to take charge of their vehicle, bending to crank it, which results in his belt breaking. This leads to his pants falling down — that old stalwart gag — as he's directing traffic. The sight of this is as a rare and much-enjoyed delicacy for Stan and Ollie in their advanced appreciation of things comic. Shortly after this they mistakenly run over the cop, causing him to become more peeved — understandably — and inspiring the clowns to new levels of histrionics. He takes charge of their car. "You're practically in jail right now!" cries the title card as he wheels it around the corner into a pondlike mud hole into which the car and its occupants — Stan and Ollie still gaily flailing the air with their frivolity, the cop still blinking with enraged incomprehension — sink completely out of sight.

"Leave 'Em Laughing" and the three films that preceded it are classics, luminous with the freshness of discovery their creators were experiencing. Less luminous, but still a solid addition to their growing canon, is "The Finishing Touch," (1928), a workmanlike comedy which has the comedians as workmen, assigned the task of finishing a house. This makes it the first of the team's films built around their attempts to fulfill a single task. It is, for the most part, an unambitious slapstick comedy — a succession of accidents and catastrophes illustrating basic laws of physics and gravity — and it's entirely successful on that level.

In terms of their evolution, we might notice here the emphatic deliberateness of its very simple gags, and the use of sustained anticipation — "telegraphing" — prefiguring their execution. "The Finishing Touch" is practically a textbook of these techniques and devices that would constitute the form of their comedy for the rest of their careers. If, in their previous film, Ollie, repairing to the bathroom to prepare Stan's hot water bottle, should have his way prepared for him by a close-up of a tack on the bathroom floor, we know that he will step on that tack, leap, howl with pain, extricate the tack from his foot, and throw it disgustedly to the floor. And if, after then fulfilling his purpose in the bathroom, this is followed by the shot of that tack lying on the floor where he threw it, we know he will once more step on it, howl with enraged pain, throw it away....

This is enlarged upon in "The Finishing Touch," with a host of gags based on anticipation and repetition. The dumbness is in full flower. Ollie repeatedly tries to transport a door into the house via a bridge he's built between a makeshift ramp and the porch. Stan keeps removing the plank that forms the purposeless "bridge" and Ollie repeatedly crashes to the ground. Ollie repeatedly puts nails in his mouth as he sets off to do some roofing. Again and again he meets with a mishap that causes him to painfully swallow those nails. Ollie keeps stepping from a door where a box has been placed as a makeshift step down to the ground. Stan keeps moving the box, sending Ollie plummeting to the ground.

At one point Stan is sawing a plank, on the other end of which Ollie stands, obliviously perched out of the window to do some roofing. Just as obliviously, Stan saws away, pausing now and then to rest, to readjust his saw, to change position, to exercise his limbs, until finally — the sawing is drawn out as long it can possibly be drawn out — the board is cut through and Ollie crashes to the ground.

There is no new gag and no twist or variation on the old one — just an excruciatingly long build-up to its firm, emphatic, deliberate, defiantly brazen execution. The laughter is in the anticipation and in the reward of that anticipation. There is no surprise — just the opposite. We watch them obliviously, casually proceed into predictable disaster.

The form perfectly matches content. They are dumb, and they cannot learn the right way of doing things. They are slow and methodical — and quite logical — in their utter incompetence. The McCarey–Laurel vision of a slower, more realistically paced comedy was being fulfilled, undoubtedly aided by the increasingly dominant naturalistic acting style of Hardy — and McCarey's desire to create comedy that could be "savored" was coming to fruition. For here, the entire point of the comedy was that the gags be examined, turned over, turned inside out, buried, exhumed, inspected — in short, savored. The intense examination, which yields untapped levels and richnesses of absurdity within the gag, itself becomes absurd and a source of laughter.

The anticipation and repetition techniques continue to be developed in "From Soup to Nuts," another "occupation" comedy that sees them as waiters sent to serve at a fancy dinner party. The plot gives Hardy a chance to indulge in many of his increasingly grandiose and grandiloquent gestures. No more refined or sophisticated than Stan on any level, Ollie is nonetheless at pains to see that Stan adheres to what he perceives to be rules and customs of the social milieu in which they find themselves. Chief among these, and occupying the first five minutes of the film, is that old bugaboo that Stan can never seem to get a grip on: the necessity of keeping one's hat off of one's head while indoors.

From there, the film is mainly a series of gags detailing their incompetence as waiters. The gags are few and deliberate, none more than the running one of Hardy taking a header into the massive cake he's attempting to transport — McCarey reportedly shouted to him while the scene was being shot: "Don't move! Just stay there!" as Hardy lay resting with his face embedded in the creamy mess.[9] The banana peel that leads to this fall shares the same dreaded ubiquity as the tack in "Leave 'Em Laughing" — after being placed in Ollie's path by a mischievous dog, it is slipped on and angrily tossed away, where it lies in wait to upend Hardy once again into another cake. Angrily flung aside after this, it then serves the purpose of casting Stan onto his backside.

They are finding their form, their rhythm. What still needs to be clarified are the characters and their relationship with each other. Here, in a film that presents them pretty much as the team we know, Stan can still angrily order Ollie around, then aggressively bully the upper-class attendees of the dinner party. He is not meek yet, not finding his strength in his gentleness. As accomplished as these comedies are, they don't yet wholly proceed from the relationship of the two characters.

That relationship gets a little more examination in "You're Darn Tootin." Stan and Ollie are musicians in an outdoor concert: their blundering causes the concert to collapse in disaster. They are terminated and repair to their boarding house, where they naturally are several weeks behind in the rent. At lunch, the landlady's son remarks that he attended that afternoon's concert, noting that the music improved immeasurably after the termination of Stan and Ollie. Hearing this, the landlady orders them out immediately, and, homeless, they become street musicians.

It's notable that the most memorable part of the first half of the film is a sequence involving just the two of them at the dinner table. Stan, unable to shake enough salt into his soup, unscrews the top of the shaker and pours some into his hand, setting the shaker on the table with its top still loose. Ollie picks up the shaker to use it for his soup, and the top and its entire contents disappear into his bowl. He angrily switches bowls with Stan to "punish" him. A moment later Stan picks up the pepper to use it, performs the same procedure on it, and returns it to the table. Ollie picks it up and now the entire contents of the pepper shaker descend into his fresh bowl of soup.

The routine has the dumb deliberateness and the completely obvious predictability of the form they've been developing. But in addition it says something important about their relationship — variations on this gag would become one of the cornerstones of the Laurel and Hardy method. Stan does something dumb, which causes pain and discomfort to Ollie. Ollie takes angry action, which is meant to correct Stan's injustice but which also attempts to secure "revenge" or a sense of balance for Ollie. All of Ollie's actions, however, only succeed in visiting more pain and disaster on himself, while Stan, who can never learn anything, in his witless innocence just keeps on doing dumb things, watching helplessly as they bring pain and discomfort to his partner. They were becoming, as Oliver Hardy described the team, "the dumb, dumb guy who never has anything bad happen to him, and the smart, smart guy who's dumber than the dumb guy only he doesn't know it."[10]

The routine is also notable in that it involves just the two of them sitting at a table — such a homely setting often provided for many of their best moments in their films to come, through to their sound productions and the elaborate feature length films beyond.

Their relationship is explored in a different way in the second half of the film, which involves them becoming progressively more frustrated at their inability to keep in time with each other in their attempt to become street musicians. Their anger grows until they destroy each other's instruments, then launch into a fight with each other, which far exceeds anything they would do in the future in terms of savagery. Ollie repeatedly punches Stan in the stomach; Stan repeatedly kicks Ollie in the shins. Like two machines, they repeat these actions over and over, and the pain they inflict on each other is portrayed with cringe-inducing convincingness— one of the few times in their films where the violence kills much of the humor in the scene. Thankfully, it isn't long before the attacks move from the body to the more familiar target of dignity: the clothing covering the body.

When bystanders happen upon the fray, Stan begins shin-kicking them, which develops into the bystanders shin-kicking others, and we are back to the social-disorder-reciprocal-destruction-device. The screen fills with men kicking each other in the shins and hopping painfully on one foot. Again instigated by Stan, the shin-kicking evolves into pants-ripping, and the screen then fills with men tearing the pants off of each other and throwing pieces of pants into the air.

In the manner by which the hostility between Stan and Ollie is transmitted into the society at large, this is clearly a look back to "Hats Off" — with the covering of one's nether regions substituting for the crowning of one's intellectual faculties. "You're Darn Tootin'" begins with the team destroying the structure of the orchestra, being rendered homeless as a result — and ends with them once again dismantling society itself. They inspire, in the usual fashion, in their fellow humans behavior that is infantile, savage, and, most important, ludicrous.

The closing shot goes a long way toward defining the team's philosophy and their worldview. A fat man is seen shouting, "Where's my pants?" and we next see Stan and Ollie, who have no home except in each other, striding along in lockstep, both ensconced in the gargantuan pants, genteelly doffing their derbies to us as they solemnly depart the film. Having expiated their frustration into the general populace, they calmly travel on, presumably to visit it upon others in the future.

The mass chaos scene must have seemed a handy device by which to end their comedies; at the same time they must have seen the danger of it becoming a cliché, that it could only be trotted out so many times. Their next film, "Their Purple Moment," sees them establishing another device that would serve them well in the future: their "married," domestic comedies. Stan and Ollie are given wives, whom they attempt to deceive, only succeeding in raining misfortune on themselves. Unfortunately, the first entry in this subgenre is perhaps the weakest of the lot.

Stan, here known as Mr. Pincher — the last such appellation before the usage of the comedians' actual names becomes firm convention — is in the habit of holding back a portion of his weekly paycheck from his wife. He puts it in a concealed pocket of a gentleman in a painting in his front foyer — a clever sight gag which is just about the only reason this comedy is remembered today.

Ollie comes to visit with his wife, and the plan is hatched by which they'll take the money, ditch the wives, and have a grand old time. They are unaware that Stan's wife has switched the money with useless coupons. They go to a nightclub and chat up some women in distress— a gambit a great deal less innocent than we will come to associate Stan and Ollie with in the future. In short order, they charge up a large bill in the club and are unable to pay it — as well, the town's gossip alerts the wives of their predicament, and they charge down to the club. The film ends with an unconvincingly motivated pie fight, the reflexive nature of which was parodied by their own Battle of the Century.

Many elements used here would be used later, and, with greater success, in the sound period: the attempted deception of the wives, in which the comedians themselves are deceived ("Blotto," [1930]), the inability to pay a bill in a restaurant where deadbeats are soundly punished ("Below Zero," [1930]), the puritan gossip carrying tales to the wives ("Chickens Come Home," [1931], Our Relations [1936]). Everything here, however, seems rather flat and uninspired. The pie fight at the end, in particular, contravenes the laws of logic, of gradual cause and effect that had been perfected so carefully in their earlier works.

The uninspired sense continues in their next work, "Should Married Men Go Home?," a story based around golf — that sport so favored by Hardy as well as by many of the other creators of these films. Ollie here is given a wife, and Stan is the obtuse friend who comes to impose himself on an afternoon of marital bliss in the Hardy household. The two men advance from there to the golf course, where they cause predictable mayhem ending in another reciprocal destruction festival, the throwing of mud being the preferred retaliatory action in this instance.

As with the preceding film, there are elements here they will return to and use more successfully later in their sound films. The business of Stan as an unwanted visitor, obliviously knocking away on the door as the Hardys cringe inside — he finally decides to leave a note under the door and depart, but notices his note being retrieved and decides to stay — would be used in "Come Clean," (1931). The routine of treating a couple of women at the golf course to refreshments, and trying to get it through Stan's head that a lack of funds necessitates that he must refuse to partake, would be used in "Men O' War" (1929), where sound and the deepening of the Stan and Ollie characters would make it manifestly richer. As in "Their Purple Moment," the fight scene wrap-up seems gratuitous and lazy — lacking the very inner logic that was the point of their large scale "wars" of the past.

Perhaps it was the dissatisfaction with these last two films — and the inevitable letdown after their first burst of inspiration — that led to the creation of their next film, "Early to Bed," one of the strangest they would ever make. In it, they willfully abandon the characters they developed over the last nine films, over the last year. Hardy here is a millionaire, Stan is his servant. Ollie comes home drunk, not in the mood to go to bed — his servant attempts to suggest otherwise. The film concerns Stan's attempts to get Ollie to bed, Ollie resisting with pranks and mischief, and besting Stan in a wrestling match, who then resolves to leave in the morning. Ollie won't let Stan go, so Stan begins to trash the mansion, so that Ollie will have to fire him.

The film consists of just the two of them. There are no secondary characters. Hardy here is truly elegant, a sophisticate, a bon vivant — in many ways a complete inversion of his usual character, whose life is an unsuccessful attempt to approximate these qualities. Hardy here is closer to his real, offscreen personality, once described by Laurel as being that of a "playboy." Laurel is more a canny, put-upon fellow than the innocent dim bulb who we have been coming to know — in enduring the whims, taunting, and indignities inflicted upon him by his master, it is he who becomes the fall guy of the team, in another inversion of the order that has been developing.

The comedy here is slow and deliberate and the gags are obvious and sparse in keeping with the form they've been utilizing. In fact, the tempo of the film is methodical and slow to a fault, making it the most ghostly and vaguely disturbing of their works. Its theme would seem to be that of power, and the necessary and delicate balance of power within their relationship — or any relationship. Hardy as master confounds his servant's attempts to — as Stan weepingly asserts — simply "do his duty." Hardy's teasing and baiting of Laurel here seems a great deal more cruel and cold than the customary bullying Ollie subjects Stan to — Hardy is in a position of unanswerable power here and Laurel has no recourse. In their standard relationship, Ollie's bullying of Stan is answered, is balanced by the fact that it is Ollie who suffers more than anyone from Stan's stupidity, from Hardy's own presumptuousness and their shared ineptitude.

Here the balance is purposely undone. Hardy is not the frustrated oaf who nonetheless regards himself as Stan's caretaker, but rather he is Laurel's callous tormentor. Laurel is simply a helpless sap. When, in the course of his attempts to put Hardy to bed the two men end up wrestling around on the ground, there is a quick dissolve and we see Hardy sitting triumphantly atop Laurel. There is a long shot of Laurel weeping after his vanquishment, Hardy ineffectually comforting him, which is reminiscent of Stan being "overpowered" by Hardy in "Putting Pants on Philip." The scene is certainly proof that there is little that is amusing — or pleasant — about a relationship in which Hardy is a grinning, all-powerful dominator, and Laurel a weak, long-suffering underling.

On another level, though, it can be said that Hardy is attempting to use his power here to, in a way, subvert that power — in tormenting Stan, he proclaims "I want to play!" He is trying to get Laurel to lay aside his false role of servant, to engage with him as an equal. Stan, doggedly clinging to the role that has been assigned him, in refusing to "play" with Hardy, can be seen to affirm a certain paradoxical power himself — this is made evident when, after enduring the mistreatment, he resolves to quit the next morning. Hardy asserts his power by saying that he won't let Laurel go — which results in Stan vowing to destroy the mansion's costly furnishings, the emblems of that power, in order to be set free from it.

They are both trapped in their roles, in the false, dysfunctional system superimposed on their relationship by society, by the material world. There is no sense of partnership, of friendship here — all that is seen are the obstructions, material and psychological, to unity. The film features only the two of them, yet they spend its entire length in battle with each other.

The battle comes to its conclusion in the nightmarish, oddly compelling final scene of the film. Stan moves through the mansion in a frenzy of destruction, and Hardy takes cover underwater in an ornate fountain. The fountain is ornamented by a circle of sculptures of the Hardy head, each spewing out a stream of water. Ollie knocks one aside and substitutes his actual cranium. Stan notes the erratic stream of water emanating from this "head" and eyes it dubiously, hitting it with a shovel in order to get it to function properly. Each time Laurel's head is turned, Hardy must duck below to replenish his stream of water. Each time the water ceases, Laurel slams Hardy on the head with the shovel — having his doubts, but never really coming to full realization about the spurious "head."

So it is that Hardy actually gets his friend to "play" after all. And in getting Stan to strike these blows with the shovel, and in patiently suffering them in the name of "play," he begins to reinstate the familiar partnership, with Hardy in the course of the films suffering blows as a result of Stan's dim-wittedness for the sake of their play, their partnership, their art. For in the purposeful divergence from the established relationship — and all its laws and rules— that "Early to Bed" represents, it could be argued that the film is the manifestation of the urge to "pull back" on the part of its creators, to retreat from the inevitability of the characters that were forming in the last nine films. It is the last attempt — on the part of Laurel?— to escape the impending and irrevocable establishment of a comic entity that would forever define all those involved. In this last part of the film Laurel has been trying to escape from Hardy, who pulls him into this game, drawing him back into equal partnership with him, ending in a rededication, of sorts, to their relationship.

This view is supported by the fact that the only scene that unites "Early to Bed" with the standard Stan and Ollie characters is the opening, wherein the two, in derbies, receive word that Ollie has inherited a fortune, giving rise to the rest of the film. The original script does not contain this scene, which was added later and personally directed by Leo McCarey.[11] Certainly one can speculate that it was McCarey's intention to ensure that this oddity would fall in line with the rest of the body of work that was being created — that the evolution of those two characters he had been at such pains to bring together and foster would not get derailed or sabotaged. Once again, McCarey took charge in his conviction that Laurel and Hardy belonged together, that the consistency of their characterizations, as far as he could guarantee it, would remain unblemished.

It has been noted that "Early to Bed" presents the basic situation at the end of their later feature, *A Chump at Oxford* (1940), in reverse. The later film sees Stan transformed through a bump on the head into the erudite and brilliant Lord Paddington, who takes Ollie on as his servant and willfully abuses and derides him. Whereas Stan is magically transformed through a freak occurrence in *Chump*, however, we are expected to believe that Ollie's complete change of character in the earlier film comes solely through money and elevated social status. The later film ends with Stan returning to character and the former relationship being touchingly reinstated. "Early to Bed" finds the two coming together again to some degree, but with Hardy pushing Laurel into the fountain and hitting him on the head with the shovel as the film fades out, we see that the relationship affirmed here is far from their customary one.

. The fact is that the characters are still in their infancy, still fragile in terms of their development. This accounts for the varying responses to the film, many seeing it as an aberrant failure, some as a meaningful exploration of what the team had created to date. In truth, the film exists in the nebulous area between the two assessments. It is far from their funniest film — it is vaguely unsettling, yet it does have power in its eerie starkness; there is something compelling in its strange rhythm. It is the last attempt to explore a form of humor quite different than that which we expect from a "Laurel and Hardy film." It is a deliberate, almost perverse, moving away from the form that was elevating them to stardom. And yet, seemingly inescapably, in the moment when Hardy tires of his "play" and reveals himself as Stan's old pal — rather than a stone approximation thereof — smiling and jollying Laurel along, offering his hand to Stan with a vow of "forgive and forget," we have a warm affirmation of the humanity at the heart of their comedy, an affirmation of the child — at times giddy with wonderment, at times savage — behind the masks of societal roles, of adulthood.

It's perhaps understandable that after this exploration they should return posthaste to the fields of inspiration that had proven so successful and had bound them together to begin with — that of the widespread reciprocal destruction orgy, or "war." From the beginning of "Two Tars" Stan and Ollie are back again, this time united as two sailors on leave, coasting along in their customary Model T. Stan fools with the controls, Ollie slaps him away, showing Stan the proper way to drive. This, of course, results in a crash into a streetlamp, the globe of which falls smashing onto Hardy's skull.

In short order they pick up some women and head off for a day's fun. In an advanced state of exuberance they head home and are forestalled by a massive traffic jam. They breezily try to drive past but are stopped by the construction site at the front. Backing up, they bump the car behind them, the driver of which then bumps their car in return. This leads gradually to the entire traffic jam becoming a vast war zone, with a crowd of human beings viciously attacking one anothers' cars.

The development here is the way each indignity leads logically to the next, greater indignity. What's not logical, though, is the way that each participant calmly observes his adversary preparing and carrying out the indignity against him — never moving a muscle to interfere with or to arrest the action in any way — doing a thorough assessment of its results before committing himself to action. Thus, a man watches Stan rip his headlight off his car and kick it away, with anger and outrage, but he won't tackle Stan before he has the headlight off as any normal person in reality would. A man calmly pulls out a penknife and gouges it into the tire of the team's Model T. Stan and Ollie simply stand and watch with horror. Then, the man stands unresisting as Stan strides to the construction site, grabs a large clump of wet concrete from a wheelbarrow, brings it over and clamps it down hard over the guy's head.

Equally as important to the ritual is the flair and creativity displayed in inflicting pain and/or indignity on one's adversary — the aesthetic symmetry of it all. Stan and Ollie smartly pull the front tires off a car in unison, sending it crashing to the ground.

The fight isn't just a chaotic spectacle of madness here, but a large organic thing, with many subsets of logical systems perpetuating themselves. The nature of the fight is to accelerate and accelerate. It gets so that when Stan and Ollie stride through this manic war zone they've created and an angry man comes up yelling at them, Ollie shoves the guy away from him with the casual disdain with which one might swat away a gnat, yet with enough force to send him sprawling over his upended car.

And so it is when authority arrives to impose order, and the mob of warring people identify Stan and Ollie as the creators of this disharmony. The cop bids the two clowns to sit tight in their car, and as the parade of the automotive deformities they've created lumber past, they are hard pressed to conceal their amusement and affect shamefaced contrition for the benefit of the cop.

"Two Tars" is a great film and a great return to form — they'd obviously realized they weren't quite done with the reciprocal destruction battle routine, that it stood to be enlarged upon and explored a little bit more. The film also benefits from the depiction of the two girls Stan and Ollie pick up, who fight their fight for them in the initial scene with Charlie Hall as the store proprietor, who egg them on into the fight at the traffic jam, and who handily slip away when they sight the policeman approaching at the end of the film, leaving the comedians to bear all blame.

After this, their next film is a bit of a comedown — though by this time they were expected to turn out a twenty-minute short every two weeks, by which standard their batting average can be seen to be very high. "Habeas Corpus" throws the comedians into the genre known as "fright comedy," and, as time would show, throwing the team into any sort of preestablished genre inevitably would lead to some of their weakest work. They are two tramps hired by a mad scientist to procure a corpse from a cemetery for use in his experiments. Most of the film seems to be an elaboration on their frightened antics in the graveyard in "Do Detectives Think?" of a year before. Everything seems a bit obvious and uninspired, with the fright element substituting for genuine invention, for the subtlety and logic they've been perfecting.

Leo McCarey had put the team together, and, in his role as supervisor over all the Hal Roach All-Star productions, had overseen the making of all their films together since that time, providing a guiding hand, assisting in the writing, in many cases providing the stories. At this point he took it upon himself to personally direct their next three films. All of the films are unique, original works bearing little resemblance even to each other. What they share are the incisive, penetrating psychological insights that are the hallmark of McCarey's style. They share an observant perception of human frailty and a strong adherence to emotional logic.

The first is, overall, the least impressive of the three. "We Faw Down" is a return to the "married" setup, and Stan and Ollie once again scheme to ditch their wives and get out for some fun. As a ruse to get out to a poker game, they tell their wives they're going out to meet their boss at the Orpheum Theatre. On their way, they become involved with a couple of floozies in a somewhat more innocent manner than in "Their Purple Moment." They return home, not knowing that the Orpheum Theatre has burnt down, not knowing that their wives have witnessed them departing from the floozies' apartment.

The stage is set for the most successful part of the film, in which they fumblingly attempt to carry out a foredoomed deception before their lividly angry wives. It is here that McCarey's psychologically perceptive style kicks in, in a scene that says so much about the team's essential innocence, sabotaging their attempts at duplicity. So strongly does the scene resound that its premise would form the basis of their later feature, *Sons of the Desert* (1933), one of their greatest achievements and the best of all their "married" films.

Both comedians do some of their finest and most subtle acting here. Their outrage at being doubted by the wives is only exceeded by their gusto in miming the various acts they claim to have seen at the theater. Every opportunity is taken to inject nuance and telling psychological detail. Their shared laughter at the growing preposterousness of the lies they're telling, while seeming somewhat out of character in light of the more frightened children they would later become, is a wonderful human touch, impeccably acted. The end of the film introduces an element that would become another of their traditions: someone — usually their wives — voicing their displeasure with Laurel and Hardy by chasing them from the film with blazing shotguns.

Their next film with McCarey is one of their greatest silents. In "Liberty," they are two escaped convicts on the run, who meet up with some conspirators who provide them with their civilian clothes. The problem is that in hurriedly changing from their prison uniforms into their standard rumpled business suits they have put on each other's pants — a variation on their standard hat mix-up. The rest of the film consists of them trying to change into their correct trousers while evading the steadfast cop on their trail.

As if in a nightmare, they repeatedly try to find a quiet corner on the busy street to exchange their pants, but are always happened upon by strangers in the middle of the procedure. A man and woman attempt to enter a taxi and find the two comedians in the process of taking off their pants; later, a woman leans out to water her flowers and sees the men pulling off their trousers in the alley. We can grasp the full implications of the bystanders' shocked surprise, and of the sheepish embarrassment of Stan and Ollie. The team is always undone in its attempts to present a respectable, dignified front to the world at large — but not usually so cruelly, so crudely and so suggestively. And just to exacerbate the problem a little bit more, a crab has fallen from atop the boxes behind a restaurant into Stan's pants, so that its periodic pinching plagues him as they make their way down the street.

In another attempt to exchange their pants, they duck into an elevator that immediately zooms up to the very top of a skyscraper under construction. They step out onto the bare girders high above the energetic city scene far below. One can see this as their foray into another genre of comedy, the "high and dizzy" routine perfected by Hal Roach's last big star, Harold Lloyd. Whereas Lloyd impressed in a similar situation with his athletic ingenuity, triumphing over the vertiginous heights, Stan and Ollie, true to form, are almost completely paralyzed by fear at being stranded at such a perilous altitude. If Lloyd was the earnest athletic gymnast clown of reality, and Chaplin was the magician — miraculously transforming banal actuality in order to serve his ends — and Keaton was the juggler ... dexterously rearranging reality on the fly in the midst of whirlwind chaos in order to triumph over it — Stan and Ollie are the helpless children of reality, the overwhelmed clown victims of material actuality. As most of us would do if placed in a similar circumstance they simply cling fast to the girders, looking down with astonishment and trembling horror.

The crab in the pants — now in Ollie's, because they've at least managed to change into their proper trousers — doesn't really help matters either. Much of the greatness of the film lies in the deliciously plodding logic that brings them, and the crab, into such an absurdly elevated place. Such logic is a hallmark of the McCarey style, as is the keen perceptiveness seen in the oft-noted detail wherein Ollie seeks to pull Stan up from a precarious position on the girder until he notices that his assistance is placing himself in peril, at which point he quickly abandons the effort in order to save himself, leaving his old pal dangling dangerously once again.

The plodding of banal logic leading to tableaus of complete absurdity is seen powerfully in their next McCarey-directed effort as well, "Wrong Again." They are stable hands who overhear that Blue Boy has been stolen, and vow to collect the reward offered for its return. The problem is that the Blue Boy that has been stolen is the Gainsborough painting, rather than the horse of the same name that resides in their stables. They take the horse to the owners' mansion and are nonplussed by his demand that Blue Boy be brought into the house, and further puzzled by his requesting from offscreen that Blue Boy be placed atop the piano. "Is he always placed on the piano?" Stan asks via title card.

There are rich psychological insights in the team's reactions to these preposterous requests. Stan is rather skeptical, but Ollie typically assures him that the directions make perfect sense, in that the very rich often are given to a "different" way of doing things—in fact it is just the reverse of the way normal people do things. He illustrates this point—"just the reverse!"—with a quick twisting gesture of his hand that Stan seizes onto, repeating eagerly as a way of comprehending this strange new world he finds himself in.

Later, Ollie bumps into a sculpture of a naked woman, breaking it into three pieces—he hurriedly reassembles it, with the middle part, the torso, haphazardly placed backwards. Stan, coming upon the sculpture later, is dumbfounded by this likeness of a woman with buttocks jutting from her groin. He stares and stares at it, first with shocked outrage, then with abject puzzlement—finally, he is able to contextualize it by retrieving the twisting hand gesture of before, to his great delight and relief. Just the reverse!

But the horse must still be placed on the piano, and their efforts in that direction are considerable. Once the horse has been enticed to stand on top of the instrument, the animal plays havoc with the two clowns as they rest against the piano. The horse begins nudging Stan's hat. Stan's reaction at first, assuming it is Ollie, is to playfully nudge his hat in return. When the horse persists in nudging his hat again—and again—Stan is moved to nudge Ollie's hat more forcefully in return, until they begin to quarrel. The horse, demonstrably more intelligent than the both of them put together, simply looks on. In the next moment, the front leg of the piano breaks, necessitating that Ollie get underneath and bear the weight of both horse and piano. Stan hurriedly tries to relieve Ollie's burden, but each time he strives to lift the piano up off Ollie's back, the horse laconically nudges Stan's hat off again, sending him off to retrieve it, letting the burden crush Ollie back to the floor. Stan returns to help him, only to have the horse nudge his hat off again....

We see here the supreme inventiveness of all involved — how many comedians would have been content simply with the situation of the horse on the piano? As well, Stan's difficulty in choosing between helping his partner and retrieving his hat echoes Ollie's abandonment of Stan on the girders in "Liberty," the film directly before. They are drawn again to this wry observation of the selfishness of humanity, the self-preservation that is pursued to the exclusion of all else even in the most intimate of relationships. As their mass chaos scenes can be seen as comically true assessments of human nature as it really is behind all the restraining laws and codes of civilized society, so here we have — presented in a paradigm of pantomimic action for all to see — the flawed loyalty, so susceptible to distraction by every fleeting occurrence, which is often the best we are capable of giving to even those nearest and dearest to us.

Stan's valuation of his hat as being equal to that of the comfort of his partner is, of course, just a reflection of his inherent childishness. The humor is in the honest and unashamed duality of his nature — he is torn between his devotion to Ollie and his devotion to his hat. As in the case of Ollie's abandonment of Stan in "Liberty," there is no maliciousness, no intentional callousness — they are easily distracted from the matter at hand, easily able to switch gears and instantly adapt to what seems to be the pressing need of the moment. Like children, they are honest and unashamed in their distraction, honest and unashamed of their selfishness, their infinite adaptability.

In the context of this, we can see their mass chaos scenes as being a similar depiction, and acceptance of the fundamental childishness of humanity. Without analyzing too much, we see enacted again and again in these comic "wars" the nature by which the contagious urge to destroy spreads from human to human regardless of justification or the root cause of the violence to begin with. What is being said is that humanity is destructive, even with all the social niceties and codes that are being observed when it is at the height of its destructiveness. What is ultimately being said — the truth at the heart of the comedy from which the comedy proceeds — is that our social niceties, our society, is a façade, a cover that doesn't always conceal the unreconstituted children that we are within, with the delight for destruction for destruction's sake we all share. The films provide relief in tearing off that cover, and when Stan and Ollie amble off casually as they do at the end of so many of their chaos scenes — or snicker joyously at the monstrosities they've created, as they do in "Two Tars" — we are provided with acceptance for our enduring childish destructiveness, we are even invited to celebrate it. And because it is seen to proceed not from evil, greed or hatred, but from simply the sheer innocent glory of destruction, we are forgiven it — or informed that there's nothing to forgive.

When Stan and Ollie engage in violence in these "wars"—which are really absurd microcosms of our own larger wars—or whether they're engaging in one of the short fights they fight with each other, there is no elaborate reason or justification for their violence, such as we require to fight our larger military actions. Often, we murder people in order to defend our way of life, a way of life that is supposed to condemn murder. What is refreshing about Stan and Ollie is how honest they are about their violence. They don't need any justification for what they do. They just get caught up in the moment: one thing leads to another, and they address the situation. Then they move on to the next thing: having released their anger and their destructive urges freely and honestly, they are now free of them — until the next time.

Again, this is the behavior of children, who have an emotional fluidity, a freedom of expression, a lack of guilt about expressing emotion honestly, which often seems lost to us as we grow older and become "socialized." The films of Laurel and Hardy say that we are still children, utilizing the system of civilization and the complex rationalizations of our incredibly thoughtful brains to justify, to explain away, to dignify behavior that is simply childish — the real motivations for which have not changed since we all were children.

It is this special sort of childish dumbness that Stan and Ollie possess, rather than the crass dumbness or ignorance that other "dumb" comedians portray. They do not want trouble, but when it arises they must meet it wholeheartedly, not passing to either side but directly though the middle. They are resilient. They give themselves to each moment as children do. Though always failing, always meeting with disaster, they have the undying capacity for believing, and believing again, that children do (as we all did before we lost our innocence and became cunning.)

It is a particular type of dumbness that leads two men into a house to put a horse on top of a piano. Yet here, as with children, it isn't just stupidity that makes them carry out such a preposterous action, but the yearning, especially on Ollie's part, to make good, to conform to what the world of pragmatic adults expects from them. If in their haste they misunderstand, if they pursue a ruinous course of action in their attempt to be part of a world they don't fully comprehend—as children do—it is not so much stupidity as a wrongful perception, a mistaken conception of the world before them. And if, as in the final scene of "Wrong Again," they are shown the folly of their ways, they are apt to smile and laugh, Ollie is apt to twiddle his tie in warm amusement at the foolishness of their error, in full expectation that their faux pas will meet with the kindly acceptance and forgiveness—even chuckling amusement—such a mistake deserves. But here, as in most of their work, the reaction of the world is not forbearance and acceptance, but rather a blazing shotgun leveled by the owner of the mansion as he chases them and their horse from his estate.

McCarey's three personally directed films with the team — he had overseen all of their "team" films to date and is credited as having written the stories for most of them — are all notable for their attention to character development. "Liberty" and "Wrong Again" are two of the best Laurel and Hardy films ever.

The next film, the non — McCarey directed "That's My Wife," is less original than the ones that preceded it. Ollie is married, and, in a situation that will occur again, his wife is heartily averse to his continued relationship with Stan. As would happen in a later film ("Their First Mistake" [1931]. *Block-Heads* [1938]), the friendship between the two men sounds the death knell for the Hardy marriage. Ollie's wife departs: this is a major problem since he's expecting a visit from an uncle who has promised to leave Ollie an inheritance — if Ollie remains happily married. Naturally, Stan is put into service to impersonate the missing wife.

Beyond the charms of the Laurel female impersonation, the most notable aspect of this comedy is its emphasis on a gag that is a variation on the basic situation of "Liberty." At a nightclub with the uncle, a stolen necklace is dropped down the back of Stan's dress. In trying to retrieve it, Ollie and his "wife" are caught in a variety of embarrassingly compromising positions around the club by strangers. As in the case of "Liberty," the presumption of the astonished onlookers is that they are witnessing contortions of an implicitly sexual nature. The repeated scenes of exposure and embarrassment simulate those of a nightmare in which one is continually, helplessly exposed before a world of strangers. The gag is even more risqué here — in the end a curtain opens on what is announced to be an act called "The Pageant of Love" to reveal Stan and Ollie writhing on the floor, entangled, in the midst of what appears to be an extended grope. One can only imagine what dear old uncle presumes.

Though the outraged onlookers who seem to find them out everywhere are convinced that the outrage is primarily sexual in nature, the aberration that Stan and Ollie's union is in the eyes of the world is beyond mere sexuality. They enrage and outrage, and sow disaster everywhere they walk, because of their terrible honesty and earnestness, because in their unseverable union they accept each other absolutely, they are one flesh and cannot be broken apart. It matters not that the provocative images they present to their fellow humans are the result of utterly innocent misunderstandings— the fact of their union alone makes them an abomination unto the eyes of the world. This is what is being said in these recurrent scenes of horror and embarrassment.

It is also underscored in the final scene where the uncle predictably huffs off, vowing not to leave Ollie a cent. Ollie laments to Stan that he's lost his wife, his inheritance — what next? — just as the drunk who's been harassing them all night comes and dumps a bowl of soup over his head. As the film fades out and we are resigned to being left with the typical Hardy stare of exasperation, Ollie suddenly, unexpectedly, beautifully, shares a smile with Stan. As with the smiles in the final scenes of "Two Tars," "Early to Bed," and "Wrong Again," something beyond the present situation is being affirmed, the continuum of their partnership and all it represents provides them the vantage point from which to look on anything, even utter disaster, with the full warmth of their humanity, and smile.

There are smiles at the end of "Big Business," their next film, as well, in addition to tears, anger, horror, repentance, and virtually the whole scale of recognizable human emotion. "Big Business" is the film where they return with full force to their standard reciprocal destruction motif and drive it into the ground. It is the most focused, refined, extended, in-depth exploration of this device that accounted for the success of many of these early films. It is their first masterpiece.

They are Christmas tree salesmen. We see them make a few stops going to doors before stopping at the door of James Finlayson who, after having faded more and more into the background as his friends have come more and more into prominence over the last seven films, is now returned to a role that approaches equal prominence with them. It is in this role that he is defined as the ultimate Laurel and Hardy foil, and this role is the ultimate James Finlayson performance.

He is reasonable enough the first time he comes to the door, if rather curt and dismissive in reaction to their pitch. Even when Stan gets the Christmas tree stuck in the door the first time, necessitating that they bother him again to get the door open, disturbing him from his newspaper and his pipe, he shows just a few signs — understandably — of impatience. By the second and third time, it's possible that even a saint would become infuriated with Stan. As in all such cases as this — as when he proves incapable of giving Ollie the right hat, provoking a seemingly never-ending scene of repetition — Stan's inability to refrain from getting the Christmas tree stuck in the door goes beyond mere dumbness into the realm of cosmic stupidity. It is an aberrant force of nature sent into the universe to create discord, to bedevil and shake up humanity; it cuts across the grain of reality and casts everything into disarray.

Finlayson's no saint and his ire visibly rises as he's forced to deal with this dark force asserting itself as the tree gets stuck three times, and then he's summoned again because Stan gets his coat stuck. One can hardly blame

Finlayson for picking up their tree and hefting it away from his house. After this, Stan and Ollie get the brilliant idea to go back and ask if they can take Finlayson's order for next year. Quite understandably, Finlayson disappears into his house — the comedians get excited, they think they've made a sale — and returns with a large pair of shears and cuts the tree in half.

From there, Stan and Ollie set out to vandalize his house as retaliation. Finlayson returns angrily, and after an exchange of a few personal indignities, the fight begins in earnest on each other's property and clothes. Like an avalanche progressing from a few trickling pebbles into a massive landslide, the attacks escalate, feeding on their own fury in a whirling upward spiral; the participants become ever more impassioned in the commitment of their ever more appalling atrocities.

The old reciprocal ritual is followed for a while, in which the adversaries stand by in mute outrage as their enemy carries out indignities upon them, but before long it is clear that the anger and passion are too strong, and the old form must be abandoned. Finlayson rushes to attack the team's car. The team rushes to attack Finlayson's home. A crowd gathers on the street to observe the spectacle. Laurel and Hardy and Finlayson are completely consumed by their respective orgies of destruction, oblivious to the crowd — and to a policeman who's just coasted up in his car, as astonished and passive as the crowd. Stan and Ollie bash down the door of Finlayson's house, fling a porch light through the window, cut down the trees on his lawn. Finlayson smashes the windshield of their car, pulls off a door, yanks out the steering wheel.

It's worth noting that just as their fight progresses into this final, terminal stage, Finlayson angrily approaches Laurel and Hardy in their car at one point, delivering his trademark one-eyed apoplectic squint of outrage. Stan returns his squint in mocking mimicry, and Ollie laughs heartily along — as though they're welcoming Finlayson and his immortal squint into their proper place, welcoming him into his new role as a unique and privileged part of their fresh entity, the position from which he will greet posterity.

The fury accelerates. It is now an organic thing, with a consciousness of its own that has nothing to do with the succession of now-forgotten trifles that unleashed it. The men are now in the mode of destruction for destruction's sake. Stan tears awnings and trellises off the house and throws them through the windows. Ollie takes an axe to the trees and digs up the lawn with a shovel. Finlayson, manic beyond the point of reason, grabs the trees in the back of their truck and wrestles with them, writhing feverishly with them on the ground. The crowd and the cop, watch on, in stunned horror. The cop pulls out a notebook and starts making some presumably salient notes.

The men are completely taken over by the frenzied need to destroy: they must be in action every moment to achieve this objective or they will spontaneously combust. Stan, inside Finlayson's house, is pitching vases out through the window for Ollie to hit and shatter with his shovel. Finlayson, breaking from his wrestling match with the trees, sets their truck on fire, causing it to explode. Not satisfied with this, he runs about striking the pieces of the dismembered truck with a hammer.

There is something terrible about the destruction in "Big Business," that makes it different, beyond all the other reciprocal destruction films, and marks it as unique among their films in general. The impulse that had animated their battles in the past is taken to its extreme, explored to its logical conclusion, with a bold faithfulness to the artistic vision pursued. In having the participants embark on separate, mad engagements of devastation against each other simultaneously, we are given a scenario much more eerily alike to reality than the pie fight in "Battle of the Century," we are given a much closer simulation of war. In the fight being focused so intensely on just Laurel and Hardy and one other person, we are given a more refined, laser-beam concentration on that impulse than are seen in the mass crowd battles in the earlier "Battle," "Two Tars," and "You're Darn Tootin'." This makes it also more disturbing than the other films. The fact that Laurel and Hardy give themselves over so demonically to destroying someone's actual home gives the frenzied last half of the film an unnerving weight and intensity the other films don't have.

There is an extremity, caused by the excessive level of hostility expressed, that Laurel and Hardy reach here that they never visited again. Certainly here in "Big Business" they needed to do it as kind of a great and awful necessity. Never again would they go so completely out of control — the film's greatness lies in its braveness and audacity in doing just that. Events give way to utter, violent calamity. The cop and the crowd who stand by and watch in astonished helplessness are our surrogates, ineffectual spectators observing a world spinning — spun — into chaos. They — we — are ever appalled by the new and greater levels of devastation that occur but at the same time are equally fascinated by the progression.

This is validated in the great moment after Stan has energetically pushed Finlayson's piano out onto the front lawn and has begun to attack it with an ax. He is unaware that the cop has finally decided to bring order to the madness. The cop has sauntered over and is standing directly behind Stan as he swings merrily away. Momentarily, of course, he turns and sees the cop and immediately becomes shamefaced and meek. He lays down the ax and sets about attempting to put the disemboweled piano back together — pocketing a piece when he can't get it back into the mechanism.

The cop angrily calls Ollie and Finlayson — retrieving the latter from his latest wrestling match with the trees — and asks, as the cops at the end of "Battle" and "Two Tars" asked, "Who started this?" Explanations are begun, but Stan begins crying helplessly, which in turn sets Ollie and Finlayson to crying, causing the cop to blubber miserably, and soon the crowd too are weeping about the horror they've all witnessed. Backs are patted, hands are shaken, and reconciliation and forgiveness between Stan and Ollie and Finlayson are seen. Stan gives Finlayson a cigar as a goodwill gesture. Moved by this, the cop folds his notebook and returns, whimpering, to his car.

Then there is a shot of Stan and Ollie ceasing to weep, mischievously smiling at each other, then bursting into uproarious laughter. The cop sees them, throws aside the handkerchief he was blowing his nose with and chases angrily off after them. Meanwhile, Finlayson settles back into a chair on his devastated front yard, leans back and ignites his cigar — which explodes in his face.

The ending follows through on the uncompromised mission pursued throughout the film. Authority can impose no order here. Life is beyond reason or sentiment. There are no morals learned. The nature of the impulse acted upon, like life itself, is ultimately beyond definition, beyond control. It can't be reduced by our presumptions, the breezy assumptions by which we do so much dishonor to life and our own inner impulses, making them less than they are, pretending they're what we want them to be, minimizing them so that we can pretend we are capable of controlling them. Like the cop and Finlayson we would like to think that everything can be calmed and explained away by a good cry and a cigar — we pretend our starkest primal problems can be ameliorated or paved over by niceties like these. Stan and Ollie's laughter affirms the vitality and authenticity of life's volatile mystery beyond the illusory "order" overlaid upon the world by "how we think things should be," by bourgeois expectations, by authority, by our faulty, frightened, ungenerous, unimaginative way of perceiving reality. Stan and Ollie's laughter affirms the meaning of the film; it affirms the unashamed violence we've watched over the past ten minutes. It also affirms that violence as being exhilarating, enjoyable — and, though it may proceed from an ostensibly logical chain of events, it is affirmed in its utter irrationality. It is affirmed as something that can't be easily put away, neatly contextualized, explained away, given a heartwarming, edifying conclusion. Their laughter, the cop chasing them off, the cigar exploding in James Finlayson's face, compose the perfect coda to the symphony — a masterful crescendo at the end of this brave plunge into madness.

Laurel and Hardy must have known that "Big Business" was the ultimate expression of the vision that had set their partnership in motion — they must have seen they could go no farther than this. The reciprocal destruction routine would always remain an essential part of their equipment, but they would never again go so far with it as they did here. Their attempts to revive it later on would be more akin to exercises in nostalgia, conscious visitations to the past, rather than expressions of unhinged glee in violence and destruction present in "Big Business."

Fittingly, it was shortly after the production of this film — it was filmed over the Christmas holidays of 1928 — that the prime creator of the destruction device, the man who had actually brought the team together, moved on from the Roach lot. Leo McCarey, who had overseen and guided all their films to date, was leaving for greener pastures, taking advantage of offers made possible by the success of the team he had created. With his departure, Stan Laurel would be the unquestioned shaping hand of the comedies from here on in.

With this change there was another, just as momentous, change. As "Big Business" wrapped, the Roach studios were closed down for a month to facilitate the installment of sound equipment. The medium in which the young partnership had gained its foothold was undergoing a complete metamorphosis. The change presented by sound was undoubtedly daunting and incomprehensible to all involved. The challenge it presented, as is well documented, inspired widespread fear throughout the motion picture industry.

As the new sound equipment was being installed, the team continued to make films. Their three final silent comedies, while all worthy efforts, break no new ground — perhaps because they were made with the consciousness that they were entries created for a dying medium. These films would be held back and released offhandedly after the premiere of their first sound film, by which time they had been effectively rendered obsolete. Not surprisingly, none of them achieve — or aspire to achieve — the intensity of "Big Business."

"Double Whoopee" is chiefly characterized by its novel setting — a ritzy Broadway hotel, where Stan and Ollie work as a temporary doorman and valet. The parallel here is with the earlier "From Soup to Nuts," in that they are sent by an apologetic employment agency ("Sorry, they're the best we can do!") to serve in the primly dignified high society environment. As in the earlier film, they predictably create havoc, infuriating the burly Tiny Sandford — back again as a cop — and arousing the hornetlike rage of cabman Charlie Hall. There is neither the abandon seen in their last effort nor the carefully observed character nuances of "Wrong Again" or "Liberty"— things simply dissolve into a minor league fracas before Stan and Ollie depart the hotel and are on their way. In addition to its setting, the film is chiefly distinguished by the appearance of Jean Harlow, who was soon to become the foremost sex symbol of the time.

Their next film, "Bacon Grabbers," is the best of these final silents. They are attachment men, sent to re-possess a radio from the poisonously dour Edgar Kennedy. As would become standard of all their best comedies, the film consists of their simply trying to do one simple task, repeatedly, and repeatedly failing — and the seemingly infinite — and infinitely imaginative — gags that are wrung, painstakingly, therefrom. Stan and Ollie repeatedly fail to serve the repossession papers to the cunning Kennedy in a variety of absurd and ridiculous ways. They are humiliated and hurt again and again. Yet still they continue to attempt to serve the papers, with the same determination and fortitude that Kennedy, in his surly belligerence, equals in his attempts to evade them. Their battle assumes, obviously, a mythic significance for both sides that is far beyond the magnitude of the actual situation.

The film consists of their trying to get into his house in a series of simple, almost childishly simple, gags — procuring a dog to scare Kennedy with, Stan infuriating Ollie by serving him with the papers, mistaking the papers for a sandwich, acrobatic antics as they try to enter house via ladder through the second-story window — to which Kennedy responds, rather frighteningly, by shooting a rifle at them. Increasingly, we see not just the characters of Laurel and Hardy evolving, but we can also see the evolution of the Laurel and Hardy world that surrounds them.

The simplicity of their best films is in fact akin to the simplicity of a child's drawing — and like a child's drawing, the simplicity is deceptive. Stan and Ollie are at war with Kennedy, yet it seems at times they are at war with each other, as well. At one point Ollie becomes so enraged with Stan that, in a brilliant and hilarious flurry of pantomime, he very nearly hits him before he restrains himself.

The film begins with them sleeping together, cramped and entangled on a too-small bench before their boss rouses them for their new assignment. Immediately following is a routine in which they spend several minutes attempting to leave the office, much to the annoyance of their boss. They are moving in their own time, which is always three steps behind the briskly efficient and ever irate world that surrounds them. Their fumbling is rather frightening in its infinitudes of repetition, once set in motion determinedly never-ending, like a sort of perverse perpetual motion machine.

The conclusion of the film presents a "switch-ending," the precursor of which formed the ending of "Big Business," and which they would return to in future works: having repossessed the radio from Kennedy — with Ollie delivering an incredible withering glance of disdain in the process — they set it down on the street, where it is immediately flattened by a steamroller. Kennedy hoots with delight at this occurrence — he "wins." His wife approaches, telling him she's just made the last payment and they now officially own the flattened appliance. Kennedy burns while Stan and Ollie whoop with joy — they "win." The steamroller continues along and flattens their car.

The endings in which expectations are raised and dashed, where defeat is unfailingly snatched from the jaws of victory, will become recurrent in their work.

Whereas the structure of "Bacon Grabbers" presages much of their best work to come, their next film, "Angora Love," is less impressive. The premise of it is promising — a goat follows them through the streets, resulting in it domiciling with them in their standard squalorous boarding room, as they attempt to conceal it from the standard irascible landlord — Edward Kennedy again. Little, however, is done with the premise. Nothing much is done with the goat after they get in the room, and things degenerate into a minor tit for tat as the team and Kennedy splash each other with buckets of water.

There are good bits in the film — Stan repeatedly hanging his clothing on a peg Ollie wants to use, Ollie mistakenly massaging Stan's foot and beaming just as rapturously as if it was his own — but none of them are as realized as they would be when recreated in their later, sound films. If, as seems to be the case, "Angora Love" was made in full consciousness that it was to be their final silent film, one can understand a certain lack of commitment on the part of its creators — knowing as they well did that their comedy would have to be reimagined anew presently in any case. There is nothing wrong with "Angora Love" — it's simply that, from the present perspective, there's nothing in it that would not be done, and done better, in films to come. There is an understandable sense of "marking time" about the film.

Over the past several years through 33 films the two comedians had entered into an unexpected partnership and had attained unexpected stardom. They had been forced together by Leo McCarey, who had bequeathed upon them a form through which they had captured the public's attention. Under the watchful eye and benevolent power of Hal Roach they had created two instantly recognizable characters, who would be continuously and lovingly refined for the rest of their lives; as defined as the characters had come to be in the silents, they were as crude outlines compared to the delineation and fleshing out they would receive in the coming years. Leo McCarey had moved on, leaving the comedians to forge ahead into a new era with their still fledgling creations. Laurel, at 39, and Hardy, 37, had both known their share of neglect and hard times. With the success of their new shared enterprise, their lives had changed dramatically. Their lives were about to change again, this time due to a technological innovation.

5

SOUND

It is perhaps difficult to understand now the magnitude of the change that sound brought to the film industry. Careers were ruined, and a particular grace and majesty unique to film were lost forever. Sound, especially for the great comedians, brought everything down to earth, made their plights more "real," afflicted their flights of fancy with terminal gravity.

The two greatest clowns, Chaplin and Keaton, were the acrobatic poets of the medium. Their artistry was fully formed in the world of silence — the coming of sound forced them to convert to prose. To observe them in their sound films for the most part is akin to witnessing the Albatross in Baudelaire's famous poem, in which that unfortunate bird, clumsy and awkward and made sport of on a ship's deck, is metaphor for the poet, trapped in dull prosaic reality, far from his soaring flights of inspired ecstasy.

Laurel and Hardy were never poets in the same sense that Chaplin and Keaton were — they already expressed themselves in sturdy, craftsmanlike, unpretentious prose. As has been noted, their homely narratives, plodding along in strict adherence to a sometimes torturous logic, assured that they were already working in "sound" time. Chaplin and Keaton, and other established comedians, had personas that had been developed so fully and completely in silence that the coming of sound limited their characters and diminished their comedy in the same way that pausing to explain a poem in concrete terms inevitably diminishes the poem. The Laurel-Hardy partnership was so relatively new that sound allowed them to explore and deepen their characters further, and to widen the scope and possibilities of their art. In short, sound had the exact opposite effect on them as it did on the others.

Aside from the newness of their partnership, being a team allowed their success in sound films as well. There was a necessity for them to speak that solo comedians did not have. Their films are about humanity's relationship with itself, where Chaplin's and Keaton's are about humanity's relationship with the universe. The words that Stan and Ollie bandy back

126

and forth between each other — the too-optimistic elucidations of ideas, the recriminations, the weepy apologies, the amiable chatter — are the continuous soundtrack we all awake to every day, as the two sides of our brains, ever in conflict, ever seeking reconciliation, attempt to negotiate and navigate their way through the fresh problems presented before us. For Chaplin and Keaton there are no words needed, there are none possible. It's telling that Chaplin's two most successful vignettes of sound comedy — his song in *Modern Times* (1936) and his speeches as Adenoid Hynkel in *The Great Dictator* (1940) — are both exercises in meaningless gibberish. As he rightly insisted, his art was beyond words. Yet sound had brought words and gravity and time and decay to film, all of which Chaplin and Keaton had heretofore existed outside of.

Laurel and Hardy were already the prisoners of gravity, of time. If the glory of the other clowns was that they succeeded in making the impossible possible, Laurel and Hardy were committed to making the possible impossible, the effortless torturous. Not only did the world of sound embrace their comedy, enthusiastically providing thunderous crashes for their frequent pratfalls, but it was the conduit for the necessary evolution of their art. Having largely attained success through their ability to stir up and give rise to the latent anger and violence of that great mob known as humanity, they retreated from their apocalyptic excesses to plumb the depths of these two childish men who so obliviously and mercilessly revealed the children in adult disguise around them. It became clear that their comedy would increasingly focus on the complexity of their characterizations. Sound allowed them to do this in a way that silence never could have. In this sense, the coming of sound was a blessing for their artistic development — and it came at precisely the time they needed it to come.

They had both spoken onstage, so verbal comedy was nothing new to either of them — the same could be said of Chaplin and Keaton. For Laurel and Hardy, the tone of their voices were instrumental in bringing one important quality of their characters even more to the fore — their gentleness. Both men had gentle and pleasant voices, reflecting their own inner qualities, and the inherent gentleness and delicateness of the Stan and Ollie characters become more pronounced with sound.

Hardy was a singer, and his rich tenor voice, often speaking in sunny musical rhythms, perfectly expresses the overdone, idiotic gallantry of his character. Yet there is a vulnerability to his voice as well. It is there in his simpering chuckle now accompanying his necktie-twiddle, so naked in its desire for approval, and so embarrassed to be so, and it is there even in his angriest shouts at Laurel. There is a musicality and a vulnerability about all of Ollie's pronouncements. From here, Ollie becomes more the fey, dainty, eternally deluded "thinking man" of the team — less seen is the more masculine, athletic Hardy of some of the silents. Words give Ollie more of an opportunity to display his pompous pretentiousness. And the long, anguished, extended wails he delivers when falling off a ladder, or being fed through a lumber machine, or tripping on a sweeper, are positively operatic.

Hardy's Southern accent was tailor-made for the grandiloquence of his character; the poetic lilt it gave his words connected them, rightly or wrongly, to that mythic consciousness of the fallen glory, the fallen honor of the Old South. Ollie's search for dignity is noble, for his pure belief in it is inextricable from his dedication to honor, to decency and civilized behavior — however much he himself deliberately sabotages these qualities.

Laurel's voice was even softer, a hesitant, lisping murmur — he pitched it a bit higher than his normal speaking voice — and it perfectly expressed the pale, frightened vulnerability of his character. The Lancashire-American accent gave his speech a fractured otherworldliness that was exactly appropriate for the strange, disconnected, 'man from nowhere' Stan was becoming. There is a disembodied quality to Stan's voice. It sounds as if it is coming to us straight from the wastes of oblivion.

As well, the words given Stan to speak open up an entire new realm of his dumbness to be explored — for Stan, it is quickly evident from even the first sound comedies, words are not a means of communication but rather another avenue by which to spread confusion, incomprehension, to inflict on Hardy and on the world more layers of his utterly useless nonsense. He is as incompetent in the use of language as he is with all other basic functions. He is as equally inept in his understanding of the simplest, most commonplace phrases used by others. It is just another manner in which Stan is lost. With sound, Stan must become, with his painful inadequacy in understanding or being understood, more dumb, more helpless and out of touch with the world. Even in many of the later silent films, he was given occasional wisecracks via the title cards; it's immediately apparent from the moment Stan opens his mouth to speak in the sound films that there will be no wisecracks forthcoming. He is capable of uttering only malapropisms, non sequiturs, Lewis Carrollian gobbledygook, and garbled, surreal aphorisms (much to the ever frustrated annoyance of his good friend).

Sound also brings us the knowledge that Stan's now trademark cry is accompanied by a high-pitched squealing that is quite unlike any other sound made by an adult male in the annals of human history. Likewise, when merriment comes, he delivers a screeching, howling guffaw, which, once heard, is never forgotten.

Laurel and Hardy made 39 short films between 1928 and 1935; it is largely on these that their reputation rests, and it is quite arguable that these films contain their greatest work. As fine as the best of their silents are, sound allowed them to perfect their technique and to bring richer detail to the two beings at the heart of their art.

Their first sound film, the cutely named "Unaccustomed As We Are" (1929), is a domestic comedy, shot for the most part on one set, as were most early sound films; it also has a stilted feel, like a photographed stage play, as did, again, most early sound films. When we first see the team, Ollie is bringing Stan home to meet his wife, describing to him the vast feast she'll only be too happy to prepare for them. Stan's first spoken words are: "Any nuts?"

The wife is Mae Busch in her first assumption of her trademark role, and her haranguing, metallic voice gives the new sound equipment a good workout. From here, the film is a situation comedy, resembling, an episode of an early 1950s television show. Ollie's wife storms off—their attractive neighbor offers to help Ollie prepare the dinner. Her dress gets set afire, the wife returns, the neighbor has to hide and has to be kept hidden further when her husband, burly cop Edgar Kennedy, appears on the scene.

Dialogue carries the plot, and along the way there are numerous gags venturing to use sound and verbal humor. The extended parody of gentility at the beginning ("And how are you, Mr. Hardy?" "Very well, Mrs. Kennedy!") is good, as is Mae Busch screaming in time to a phonograph record. There is some use of sound as an indicator of offscreen calamity in Ollie being beaten by Kennedy on the other side of a door, but the coup de grâce is in the film's final gag, which consists of Stan smartly striding off after apparently having dispatched Kennedy — he intones "Good night, Mr. Hardy!," turns, and trips at the top of a staircase, leaving the frame at a perpendicular angle. Ollie rushes to the top of the stairs, wincing as he observes what we can only imagine, and the soundtrack describes a clattering catastrophe of train-wreck proportions. The film fades out. It is a uniquely aural gag that sets the slapstick free in an unexpected, audacious manner — paradoxically and psychologically more vivid than its silent predecessors. Reportedly invented by Laurel on the set, the gag is the first appearance of their use of sound to liberate their audience's imagination, forcing it into complicity in the creation of their world of bizarre fantasy.

"Unaccustomed As We Are," with its setbound action, its chatty talkiness, its tightly controlled situation comedy, was obviously contrived with great care as their first sound film, designed to display all the unique properties of the new medium. Strangely, their next film, as if to test the degree to which the talkies would allow them to "be themselves" and practice their craft in the same leisurely manner as they had in their silents, is comparatively lax in its construction, containing little scripted dialogue and rely-ing for the most part on one threadbare situation for its comedy.

"Berth Marks" has gained a reputation as being one of the worst of all their comedies. In it, they are vaudevillians, boarding a train to their next engagement. The first segment with them attempting to meet each other at the station and repeatedly missing each other with uncanny ineptitude is amusing — they would use it as the beginning of the Music Hall sketch they performed in Britain in the 1950s. Once aboard the train they attempt to undress and settle in for a night's sleep in a very narrow upper berth — their struggles to do this comprise the remainder of the film.

The wrestling, the writhing, the entanglements of clothes and limbs, the contorted claustrophobic discomfort of the two men are extended and stretched out to what becomes an oppressive degree. For those who have endured the film, it is difficult not to harbor the suspicion that somewhere, somehow in an alternative universe, Laurel and Hardy are still struggling in the tiny berth, one still entangling one's foot in the other's vest, or vice versa. The oppressiveness here, though, is entirely intentional, not so very different in intention from the more challenging affronts of the avant-garde (though positively merciful when compared to something along the lines of Warhol's *Sleep*). Stan and Ollie squirm and struggle to undress in the minute berth, undaunted by the obvious impossibility of the task, for the same reason that they cannot place the correct hats on their heads. They cannot, or will not — cannot in Stan's case, will not in Ollie's — recognize the preposterousness of what they are attempting to achieve. Every infuriating and frustrating new twist on the hopelessness of their predicament only ratchets up their deter-mination to achieve the impossible. Naturally, when they do achieve a mod-icum of comfort, the train arrives at their destination.

Though undeniably correct artistically and in complete accordance with the characters, "Berth Marks" is torturous — there is a sense to it that it had to be made, if only to follow one strain of the team's plodding, idi-otic logic to its ultimate conclusion. To ascribe the film's only value to necessity, however, may be to give it short shrift, because there are indica-tions that it was received with considerable amusement in its day — and the fact that its basic situation was used again twice — in *Pardon Us* (1931), where they try to share an upper bunk, and in *The Big Noise* (1944).

Laurel and Hardy attempting to undress in a cramped berth does have the potential to be amusing — just not for 15 minutes. The film is not helped either by the fact that most of the dialogue seems improvised, with Ollie imploring Stan every few minutes to "Stop crowding!" In their next film they are back to scripted dialogue, and it is the verbal humor that accounts for most of the comedy.

In "Men o' War" (1929), they are sailors out on a day's leave, coyly chatting up the standard enthusiastically flirtatious girls. The first segment is based on risqué double entendre as they embarrassedly yet naughtily discuss a pair of knickers they've found with the girls, who are under the impression that the team is referring to a lost pair of gloves. In the second segment they adjourn to a soda stand, where they perform the routine already seen in "Should Married Men Go Home?," in which Ollie attempts to impress on Stan the necessity of refusing a refreshment, in view of their impoverished bank roll. With sound — and James Finlayson as the soda jerk — the scene in "Men O' War" becomes one of their greatest dialogue routines ever, and certainly their best so far.

Ironically, the least impressive scene in "Men O' War" is that old faithful standby of their silent films — the mass chaos ending, in which the team sets off a battle among a crowd of people. Here, one boat bumping another leads to a war between various pleasure seekers until the whole mob of them go on beating each other as they sink beneath the waves. The "reality" that sound imposes — the need for angry dialogue, the inability to quickly cut from vignette to vignette — makes the scene inevitably less intense than most of its silent counterparts.

Still, "Men O' War" is the best of their sound films so far. It is equaled, if not surpassed, by "Perfect Day," their next entry. Returning to the standard formula of the team simply attempting and failing to do one thing, Stan and Ollie here are merely trying to set off on a picnic with their wives and Uncle Edgar Kennedy. They are forestalled firstly by their own stupidity and arguments with each other, then by various automotive difficulties, conflagrations with neighbors, and other attendant misfortunes, all of which are somehow symbolized by and find their essence in the large bandaged, gouty foot of Uncle Kennedy, which is slammed, kicked, sat on and otherwise pummeled throughout the duration of the film. Here is one of the greatest Laurel and Hardy running gags, in which they take it upon themselves to display, almost boastfully, the many ingenious and utterly logical ways by which they can cause pain to Kennedy's foot. Stan pulls away the chair it rests on so that it falls on the dog, who immediately leaps up and bites it. Stan steps on the foot. Stan sits on the foot. Stan slams a car door on the foot. In changing the tire, the entire weight of the car comes to rest on the foot.

One of the great aspects of the simplicity of a film like "Perfect Day" is the element of satire it easily contains; in typical fashion for the team it is always deftly hinted at, never overdone. From the first scene in which Stan and Ollie bring in the sandwiches they have made for the picnic, beaming with pride, and the expected upset soon occurs with the sandwiches being angrily thrown at each other, the wives intone: "Boys! After all, this is the Sabbath, you know!" It is established that they will adhere to the standards of civilized behavior in their pursuit of leisurely fun on this day of rest. When later, a window-smashing free-for-all begins with some of the neighbors, there is a sudden truce as all participants lay down their arms and rush madly into their houses; we then see the local pastor striding piously by. After his departure, the citizens emerge once more.

Of course, Uncle Edgar isn't taken in from the beginning — his corrosive sourness is beyond conversion, and he will not enter into the increasingly strained pretense of enthusiasm all involved are attempting to maintain for this day of good wholesome fun (Ollie's savage bellow of "Shut up!" to the wives at one point indicates he might just about be reaching his limit). We assume that once the car finally does set off on its joy ride, Kennedy isn't surprised at all — or disappointed — that it promptly sinks to the bottom of one of those handy ten-foot-deep mud puddles.

Compared to this classic, the team's next effort seems a retreat to the claustrophobic stiffness that marked their first sound film. "They Go Boom" returns them to the confines of their tiny boarding-house room, complete with the shared, cramped bed and the white nightshirts — and the hateful Charlie Hall as landlord. Ollie has a cold, and Stan attempts to nurse him back to health with his usual competence. It's a pedestrian film, and one in which the dismal, dingy surroundings, and the unpleasant nature of some of the gags — Stan steps on flypaper, resulting in a thick layer of glue stuck to the bottom of his sock; brightly, he solves the problem by turning the sock inside out and wearing it that way; a punctured water pipe spews water down on the chest of the flu-stricken Ollie as he lies in bed — affirms the team's predilection for wry, hoary, dark-tinged humor and the essentially bleak view of existence that overtakes their films at times. Typically, this touching tale of a man nursing his stricken friend in the dead of night in a poverty-stricken hovel concludes with the cataclysmic blast of their air mattress being blown to pieces.

In contrast to the dark confines of "They Go Boom," "The Hoose-Gow" takes place entirely out of doors. They are convicts, sent to a prison camp to work on a highway gang. We see here the method by which they were growing in their ability to work in sound in pretty much the same way as they had worked in the silents. There is little in "The Hoose-Gow" that depends on sound, but one doesn't notice the lack of verbal necessity. Virtually all the humor is physical — there is little that differentiates it from their later silent comedies. They have mastered sound, incorporating it into their form, giving it precisely the right amount of weight — no more and no less — in their art, allowing them to maintain the spontaneous sense of freedom of their silent films. As adept as they've shown themselves to be with purely verbal humor, in the main they use sound to motivate and punctuate their essentially pantomimic comedy.

Here, as the paddy wagon pulls up to discharge its prisoners, and the scar-faced, sinister criminals disembark, leaving Stan and Ollie to disentangle themselves from each other's bodies in the corner of the wagon where they've been wedged, we see the increasing innocence of the characters in comparison with the world around them. When they go for dinner in the prison camp and find no place to sit, their fellow convicts maliciously direct them to the warden's table, and they unquestioningly avail themselves of the fine delicacies there. We see their dumb trust, but also that they are no more part of the criminal world than they are of the world of authority and discipline — "society." As displayed in the image of them seated happily at their own private table, separate from the mobs at the prisoners' table — Stan again unscrewing the top of the salt shaker, Ollie again sending its contents cascading into his soup — they exist on their own plane, in their own world, with its own pressing concerns and dramas far from the stark, yet mundane, conflicts between the powerful and powerless that characterize the reality around them.

Unlike their earlier tenure as jailbirds in "The Second Hundred Years," Stan and Ollie do not cook up a clever ruse by which they will escape. They have become far too dumb for that, and it's telling that when they do become involved in an escape plan that results in them finding themselves outside the gate of the prison, Stan knocks on the door for re-entrance. Again, their conflicts, their concerns, are mostly with each other: Stan is unable to use his pickax without getting it entangled in Ollie's jacket or hat; Stan interferes continually with Ollie's frustrated efforts to cut down a tree. At the end, when they have punctured the radiator of the visiting governor's car with a pickax, one of the prisoners maliciously tells them to plug the hole with rice. When the rice burbles up and floods forth as the car is started, they are in their innocence the instigators of a rice-throwing free-for-all between the prisoners, the warden, and the governor's party. They don't fit in anywhere, and when their own little world comes in contact with the larger one, mayhem and strife is the order of the day for all parties concerned.

Typically, the rice melee is started by Stan. The warden, demanding to know who's responsible for the vandalism to the governor's car, beckons Stan over. The warden kicks Stan face first into the large blob of rice. Stan arises, and with great deliberation flicks a handful of the rice into the warden's face. Ollie ineffectually tries to forestall Stan from striking back, and winces when he does so, but in such moments Stan is alive to the moment and beyond the constraints of societal roles in a way Ollie can never be. He is not a prisoner, and the warden is not the warden — just a man who's kicked him into the rice and who therefore must suffer vengeance. It only takes one person acting outside of established societal roles— that person usually being Stan — and, as we have seen repeatedly in Laurel and Hardy films, the entire structure of society collapses.

"Night Owls" (1930), their next film, shares with "The Hoose-Gow's" a reliance on mainly silent, physical comedy, with sound used appropriately — sparingly, not pervasively. The plot, with the team as two tramps who are convinced by a cop to rob the police chief's house, allowing the cop to catch them so as to improve the cop's standing with the chief, seems to be based at least in part on one of Laurel's old vaudeville sketches. In converting the sketch to a two-reeler, its creators seem to have been deficient in constructing any new, fresh business, for "Night Owls" is one of their least inspired comedies, containing nothing that is particularly memorable. For them to spend an entire film trying to break into a house is entirely in character, but there is no build or momentum to the film, so that it never rises above the level of the banal.

Looking to the past for ideas proved more successful for "Blotto," which is clearly inspired by their silent short, "Their Purple Moment." In the earlier film they were two husbands who make off with Stan's "held back" money to a club for a rousing good time, only to discover that Stan's wife has replaced the money with worthless coupons. Here, they attempt to make off with a bottle of the wife's liquor to a club — during Prohibition times— to find, in the end, that Stan's wife has replaced it with a concoction of cold tea and spices.

This is the film that allows, for the first and only time, the spectacle of Stan in the bonds of matrimony and Ollie in the role of the "outsider" who seeks to entice Stan away from home and hearth. Stan can't get out, so they devise a ruse by which Stan sends himself a telegram that, he tells his wife, says he has to go out on "important business." Here, more than in the silent "fool the wife" films, their innocence is seen — the joy in their attempt to deceive the wife is the innocent joy of children play-acting in their roles as adults. "She's so dumb she'll never know the difference!" snorts Stan with hysterical scorn, as Ollie chortles with merry conspiratoriality. They are, in their dumbness and their innocence, two children attempting, with great passion, to act like what they believe adult males act like. But what they are acting like is two children's conceptions of what adults are.

In this sense, Laurel and Hardy films are comic expressions of what a child's view of the world is like, the world we all, to varying degrees, are still in touch with — the world in which, more than we often care to admit, we still live, still react to the larger world from. Stan and Ollie are like children: always falling down, always making mistakes and making messes. The world around them and the people in it, for the most part, is the world of adults, which is grim, sober, unkind, hard. Stan and Ollie, for all their faults, are kind and gentle men, and in the purity of their emotions, and in their innocence, are alive to wonder where the world around them is not. The world around them is cynical, angry and violent, and has nothing but scorn for the team. This is the experience of the child's idealism as opposed to the "closed," unloving corrupt world of the adult. Their films are comic visions of the trauma of our own leaving of Eden, our own loss of innocence. In the topsy-turvy world of Laurel and Hardy however, disaster, misery, humiliation, and pain only lead to more innocence — not the wisdom that brings grim prudence and impoverishment of the senses. They strike out anew, undaunted, unbroken by their apocalypses, children unbowed by the brittle, hard-hearted world of the adults— as we wish we could be, and never can be. Experience has claimed us.

This sense of acting like adults is seen in the joy they take in their deception here and made explicit in the final half, when, settling in at their table, they begin to partake of their purloined "liquor." Drinking it, they smack their lips, attesting to its strength and potency. They become "drunk." The singer in the club sings a torch song, "The Curse of an Aching Heart." Over its course Stan and Ollie take it increasingly to heart, until by its end, both are unashamedly bawling, overwhelmed with sorrow and grief. They offer the singer a drink, who takes it and spits it out, saying, "That's terrible!" and departs.

But a very short time from this, Stan begins laughing, seemingly apropos of nothing. Ollie, puzzled at first, soon joins in the laughter. "Wait'll my wife finds out we drank her liquor!" Stan cackles, as Ollie surrenders to the hysteria. As in the closing moments of "Big Business," unrestrained merriment follows close on the heels of unrestrained tears— in their "drunkenness" they are freed from everyday behavior to run the gamut of human emotions, from one far extreme to the other. Part of the joke, of course, is based on the power of suggestion — they believe they are drinking liquor, and so they come to believe they are drunk, and act accordingly. But their ecstatic and emotional drunkenness exceeds that of anyone who has merely drunk liquor. The great joy they take in their freedom to laugh, to cry, is liberating to behold, for in these moments the "children" transcend and triumph over the sober, confining, disapproving adult world around them.

This adult world runs parallel to their child world and is seen in the cutaway shots inserted during their bacchanalian revel. We might be forgiven for having thought Stan's wife (Anita Garvin) to be the wry, forbearing sort, disapproving of the team's actions, yet observing them with a sort of maternal, cynical bemusement — as seen in her replacing the liquor with her own bizarre concoction, or in her taunting "Good night, Mr. Hardy!" to the furtively "hidden" Ollie. In the midst of Stan and Ollie's hysterics, however, the film cuts away to Mrs. Laurel in a shop purchasing a shotgun and some bullets. It isn't long before she is seen sleekly sliding into the background of the club where the team sits in the throes of merriment. And it isn't long before she unwraps her new purchase. Laurel and Hardy leap up and scramble out of the club in horror; she chases them outside where they escape in a cab. She fires the shotgun, and instead of a rear window being shattered or a tire exploding, we see the entire cab fly to pieces in the middle of the street, its occupants rolling into the gutters at each side. As the film fades out, Mrs. Laurel is striding purposefully with her firearm toward the men lying prone on the pavement. As in many of the team's other visions, liberation and exhilaration are followed by punishment and horror. The adult world is relentless and implacable.

Certainly the awareness that the dumbness of Stan and Ollie was not the mere stupidity of dolts, but in large part the inexperience and innocence of children, contributed to the conception of their next comedy, "Brats," in which they play their own children. The charm of the premise of "Brats" and the cleverness of its execution — amazingly seamless for such a small, unpretentious studio—contrive to make the film, in a way, beyond criticism. The team play themselves as fathers, and they play their children (Ollie sans moustache) on sets constructed three times larger than the one utilized by the "adults." The device by which two Laurel and Hardys are able to share the screen attracts no attention to itself, allows us to be convinced by its illusion. The scene in which the two men sing their sons to sleep, for instance, is great for the reason that all their best scenes are great — the interaction of the two characters, or, in this case, the four characters. The technical gimmickry that allows the scene to take place is taken for granted and doesn't distract from the performances.

It is the first film since "Early to Bed" that is essentially a two-man show — there are no other actors. Not surprisingly, there is little difference between Laurel and Hardy Senior and Junior. Big Stan and Ollie cause trouble for each other and fight amongst themselves, and Little Stan and Ollie fight amongst themselves too, perhaps more aggressively and honestly than their adult counterparts. The big difference between fathers and sons is that, understandably, the sons have more energy in pursuing their conflicts. In this more obvious aggressiveness, the sons bear more resemblance to the silent Laurel and Hardy — the adults are the more mannered, more thoughtful sound incarnations.

As with "Blotto," "Brats" concludes with a devastating gag of disaster that is carefully foreshadowed, "telegraphed," and made logical by its meticulous preparation. The sons have left the tap running in the bathroom, and throughout the last quarter of the film we see cutaway shots of the bathroom slowly filling with water. When, as they inevitably must, the boys ask for a glass of water, Stan moves to comply, but Ollie checks him: "You might spill it," he observes haughtily. Ollie moves to the door, opens it, and a tidal waves emerges, which washes the two men to the other side of the room.

The sense of grotesque fantasy continues with their next film, "Below Zero," which is one of the most dismal, desolate, relentlessly bleak films ever to be designated as a comedy. They are street musicians, playing on a snowy, pitiless stretch of street populated by angry, monstrous human beings. Great care is taken to convey the frigid grayness of their surroundings. Unlike their previous sojourn as musicians in "You're Darn Tootin," they suffer not from the inability to get in time with each other but from their inability to do anything that does not annoy and enrage their prospective audience. Certainly their cause is not helped by playing "In the Good Old Summertime," which arouses the waspish wrath of the frostbitten Charlie Hall. Yet they do comparatively little to incite an Amazonian hag, played by Blanche Payson, who strides over and in short order smashes Ollie's bass over his head and throws Stan's harmonium into the street, where it is naturally soon run over by a truck. In reaction to this, we are given a plaintive shot of Stan looking into the street and weeping.

Their luck seems to change when they find a lost wallet in the snow. A thief tries to take it from them, but they are saved from the thief by a chance collision with a cop. Ollie typically insists that the cop join them in a feast at a local restaurant. After the meal, they take out the wallet — and notice the picture in it is the cop's. Unfortunately, the cop notices too, takes the wallet, and leaves them to face the pugilistically ferocious waiters we've previously seen deal with deadbeats. The lights go out — the soundtrack invites us to imagine a calamity somewhere between a runaway freight and an earthquake.

We see the back door of the restaurant, through which the apparently unconscious Ollie is carried and dumped in the dirty snow of the alley. We see Stan's body carried out and dumped into a full rain barrel — with the carefully observed eye for gruesome detail often found in these films, it's necessary for the thug to break the ice on the surface of the water before he dumps Stan in. Ollie regains consciousness and immediately begins calling for Stan. Panic-stricken, he looks around for his friend, then grabs a stick and resolutely knocks on the restaurant door. Stan makes himself known, hiccuping profusely from within the barrel. Ollie asks where the water in the barrel has gone, and Stan replies that he drank it. This is verified when he is tipped out of the barrel and he waddles around with a belly distended to ludicrous proportions. As the film fades out, he is whispering urgently into Ollie's ear.

Certainly it is difficult to think of another of their films where the world around them, and by extension life itself, is portrayed so nihilistically, so bereft of mercy or hope. The futility of their efforts is seen in one of the film's first gags, which has them discovering that they've been playing enthusiastically for some time in front of an institute for the deaf. The people in the frigid world around them are not just indifferent, but actively hostile. When hope does come, it is pitilessly snatched away and leaves them in even more dire straits than before. Even their burgeoning friendship with the cop is not allowed to come to flower, and must be destroyed by unfortunate coincidence. After a time the bleak malevolence of their universe becomes so pervasive that it finds release in the grotesquely bizarre vision of the film's final frames.

It is a film about suffering, which offers no consolation, except perhaps to observe that excess of suffering, like the excess of anything, ultimately becomes absurd: that misery taken to its final conclusion ultimately becomes a source of laughter. But the laughter aroused here is manic, desperate, stopping just short of the demonic.

There is a pulling back, a return to a more moderately hostile world, in their next film, "Hog Wild." This is a return to the classic premise of Stan and Ollie attempting one simple task: to put up a radio aerial at the behest of Ollie's wife. The wife here is allowed, thankfully, a rather more tolerant attitude toward the team's incompetence: at one point she looks out the window and half-smiles in an expression of bemusement and love as they go up the ladder for the umpteenth time.

The wonderful simplicity of the premise is evoked consciously in the dialogue of the film when Stan asks: "Can I help?" and Ollie says: "Yes — if you'll help me." The skeptical qualification in Ollie's acceptance of Stan's help testifies that he at least half-knows what he's letting himself in for here. The characters, and their ritual, are so established by this time that even Ollie in his density is beginning to clue in to the way things have to go.

The only reason for them to install the radio aerial is as a pretext for Ollie to repeatedly fall off the roof of his suburban home into its accompanying decorative lily-pad pond. As with earlier variations on the never-ending running gag, the enthusiasm of the creators in inventing one more manner by which Ollie can be jettisoned from the shingles of his domicile is contagious, infecting the viewer. Each time we never see Ollie land in the lily pond — he merely bellows, waves his arms before helplessly disappearing out of frame. We see two splashes of water leaping into the air, looking rather more like the result of two men tossing buckets of water into the air from off camera—from opposite directions—than the result of Oliver Hardy's body plummeting into a pond. Then we see, naturally, Ollie lying in the pond, gazing disgustedly at us, perhaps with a lily pad in his mouth, which he pulls out and throws away angrily.

Ollie first falls when he slips on a pole Stan has laid on the roof. Then he falls when Stan trips him with a wire. Next, they both fall, bringing the chimney down on their heads as well. After this, Ollie falls down the chimney hole into the fireplace after Stan electrically shocks him. Each time the gag is done in a new, inventive way. Each time we are given the shorthand of the plumes of water splashing into the sky. An enthusiastic contemporary reviewer may have been overstating the case when saying that finally Hardy's falls passed "entirely into the realm of cutting,"[1] but the effect is similar—we are being beckoned into the abstract realm of sophisticated, symbolic slapstick.

And at the very moment when the gag is on the verge of being exhausted—and to stop anywhere short of that very last moment would be in complete contravention of their style—the scene shifts into a crazy car ride that concludes the film. Ollie is balanced at the top of the ladder in Stan's car; Stan is trying to drive and hold onto him at the same time. In the end, Ollie is mercilessly dashed against the pavement. His wife comes running to him, weeping; taking her tears as indication of concern for him, Ollie is momentarily heartened. Then she tells him she's crying because the radio's just been repossessed. Again, the switch.

They clamber into Stan's car, which is soon squeezed between two streetcars. The film ends with the image of them driving the grotesquely deformed automobile—riding high at the peak of its squashed accordion-like coils—from the scene. This final humiliation is like an emphatic exclamation point that fate delivers with a flourish at the end of 20 minutes of frustration. For it isn't just Stan and Ollie's stupidity that is to blame for their misfortunes—reality itself is seen to be rather steadfast in its refusal to bend to their wishes. Simply put, existence itself is malevolent toward them. Still, they are determined to strike out again, even more determinedly, such as when even Ollie's wife pleads with them to forget it for the day, and Ollie retorts, "I'll put that aerial up if it's the last thing I do!" The team's greatest stupidity, perhaps, is that they are unable to realize how thoroughly reality is against them.

With "Blotto," "Brats," and "Hog Wild," made one after the other, Laurel and Hardy hit their stride in sound film—these three films are some of their greatest work. It was only natural that after such a streak a letdown would come, and that is "The Laurel-Hardy Murder Case." As is the case with many of their inferior films, the characters here are injected into an established genre, in this case the horror-whodunit category, without any apparent care taken to create fresh material for the occasion. Most of the film's energy goes toward parodying — tiresomely — murder mystery films. "Murder Case," like "Blotto," is a three-reeler, but here the extra length seems unjustified. The reason for the film's existence — the "scare" scene, in which Stan and Ollie run amuck, thinking a ghost is pursuing them, is good. But after the bold visions of the last three films, it seems contrived and bland.

Lack of inspiration seemed to continue through the creation of their next film, which might explain why it's a remake of their first important work together at the Roach studios, the silent "Duck Soup"— which itself was based on a turn-of-the-century music hall sketch by Laurel's father. As before, the team, on the run from the law, seeks refuge in a deserted mansion and are forced to impersonate the owner and butler when prospective renters come by. Another three-reeler, "Another Fine Mess" is better than "Murder Case," but it is only tepidly amusing until Stan and Ollie begin their masquerade as the colonel, his manservant, and his maid — the last two played by Stan. What is captivating is the ease with which the two clowns flow into these new identities. Ollie is suave and courtly as the good colonel, and Stan coquettishly giggles in his new persona of Agnes, the maid — his scene with Thelma Todd is one of his greatest ever. "Another Fine Mess" is a good film that displays how the exuberance and skill of its two star performers could triumph over mediocre material.

However, their exuberance and skill couldn't save "Be Big," another three-reeler, and one whose extra length is entirely unjustified. The film begins as another "fool the wives" domestic comedy — they're preparing to leave with their spouses to go Atlantic City (Stan makes sure to take his toy sailboat and shovel and pail). A call comes from their lodge, informing them that a special dinner, with all manner of hijinks, is being planned for them that night. They decide that Ollie will play sick, opting out of the vacation, so that they can attend the wild party instead.

These opening scenes, which look back to "We Faw Down" in their enticement away from the wives by the promise of male comradery, are good. When they change hurriedly into their lodge uniforms, however, and mistakenly put each other's boots on, the remainder of the film veers from the "fool the wives" scenario to the "Stan tries and fails to remove Ollie's boots" dilemma — for nearly 20 minutes. It is entirely in character for Laurel and Hardy to spend twenty minutes attempting to remove footwear, as it was entirely in character for them to spend almost the same amount of time trying to undress in a cramped berth in "Berth Marks." The question is whether it is entertaining or edifying for us to be taken into this particular circle of hell. Even clowns as ingratiating and skillful as Laurel and Hardy are hard-pressed to wring laughter out of one basic situation for as long as they try to do here — and the extra 10 minutes the three-reeler format provides doesn't do them any favors. As is often seen, their characters, when left to their own devices, can often get stuck in a sort of demonic loop — the hat mix-up routine, their attempts to leave the office in "Bacon Grabbers," their attempts to row the boat in "Men O'War." In their incompetence they are drawn into a self-perpetuating cycle that seals them off from the rest of the world, which can spiral into a nauseating vision of infinite futility. In their best works, this vision is indicated — just enough to be funny and meaningful — rather than imposed on us to the degree that it becomes as oppressive to us as it is to them. At their best, we gaze into their vertiginous vision of infinite futility, standing close enough to relate to its truth, rather than being held hostage to it.

Evidently still in a period of creative malaise, for whatever reason, their next effort is again a remake of one of their silents. "Chickens Come Home" reheats the plot of "Love 'Em and Weep" — with Hardy now taking the role of a mayoral candidate who finds himself compromised by the return of an old flame, and Finlayson as his butler (in the earlier film, their roles were reversed). As in the earlier film, Laurel is the friend and assistant of the candidate.

What's fascinating is how well this film works, given that its basic plot comes from a period prior to when the team as an entity had been fully formed. Yet the team shows its versatility, now with their fully formed characters, in the way they make the plot work for them. The mammoth pretensions to dignity of the Ollie character are perfectly suited to the role of the nervous candidate who could lose all. And the Stan character is equally at home in his role as the assistant who mostly does everything but "assist" his associate. As always, his very existence carries the seeds of destruction for the false personality Ollie clings to. When we first see Stan he comes with flyswatter in hand, having just visited their business's fertilizer sample room (they are "Laurel & Hardy — Dealers in High Grade Fertilizer").

The form of comedy here is farce, and it is here that Hardy is really at home. From the first moments he dominates the film — there's a long scene of him at his desk, lighting his cigar, every inch the child acting out the role of a big, important businessman. The frenzied, almost unhinged embarrassment at being exposed before the world, and his panicked attempts to remain composed in the face of this embarrassment, are anguished expressions of the Ollie character and are some of the high points of Hardy's performing life. By contrast, Laurel fades more into the background here, more the ineffectually dull fumbler, as he seeks to keep Ollie's old flame out of the picture.

The concluding scenes provide a fair amount of fun, with Finlayson doing a fine job as the skeptical, scornful butler, squinting disapprovingly at each new proof of Mr. Hardy's indiscretions, yet proving more then amenable to accepting bribes for his silence. There's lots of frantic running around, and it's all well done — "Chickens Come Home" is the best of their three-reelers since "Blotto" — but it, like the films immediately preceding it, doesn't really follow up on the unique Laurel and Hardy vision as put forth in "The Perfect Day," "Hog Wild," or "Blotto." There is not the focus found in these earlier films, the sense of their illogical logic; they aren't saying anything new about the characters. With a few notable exceptions, the three-reeler format just didn't fit Laurel and Hardy. The basic, simple situations they were apt at developing into disasters could be efficiently and entertainingly explored in 20 minutes. That extra 10 minutes from the third reel often results in a sense of fatigue, of an overstayed welcome.

It's somewhat of a mystery why they persisted in the 30-minute format around this time — probably it was a novelty, an experiment for them. But it seems undeniable that alongside of this was a paucity of inspiration as evidenced by the high percentage of remakes they were doing of their silent comedies. They were casting around, at a loss for new ideas.

Then again, reusing, and improving, old material often gave birth to new inspiration and was one of the mainstays of their art in any case. Their repetition of old routines was often like musicians bringing back an old song, recreating it, and finding new life in it. Their next film proved this, in that it was a return to form as well as being a remake of the basic situation used in their very last silent, "Angora Love." They are back in their cramped bed, in their dingy, squalorous apartment, but this time they have allowed themselves the luxury of a pet dog, whose curious name, "Laughing Gravy," gives the film its title. It's a frigid, snowy night outside, and their irascible landlord is, again, Charlie Hall, who, naturally, is dead set against the presence of their canine friend.

Sentiment is lightly touched on here, in the obvious concern and love Stan and Ollie display for their little dog, who is shown to be their intellectual superior. If Hall, in parody of every melodramatic cad from time immemorial, kicks the dog cruelly out into the snow, Stan and Ollie must determinedly set out to rescue Laughing Gravy, causing no end of harm to themselves and to Hall in doing so. Yet the sentiment is leavened by such wry observations of psychological reality as Stan shutting the window after one of their rescues, thoughtlessly leaving Ollie to shiver in the cold night below.

"Laughing Gravy" is one of their most beautifully simple and elemental films. There is a humble craftsmanship in the way they mine the laughs from their very basic situation. And if sentiment is hinted at early on, the memory of it is totally expunged by the closing scene. Hall, having finally had enough, evicts them, escorting them to the door with shotgun leveled. Just as they're about to depart, a policeman is found to be nailing a Quarantine poster to the door — no one's allowed to leave the premises for the next three months. Hall notes: "This is more than I can stand," and leaves the frame with his shotgun. We hear two shots, and Stan, Ollie, and the cop respectfully doff their hats.

The focus is still there in the next film, "Our Wife," which concerns Ollie's enthusiastic plans to get married to his sweetheart. From the beginning, Ollie is in utter bliss, envisioning his approaching ceremony, and it's obvious he has nowhere to go but down. Stan is there to help him on the way. The opening scenes in which Ollie tries to have an intimate conversation with his beloved, the privacy of which is repeatedly violated by Stan — who is really quite ignorant of all such proprieties— points out some of the more disturbing implications of the film's rather strange title.

As noted before, Laurel and Hardy really can't be married to anyone else — they are both already married to each other. Their wives, and the world, take revenge on them for their lack of commitment, often with blazing shotguns. Yet Stan and Ollie bear no malice toward their wives. It's just that their ultimate loyalty is to each other.

"Our Wife" gives a different perspective to their domestic comedies in that it shows the beginning of one of their marriages. Because Ollie's prospective father-in-law — James Finlayson at his double-taking best — strenuously objects to the marriage after seeing a picture of Ollie, plans are made to elope. Stan is entrusted with the procurement of a vehicle and shows up with a minute car the likes of which a multitude of clowns might have miraculously disembarked from in an old circus routine. The routine here is performed in reverse, with Stan, Ollie, and Ollie's robust fiancée all trying to squeeze themselves into the absurdly small car. As in the case of "Berth Marks," the humor is in their attempting, with fervor, to do something that would seem to be obviously impossible. The routine here, however, goes on to just the right length — they do, somehow, all wedge themselves into the cramped confines, with Stan's head popping through the roof, and they set off jauntily for the justice of the peace.

Stan's conversation with the justice of the peace's wife can't really be illuminated by mere transcription — it is one more example by which his thought processes transform standard everyday communication into labyrinthine confusion. There really is something demonic about the way his use of language sabotages any form of clarity, and it isn't surprising that the judge's wife — the Amazonian Blanche Payson again — is only able to take several minutes of his nonsense before clouting him in the nose. And if Ollie, for his part, becomes so weakened and exhausted by Stan's stupidity that he can only sigh and accept it with sad resignation every so often, who can blame him?

This confusion and miscommunication are nothing compared to what happens when the Honorable William Gladding appears on the scene to officiate the proceedings. Gladding is played by that stalwart Keystone clown and Chaplin confederate Ben Turpin, arriving as a blast from the not-so-distant yet somehow immeasurably distant past of 1911. His cockeyes scanning both sides of the universe simultaneously, he picks up his book and begins muttering a string of incomprehensible gibberish. After conducting the ceremony, he shakes Stan's hand and asks to kiss the lovely bride, then steps forth and plants a wet one on Ollie. His wife calls out "William!" and snatches him away — this has evidently happened before — as the film fades out.

It is, of course, entirely appropriate that the two men should end up married to each other. If "Our Wife" isn't one of their classics, it is a film that is incredibly rich in so many of their idiosyncratic touches, the strange details that are part and parcel of their vision — the gag at the beginning in which Stan solves the problem of the wedding cake being infested with houseflies (and what a hoary close-up that is) by spraying the cake liberally with pesticide, leaving the tiny corpses to litter the icing; the forlorn resignation of Ollie's intended, Dulcy; the churlish scorn of the judge's wife; the ever-apoplectic contortions of James Finlayson; the bizarre natterings of Ben Turpin — which all combine to provide a glimpse into a homely, disquieting, out-of-kilter universe.

The strange darkness lapping at the edges of reality is also seen in "Come Clean." the film they made immediately after. It is a "married" film, and Mr. and Mrs. Hardy are shown enjoying a cozy night at home in connubial bliss, without "those awful Laurels." The Laurels show up outside the door shortly after; Ollie and his wife pretend they aren't home. Stan's wife is all for going home, because, as she says disgustedly, she didn't want to come anyway, but Stan wants to leave a note and he is quite interested to see that it is fetched from beneath the door. Finally forced to admit their unexpected guests, the Hardys feign delighted surprise, as does Mrs. Laurel — though the only one who truly desires the social event is Stan.

And naturally, all pretense of marital happiness fades for poor Ollie, for, with the arrival of Stan, his wife immediately becomes the scornful, spiteful wife of all other Laurel and Hardy films. Both wives go off in the solidarity of disgust they have for their husbands as Stan continues to bedevil Ollie with his complete ignorance of all social graces: when asked if he'd care for refreshment, Stan requests ice cream. When told they have no ice cream, Stan replies, "Well, you could get some ice cream." Stan and Ollie go off on their quest for the treat and Stan nearly drives the soda jerk (Charlie Hall) mad with Stan's inability to comprehend that there is no chocolate ice cream.

All this leads up to their encounter with an actual mad woman, Mae Busch, who is playing the quintessence of all her roles with the team, letting the hysteria flow unabated. She's a suicide, standing on a balustrade shouting, "So long world, I'm leavin' ya flat!" before leaping into the waves below. Stan and Ollie run to save her, but their bravery wins them not gratitude but scorn — she informs them her life is now their responsibility, and when they try to run from her she lets out a series of bloodcurdling screams. Reminiscent of their situation in "Chickens Come Home," they try to hide the existence of the crazy and dangerous Mae Busch from their wives — and Hardy in particular is in the panic-stricken embarrassment mode he plays so well in virtually all their domestic comedies.

Their fights, the actual wrestling matches they have with Mae Busch, are their frenzied attempts to maintain at least the illusion of domestic harmony they had enjoyed at the outset of the film. Just as it is standard in their world that if they are seen motoring off to work at the start of one of their adventures, the complete destruction of their job and of the workplace will be the order of the day by film's end, so it is with their marriages— which, like their jobs, allow them to have an acceptable identity in society. As always, they strive to maintain the fiction that they belong, that they have a place in the world, but all the while forces from without and within — and often the forces from without are but manifestations of the forces within — are working to depose them from the false place they've managed to wrangle themselves in society, are reaching forth to destroy their tenuous, false identities.

Here the Mae Busch character turns out to be wanted by the police and is taken away by the end of the film. Stan, it turns out — who, as a result of the recent action, is sitting fully clothed in a bathtub full of water — has earned a $10,000 reward for her capture. "Gee, that's a lot of money," Ollie notes, smiling, sidling up to Stan: "What are you gonna do with it?" "I'm going to buy ten thousand dollars worth of chocolate ice cream!" Stan says proudly. Disgustedly, Ollie reaches down and pulls out the plug. We hear Stan's cry, a gurgling sound, then see an empty bathtub. A wife enters: "Where'd Stan go?" "He's gone to the beach," Ollie observes sweetly. The madness swirling around the edges of banal reality has become manifest.

"Laughing Gravy," "Our Wife," and "Come Clean" are three very rich comedies—the first is perhaps the only genuine classic among them, but they are all bold, original visions. At their best, there is a view of reality articulated in them, which might exist just at the periphery of our comprehension or that might dwell closer to home than we are ready to acknowledge: two of the films deal with suicide, one ends with two men getting married to each other, and another ends with a man getting sucked down a bathtub drain. This last, it might be relevant to note, is a recurrent fear of young children.

Their next, film "One Good Turn," previously discussed in detail in this book, is somewhat too over-plotted to have the power of the three before it. Yet it does deserve credit for being an experiment, in that it seeks to explore the characters in a new way. They are hobos, "victims of the Depression," who beg at a kindly old woman's door for food. They overhear her rehearsing a play and assume she's in dire straits, so they auction off their old Model T — through a misunderstanding, Ollie comes to believe that Stan has stolen the old woman's money and forces him to make a confession to her. When he's shown to be innocent, Stan exacts revenge on Ollie for his false accusation, giving him a beating that has no parallel in the team's career.

The end, it is said, was devised for the benefit of Laurel's real-life daughter, who was understandably disturbed to see her father pummeled by his large partner in film after film. The fight is well done and says much about their relationship, particularly as it concludes and we can see their old order returning — we see that the constant fight between them is their relationship. There are many good moments throughout the film, but in the end it is more interesting than entertaining. As in "Laughing Gravy," the decency and compassion of the two men are shown in their concern for the old woman — even Ollie's wrongful accusation of Stan is based on his insistent, though wrongly pursued, ideas of honor and virtue.

"Beau Hunks" is in a way an experiment as well, as it is four reels (40 minutes) long, twice the length of their standard short. By this time they had already completed their first feature film, an experience they had been distinctly uncomfortable with, so perhaps this was conceived as a compromise between the forms. Or, more likely, the film started as a two-reeler and was found to be so full of possibilities that it expanded to 40 minutes — as Hal Roach recalled.[2]

It is a satire of *Beau Geste*, a popular foreign legion film of the time. As with the earlier "Murder Case," the film is at its least interesting when it is attempting to satirize the genre. The film's best parts are in its first half: the later "patrolling the desert" scenes seem protracted and long.

The film begins with Ollie in love — he displays much of his soul, and much of his creators', as he passionately sings "You Are the Ideal of My Dreams." Ollie has romantic attachments or yearnings for them, in a way that Stan does not and cannot have. This scene is a good indicator of the difference between the characters: Ollie sings in a rapture of romantic love, while Stan busies himself with snipping an advertisement for fertilizer out of the newspaper.

Ollie describes the great affair of his heart and Stan is utterly bemused. Ollie is given the heave by his loved one and resolves to forget his broken heart by joining the foreign legion. They both join, and the last half of the film is a prelude to all their "martial" comedies in uniform to come. The best parts, aside from the opening dialogue scene, are routines last performed in a couple of their silent films. They do the "leaving the office" gag from "Bacon Grabbers," in which they take around three minutes trying to leave the office of their commandant. First Ollie leaves behind his hat, then Stan leaves behind his hat, then he gets it stuck on the paper spike, then he puts the paper spike on his head, ad infinitum. It is performed splendidly here, even including the separate shot of them going puzzledly into the bathroom at one point, as seen in the earlier routine.

The other bit is the foot massage scene lifted from "Angora Love," in which Ollie, exhausted, sits beside Stan on a bed. Complaining that his feet are killing him, he reaches down to pull off his boot and tenderly massage one of his feet. Unbeknownst to himself, the foot he has lifted and is now daintily rubbing and blowing on is Stan's — yet Ollie grimaces and smiles, moaning "Oh, that feels so good!" in a sort of ecstasy of relief. Ollie really seems to feel the gentle care he's giving Stan's foot, with that unthinking persistence of conviction that so defines him — he's set out to treat and relieve the pain of his abused feet and to luxuriate in the tender care that brings the cessation of that pain, and that's exactly what he's going to do. It's like becoming drunk on the false liquor in "Blotto" — Ollie's reality is shaped by his will. Only when events conspire to bring his illusions painfully into collision with reality will he wake up and react with his customary anger and disgust.

On another level, his "feeling" Stan's foot is in line with the sort of floating disconnectedness with their bodies that both men experience. In *Block-Heads* (1938), Ollie will carry Stan around, put him down, hoist him up again, all the while believing that Stan has one leg, because that appeared to be the case when they first met. In *A Chump at Oxford* (1940), Stan is nonplussed by the extra hand he seems to have, courtesy of a prankster hidden in the bushes behind him — he accepts the hand for a while unquestioningly, putting it to use. Stan and Ollie are both child souls, not entirely conversant with the bodies in which they are contained or with the laws that govern those bodies.

Stan, for his part, mutely accepts Ollie's massage. He does not question Ollie's assumption of the task and he does not seem perplexed by the great, sensual joy Ollie seems to derive from carrying out the task. Stan simply leans back and enjoys the special treatment that his friend, for reasons unknown, is driven to give him. It's only when Stan is moved to ask "Can ya rub my back, too?" that Ollie is shocked from his reverie and angrily shoves the foot to the floor.

"Any Old Port," finds them once again wrestling with plot, though at the standard two-reel length. They are sailors, coming ashore on leave, and they check into a waterfront dive run by the thoroughly disreputable Walter Long. They soon find out that this repellent, unshaven, drunken lout is in the process of forcing his sweet, young skullery maid to marry him. The gentlemanly Stan and Ollie intercede, the lout is dispatched after a battle, and the servant girl goes free. Now bereft of money, Ollie decides that Stan will fight in a boxing match for $50. Stan enters the ring — and his opponent is the furious Walter Long.

There is the inescapable impression that there are two distinct parts of this film, and neither of them has much to do with the other. The first part sets up the melodrama in which the team displays much of the decency we had seen in their concern for their dog in "Laughing Gravy," and for the old woman in "One Good Turn." They save the girl from Walter Long, she escapes, and that's the last we see of her. The second half of the film, with the boxing match, doesn't grow organically out of what came before.

Apparently, an entire 10 minutes was shot detailing action taking place before the start of the film as we now know it. It was deleted after previews, and the boxing section was conceived and added later.[3] This accounts for the disjointed quality of the film and attests to the difficulty the team often had in arriving at the right structure with the right amount of plot for their comedies.

Though the concluding boxing scene is amusing, with Stan realizing that if he stays close to his opponent he can't be hit, thereby clinging to Long with his arms wrapped around his torso, the greatest value of "Any Old Port" is that it contains the best rendition of the team's "signing the register" routine. After Ollie with a great flourish graces the register with his signature, Stan makes his attempt to do the same, all the while bedeviled by Ollie's insistence on keeping his hat off his head while doing so and by his own paralytic clumsiness. Stan drenches the register in ink and ends up tearing pages out of it, to Ollie's mounting frustration and Long's disbelieving anger. This long, silent interlude — time really does seem to stand still — is classic in itself and makes the entire film worthwhile. Stan tries, fumbles, messes up, tries again, while Ollie and Walter Long stare at him. Finally, Stan does succeed in leaving his mark on the page: proudly he displays the "X" he's inscribed there.

The evident difficulties in sorting out the story of "Any Old Port" must have made the team newly aware of the necessity for simplicity in their structures. Their next film is as simple, to the point, elemental, and intimate — vis-à-vis the characters — as "Any Old Port" is not. The plot can simply be described as Stan helping Ollie clean up after a wild party he's had before his wife comes home. It is aptly named "Helpmates," and it is their first sound masterpiece.

The film is a cosmic meditation on the nature of the characters. As it opens, we see the essential Ollie, addressing us directly apparently — in what seems to be a new evolution of his by now-familiar camera look — before we see that he's staring into a mirror, reprimanding himself for his conduct of the night before. He is furious at himself for not living up to the high standards he has set for himself. The scene is the quintessential portrait of a man tormented by the chasm that exists between his ideals and the reality of his existence. He shakes his head in chagrin at his reflection: "I'll tell you what's wrong with you in two words: im-possible!"

By contrast, our first glimpse of Stan, once Ollie has phoned him to get him to help with the clean-up, is of a man submerged deep in the realms of the subconscious (or, it should be said, the unconscious). He slumbers in his disheveled bed; even when awakened by the phone, he is little more conversant or engaged with the laws of reality than when he was asleep. He talks nonsense into the phone, light years away from the tormented "self-consciousness" of Ollie — that is, when he's actually speaking into the phone and not into the buttocks of the curious trophy he's prone to mistake for the phone.

Ollie orders him over and hangs up the phone; a knock comes to the door, and Stan is there, fully dressed. It's one of the little cinematic jokes they enjoyed throwing into the films, and at the same time, like the "magic" Stan performs in the later films, and which this is a precursor of, it's simply an extension of the thoroughly "unengaged with reality" aspect of Stan's character. Stan is far away from even beginning to understand the troubles of Ollie, and the mundane struggles of the rest of us. The universe is kind to him because he expects nothing of it. When Ollie implores him to help him clean up before his wife's arrival, he tells Stan, "I'd do the same for you!" "No, you wouldn't," Stan demurs. "Yes, I would!" Ollie insists. "No, you wouldn't," Stan says proudly, "because I'm not going to get married!" And the beatific smile that follows after these words bespeaks an essential truth of the Stan character. Stan is truly simple and truly innocent, and in his guilelessness is quite unable even to conceive of the complex problems the rest of us face as a result of our constant attempts to dominate and manipulate reality. Stan in his simplicity is cheerfully free of the anxious deceptions Ollie, and the rest of us, are imprisoned by.

Ollie fears his wife's reaction to his devastated house, and to the fact that he's lost all his money in a poker game. He is overwhelmed with fear and anxiety and so solicits Stan's help in cleaning the house, in concealing the fact that he ever had the wild party, seeking to deny even to himself his "fall from grace." It would be obvious to just about anyone — except Ollie himself, of course — that he is embarking on a losing battle. But his panicked certitude that his house can be restored in time for his wife's arrival — that he can succeed in his great deception about his own nature — is matched in its delusion by his confidence that Stan is the man to carry out the task. As in all the other films where Stan "helps" him, Ollie never sees that he is seeking the assistance of one whose complete incompetence has caused him so much pain, whose density infuriates him even as he's trying to explain to him what he wants him to do. He seems to have utter confidence, unfounded in past or present experience, that Stan is capable of doing something right — or of even making a move that will not result in disaster for Ollie.

Then again, who else but Stan would tolerate Ollie's bullying, accede to his imperious demands, and carry out the thankless tasks assigned to him so uncomplainingly, for the most part? Occasionally, of course, Stan does rebel, such as when Ollie frantically orders him about after one of their catastrophes, shouting, "My wife'll be home at noon!" Stan retorts: "Say, what do ya think I am. Cinderella? If I had any sense I'd walk out on ya!" "Well, it's a good thing you haven't any sense!" Ollie shouts. Stan agrees: "It certainly is!" Stan is left to contemplate, fruitlessly, the meaning of the exchange for some minutes after this. The meaning, so beyond him, so beneath him, so evident and yet so incomprehensible (to him), goes to the very heart of their relationship. Stan is bound to Ollie because he has no sense, yet Ollie is bound to Stan and suffers because of it due to a far greater ignorance. Ollie does not know, yet is unwilling to admit that he does not know, and so pretends to know, the nature of reality. No one but Stan would entertain Ollie's pomposity for a minute and no one in the universe but Stan could innocently rain down such destruction on Ollie's head or mercilessly puncture each and every one of Ollie's pretensions.

"Helpmates" is the film beyond all others that articulates these truths of their relationship. As excellent as the dialogue quoted above is — and the film contains much of the team's best dialogue ever — "Helpmates" is mainly a slapstick comedy. The simplicity of its premise and structure, while being so meaningful and revelatory of the characters and their relationship, is also utterly functional as a framework for a series of very basic slapstick gags. Stan succeeds in washing and stacking a tableful of dishes; Ollie emerges, dressed to pick up his wife, but slips on a sweeper and is catapulted into the dishes. A bag of flour falls on Ollie's head. A stovepipe deposits a bunch of soot onto his head. Later, Stan throws a bucket of water into his face.

The running gag here is that Ollie repeatedly tries to get dressed to meet his wife. Each time he emerges from his bedroom, a new disaster befalls him and his wardrobe. At one point the light-the-match-and-stride-into-the-already-gas-filled-kitchen-and-get-blown-into-the-living-room gag is resurrected from "Unaccustomed As We Are." With each new indignity, the level of Ollie's frustration and panic rises — it's one of Hardy's greatest performances, giving the film its tempo and momentum — until Ollie laments in anguished tones, "Do you realize this is the last suit I've got left? It's enough to make a man burst out crying!" All along, Stan is ineffectual and fumbling — he can only watch the disasters accrue at an ever more accelerating speed, only puzzledly observe his every intention to help turn into another debacle for his friend.

Finally Ollie's wife calls and says she's at the train station, bellowing for him to get down there and pick her up pronto. Notably, this insert shot of the wife, and the fleeting appearance of a telegram delivery boy at the beginning of the film, are the only other performances in the film — otherwise it's virtually a two-man show. Ollie hurriedly changes into his lodge uniform and leaves Stan to finish the job. We see Stan miraculously clean the house, and, as a finishing touch, he endeavors to start a fire in the fireplace. He strikes a match, can't get the logs going, brings a can of gasoline, douses the logs, leans in closer with the match, the gas container overturns, the fuel spilling on the floor, he leans in with the match. . . .

Ollie arrives home later with his eye blackened and his ceremonial sword bent. He opens the door and is astonished to see that it is virtually the only part of his house still standing. Stan is hosing down the charred remains of his domicile. In response to Ollie's aghast "What happened?" Stan weeps, blubbering, "I wanted to start a fire . . ." After a moment, Ollie signals for his silence, gravely, stoically. What can it matter now, anyway?

"Well, I guess there's nothing else I can do," Stan observes reasonably. "No, I guess not," Ollie notes, now sitting in contemplative silence in his ruins, in a chair mercifully still serviceable in spite of the devastation. "Well, I'll be seeing you," Stan says, taking his leave. "Hey, would you mind closing the door?" Ollie asks. "I'd like to be alone." And alone Ollie sits, and thunder sounds from above, and a sudden cascading rain comes pouring down on him. He meticulously removes a piece of lint from his trousers as the film fades out.

There are images of devastation in the films of Laurel and Hardy, at once so bleak and catastrophic, at once so ridiculous, that they attain a sort of poetry, a sort of majesty in their hopeless depictions of destruction. We see this in the finale of "Helpmates," which has something at the heart of it that is terrible but also has beauty in it, and the joy of seeing things brought to their final, absolute conclusion. The proud unrepentance of its creators who took it as far as it could go is evidenced by the ultimate indignity afforded to Ollie as a parting shot after the destruction of all he has in the world (his marriage, his home)—the clouds part, and the heavens send down a vigorous rain on his head. The beauty and joy are inseparable from the terribleness, the real terror at the heart of this conclusion. We have seen the bleak side of things with them before, and we know now the degree to which Ollie must suffer for Stan's (and his own) stupidity. But this is beyond all previous downfalls, this outstrips anything we've seen before. It is a defining moment. Their characters have reached their absolute definition.

But the scene, and by extension the entire film, would not be as great as it is, would not be as near perfect as it is, without the one small gesture at its very end, said to be one Hardy himself devised and suggested on the set. As he sits getting drenched by the rain in the roofless interior of his house, he reaches down and picks the piece of lint from his pants. The film does not end with him sitting merely forlorn and overcome in his ruined house. It ends with him attending to his wardrobe. The lint removal signifies that whether he loses everything he owns or not, or whether even God Himself seems against him, punishing him with a rainstorm, Ollie will still be Ollie. He will still seek to maintain his ideal of decorum, his sense of being a gentleman, and take interest in the state of his wardrobe, as a gentleman does, even while soaking wet and newly homeless. It is an act of defiance against fate, against reality; it affirms Ollie in his all-too-human delusions, affirms his dignity and heroism in communicating in so many little gestures, all dainty and graceful and baroque, imprinting on the world his own little conception of beauty, his own "art," against the backdrop of a bleak and ruthlessly cruel existence. It is absurd and at the same time heroic. It is the human condition.

It is notable that "Big Business," their silent masterpiece, ended with a ruined home as well. In the earlier film, the home was destroyed by the frenzied battle device, which was the main tool in their arsenal at that time. In the later film, Stan destroys the house through incompetence, and most important, it is Ollie's house. The films have shifted their emphases to the dynamic between the two characters, rather than on how they affect the outside world. All of their art has led to this moment, this unabashedly tragic ending, and all the future of their art would proceed from this moment, this intense and unmistakable stating of the idea of Laurel and Hardy.

Astoundingly, they moved from this and, after spending three days shooting some new scenes for the troublesome "Any Old Port," went on to create their second and final sound masterpiece, "The Music Box." It's a remake of the film that had given birth to their career together (and from all accounts had been a classic, a defining and monumentally important film), "Hats Off." "The Music Box" returns to the geographical centerpiece of that film, the impossibly long and steep set of steps ascending from a sidewalk. In the earlier film they had been salesmen; now they are humble deliverymen, or laborers. In the earlier film they carried a washing machine up and down the stairs, a cumbersome object they seem to have taken turns carrying. Now, in sound, they carry a piano, which often jangles as they transport it, and which requires both of them, one at each end, to carry it, both bearing the weight equally. They are no solicitors, and they entertain no grandiose ambitions, other than to transport the piano to the top of the stairs. This is their duty, which they are utterly united in. But for the longest time, its fulfillment is denied them.

Again we see the simplicity of the premise, and again we see that this is a film based around one basic gag—the piano keeps sliding back down the stairs. It is repeated over and over, because it must be: the characters demand it. Yet each time it goes down, there must be a reason and an imaginative variation on the basic gag. They lose their grip on it when moving it to the side for a nanny and her baby carriage—it slides down the stairs. It slides down later, chasing Ollie down the stairs, then sliding over his back when he falls. They get to the top, knock at the door of the home; the piano, seemingly of its own accord, shifts, turns, and slides joyfully down the stairs. Ollie runs behind it to retrieve it, and it drags him down the entire flight of stairs. They carry it to the top again, and a mailman informs them they needn't have carried it up that way: there's a road running around to the top of the hill so they could have carted it up that way. Painstakingly, they carry the piano down the steps again, in order to bring it up the "right" way.

Granted, it's pretty idiotic even for Laurel and Hardy to carry the piano down the entire length simply to bring it up again by carriage. It's a pretty far-fetched expression of their "logic," yet it is done in service to the mythic entity at the center of "The Music Box," which is those stairs. The sheer intractable daunting fact of them and the sweat and toil they demand are a metaphor for life, for every torturous journey and impossible task Stan and Ollie face. The piano, borne between them, is their burden, and as each needs the other to carry it, working in tandem, with full cooperation, as they do here, we see it represents their relationship — it is their birthright, which they must transport unharmed to its proper destination.

It is not only the stairs that thwarts them in their mission but also fate, gravity, physics, geography, humanity. Their horse is against them. The piano itself, churlishly, almost demonically, seems to be against them. The nanny they encounter, with her infant charge, who they accommodate in the most gentlemanly manner possible, inconveniencing themselves terribly on her behalf, is against them, laughing at the misery they've brought on themselves. The policeman on the beat is against them. Professor Theodore Von Schwarzenhoffer — Billy Gilbert in his first and greatest role with them — is most vehemently against them. Still they start out again from the bottom of the stairs each time. "Heave!" "Ho!"

Their determination is not entirely stoic, however. In their encounter with the nanny, they are only able to stand so much of her mocking laughter before Stan — typically — hauls off and kicks her in the ass. We note that the entrance into violence is only made after extended provocation, and that the retaliation for it is lightning-swift — Stan receives a punch in the nose and Ollie gets a baby bottle broken over his head. In their encounter with the professor, we see him attempting to bully them into making way for his most esteemed self, disregarding their exhausted pleas for him to walk around with an outraged "What?! Me, Professor Theodore Von Schwarzenhoffer, walk around?" It is only after he has called them "blithering idiots" and has begun to jostle their piano that Stan — again — reaches out and sweeps his top hat off his head. How many times has the appeal of slapstick comedy been described through the metaphor of a child knocking the top hat off of "dignity?" And the image we are given of the top hat bouncing and wafting down the entire length of those stairs, in one long unbroken shot, finally coming to rest on the street below, where it is immediately run over by a leisurely moving truck, is one of the most poetic and beautiful in all of Laurel and Hardy.

"Hats Off," we might remember, ended with the first of their full-scale battles, and was in fact the introduction of their reciprocal destruction routine: the staple of so many of their silents. The emphasis of their art, as we have seen, has moved from these wars to the struggle of the two characters against a hostile reality. And so "The Music Box," focused much more on the stairs and the journey they represent, goes on with a continuation of that journey once they have reached the top — the climax of the "battle" by this time being far behind them. Finding the door of the house locked, the team tries to deliver the piano through an upstairs window — there is by-play with a fountain, a block and tackle, a lot of wandering up and down the stairs in the house, even some nostalgic hat switching, perhaps in homage to the earlier film.

This is one of the few of their comedies that benefits from its three-reel length. The first 20 minutes document their trip up the stairs and their encounters with various hostile individuals. The last 10 minutes consist of their struggles to place the piano in the house and focus more on their relationship and their conflicts with each other.

Their success in setting up the music box and getting it functioning — and doing a little soft-shoe shuffle in time to its music into the bargain — is quite unappreciated by Professor Theodore Von Schwarzenhoffer, the owner of the house, and the recipient of the eponymous musical device. He repairs posthaste to the back of his house, emerges with an ax, and hacks the piano to pieces with a murderous fury. "Pianos? Pianos? I hate and detest pianos! They are mechanical blunderbusses!" Stan and Ollie observe this behavior with perplexed alarm.

Their perplexion continues with the arrival of the Professor's wife, who is aghast at seeing him in such unhinged savagery. She tells him that she had the piano delivered as a surprise birthday present for him, and he becomes immediately, ludicrously contrite. "I wouldn't have had this happen for a million dollars!" he insists. "But you just said you hated pianos!" the wife notes. "Hate 'em? Hate 'em?" the professor insists. "Why, I'm nuts about 'em!"

In this same suddenly expansive mood he turns to Stan and Ollie and asks them, "What can I possibly do to repay you?" All that's necessary is to sign the delivery receipt, Ollie humbly notes. "Stanley, the pen." The professor, sobbing with remorse, takes the pen's cap off, and it spurts a jet of black ink into his face. His rage instantly begins anew, and he runs, grabs our old reliable friend the shotgun, and chases Stan and Ollie out the door, shouting "Get out of my house! Get out of my house!" The film ends.

This is the switch again, from reconciliation to renewed hostility, that we had last seen at the end of "Big Business" — the active rejection of truce, of sentimentality. People are essentially irrational: this is a common observation of the team's films. Stan and Ollie believe that things and people do make sense if only they had the capacity to understand how they make sense. Their earnest, steadfast pursuits and their sincere belief in the attainability of dignity, are mostly unreflected, unencouraged, and unappreciated in the world around them — here, even the simple dignity of a job well done is assaulted, eaten away by madness as the piano is axed into kindling wood (an image also seen in "Big Business.") With "The Music Box," Laurel and

Hardy create an indelible image of struggle and pain on those mythic stairs—their skyward journey on them is their journey of guileless, unfounded optimism, of diligent service to an ideal that vacated the premises long ago, these sentiments confounded by a universe dead set against them.

Although there was much great work to come, it's impossible to escape the conclusion that with the productions of "Helpmates" and "The Music Box," the team had reached the peak of their art, setting the standard by which all of their works would be measured.

After the creation of these two masterworks it's understandable that their next effort is slight and unambitious but still fun in its childlike, or childish, silliness. In "The Chimp," they are workers in James Finlayson's circus, which is one of the saddest, most woebegone and pathetic depictions of a circus ever committed to celluloid. The circus goes bankrupt, and its workers are paid off in pieces of the show—Stan gets the flea circus, Ollie receives the Ethel the chimp (she's actually a gorilla). Some fun is had in displaying the completely effortless rapport Stan has with the ape, even conspiring a bit with the animal against Ollie.

They go off and seek shelter with the chimp, trying to sneak into the boarding house of Billy Gilbert (who is only slightly less histrionic here than in the previous film). Naturally, Gilbert is mourning the disappearance of his unfaithful wife, whose name is Ethel. When the gorilla starts dancing around in the middle of the night, going into her circus routine, hauntingly, mesmerizingly, the team's cries of "Ethel! Stop it and come to bed!" are not lost on Gilbert, who comes charging into the room. The gorilla now hiding under a blanket on the bed, Gilbert addresses her form bitterly: "You, who I've loved more than life itself . . . the mother of my children!" Stan and Ollie look on in blinking confusion. When the gorilla's exposed, Gilbert goes further into apoplexy: "Get her out of here!" "But you said you loved her!" Ollie notes. The gorilla grabs Gilbert's handgun and begins shooting it, jumping up and down on the bed in a frenzy, as all run out at the end of the film.

"The Chimp" is one of those three-reelers that drags a bit, but it has its own homely and bizarre charm. "County Hospital," their next effort, has all the makings of one of their greatest films, but it fails in its execution of its final quarter. A two-reeler, it concerns Stan's visit to Ollie, who is laid up in the hospital with what appears to be a broken leg, encased in a gargantuan cast. When first we see Ollie, he is leisurely reading a book. Later he tells his doctor (played by Billy Gilbert) that this is the first time in years he's had a rest, that in view of that he doesn't mind his hospital stay at all.

Stan arrives, informing his friend he came to visit him because he didn't have anything else to do—he brings him hard-boiled eggs and nuts. Ollie reacts with distaste—couldn't Stan have brought him some chocolates? Stan points out that Ollie never paid him for the last box he brought.

There is a poignance in Ollie's relationship with Stan in that Stan can never be the friend Ollie so manifestly desires—in this, as in so many other ways, Stan fails him. Even with Ollie incapacitated as he is in this film, with a broken limb, Stan finds a way to make his situation that much worse, and uncomfortable. The visit starts out with the comparatively tame annoyances and frustrations Stan brings by sitting and eating his hard-boiled egg with a vapid expression on his face. Later, when he uses the counterweight for Ollie's suspended leg to crack nuts, he drops the mammoth cast-encased leg on the florid doctor's head. The good doctor grabs the weight and promptly falls out the window, causing Ollie to be pulled into the air, hanging by his broken leg, in one of their most brilliant gags ever. With Stan scurrying back and forth between the two sufferers—his suspended friend and the doctor hanging on for dear life—we see just how deep Stan's failures as a friend can cut. Once the doctor's been retrieved from the window, he orders Ollie out of the hospital at once.

"So you had nothing better to do," Ollie notes grimly, reproachfully, to Stan in the aftermath of this, "and you thought you'd come visit me." Stan looks down, on the verge of tears. "Here I was, for the first time in my life, enjoying myself, and you had to come and ruin it." The pathos inherent at the heart of their relationship is touched on here, lightly, as it always would be—they never ask for our sentiment or our pity. Ollie is always remarkably quick to forgive Stan, no matter what disaster Stan visits upon him. For that matter, Stan, in his rare flashes of temper, rarely stays angry at Ollie for long. But there are moments such as this, when Ollie's disappointment is so deep and so raw, the consequences of Stan's ineptness so tragic, that we can only marvel at the loyalty that holds this friendship together.

They get Ollie's things and depart the hospital. Stan has sat on a hypodermic needle full of anesthetic, so he falls asleep while driving Ollie home. Unfortunately, the thrills and chills of the crazy car ride are facilitated by crude and unconvincing back projection work—its obvious falseness is jarring and doesn't succeed on any level. In the end, their car is squeezed between two streetcars and emerges accordion-shaped. The first part of "County Hospital" contains some of their finest and most evocative work, but the film as a whole is ruined by its shoddy final act.

By contrast, much of the first part of "Scram!" is rather slow, but it builds to a glorious finale. In it, Stan and Ollie are vagrants, banished from the town by the local judge because the jail's full. In a rainstorm they encounter a drunk (the first appearance of the perpetually slurring, wavering drunk of their films, Arthur Housman). With typical kindness, they help him find his lost key. He offers to take them to his house to get out of the rain. But he can't find his key again, so they help him break into his house. Naturally, it's the wrong house, as the drunk finds when the butler comes and escorts him — bodily — out the front door. Stan and Ollie, meanwhile, have, at the drunk's invitation, availed themselves of a bedroom on the second floor, and of the silk pajamas and cigars found therein. The lady of the house discovers them, screams, and faints. They revive her with a tumbler of water — into which the drunk had lately poured his bottle of gin. She comes to, inebriated, and with a powerful urge to dance, wrestle, and laugh. She has a gay old time with her new friends— until her husband arrives home, who is the judge that banished them from town at the beginning of the film.

We see here the same device used in "Any Old Port," "The Music Box," and their concurrent feature "Pack Up Your Troubles," all made within a nine-month period. The device is that a person they had antagonized in the earlier part of the film reappears unexpectedly at the end, just when we, and they, had forgotten about them, just as the team seemed to be in the free and clear. Like some perverse manifestation of karma in reverse, or a grim meditation on the inescapability of the past, these embittered ghosts come to collect their dues.

It is used most strikingly here, in that the judge is the voice of sober moral responsibility in the film. When he orders Stan and Ollie to get out of town in an hour, he snarls, "Scram! Or I'll build a jail for ya!" When his wife hears the disturbance of the drunk being taken from the house, her butler informs her of what happened, and she states, "It's a good thing my husband wasn't here — he hates drunks!" Stan and Ollie are brought to the judge's house as a result of their committing an act of kindness. When the judge's wife sees them and faints, and they scurry with concern to revive her with a glass of water, it is another in a long series of twists of cruel fate that ever plagues them that the water has been spiked with gin.

Certainly since she's the spouse of one so morally upright and severe, we might wonder at her sudden enthusiastic casting off of dull care. But we see here a fascinating depiction of a moral universe, the social satire lurking just beneath the surface: Authority, or Societal Justice, banishes Stan and Ollie, and through a completely innocent chain of events, they cause Authority's worst nightmare to come to be. The judge's wife is laughing, unhinged in her nightgown, trying to get Stan and Ollie — two strange men she's found in her house in the middle of the night — to dance with her. "I don't want to dance!" Ollie cries helplessly, and Stan just cries. They are frightened by her absence of control. "Let's wrestle, then!" she says and leaps on them. They are mortified in their innocence by her behavior. Notably, there is nothing sexual here. The woman wrestling with Stan and Ollie is the equivalent of children playing on the floor. They're simply afraid of someone acting so strangely. And she is innocent, seemingly only looking for fun, for the freedom to roughhouse, and be silly.

Such is her desire for these things, that even Stan and Ollie with their caution and fear are caught up in its contagion, and they are joined with her in a thoroughly unprovoked jag of laughter that she suddenly goes into. She begins laughing, and they begin to smile and titter along, then they proceed to chuckle, then go forward to outright stomach-clutching guffawing. The laughing goes on for a protractedly long time — they all three partake of it and create it together, in a union of enjoyment that is in some ways more intimate than if it were a sexual one. Their laughter leads to more laughter, feeding on itself.

There are no other laughing scenes in movies that are like Laurel and Hardy's. Ultimately, there is something subversive about them, obviously in the case of "Leave 'Em Laughing," but here as well, where the laughter and the deep enjoyment of that laughter are depicted so joyfully and convey so much joy that they are a vivid and triumphant protest against the dismal grayness and misery of our everyday world. Simply to laugh for no reason, or for some silly reason, is seen here as an end in itself. It affirms the raison d'être of these films. It is in these scenes that the laughers achieve a sort of transcendence, or a freedom, from the world, from themselves and the roles they are made to play by the world. Of course the laughers also could be said to be very near the point of madness as well, but who can deny that the judge's wife is inebriated as much by her sudden rush of freedom as by the gin?

Yet here, as in other laughing scenes, the harsh, constraining forces of the world will not allow this freedom to stand. Never has it had a nemesis more formidable than the judge here, sullen and scowling in his moral rectitude. He arrives at his home, notices things out of place, mounts the stairs to the second floor. He sees Stan, coming out into the hall to procure a drink for the lady of the house from the same gin-spiked pitcher of water — after Stan departs, the judge sniffs the pitcher, confirming its contents. He moves to the bedroom, seeing his wife on the bed with Stan and Ollie, sees them bringing the glass of what he knows to be liquor to her lips. They enter into another laughing jag — their uproarious merriment is sharply contrasted with close-ups of the judge's face, which is seething with silent anger and righteous hatred. These contrasts echo those in "Leave 'Em Laughing," where the near-paralytic hysteria of Stan and Ollie is played against the dis-approvingly scowling face of the policeman (Authority) played by Edgar Kennedy.

We are given a shot of the three of them on the bed from the judge's perspective. We see what he sees—two men in his own silk pajamas, ply-ing his wife with alcohol in the middle of the night, reclining on a bed with her. He can only imagine what they've gotten up to before his arrival. They are laughing in the throes of what seems to be well-advanced intoxication— that state he despises and disapproves of so heartily. And they're the two bums he personally ordered out of the vicinity that very day! His glower-ing face shifts its expression from anger to real anguish, murderous rage.

From his perspective, we see the revelers flop back and disappear behind the headrest of the bed. Suddenly Stan does a double take, looking straight into the camera with an expression of shock, then fear. Then the wife looks, and quickly beats it out of there posthaste. Then Ollie looks and gulps with fear. We see the face of the judge advancing toward the camera, his sullen fury contorting his features. His expression tells us he's not just angry, he's emotionally destroyed; his eyes are glittering with real pain, with depthless, primal hatred. We see Stan and Ollie up against the wall, help-less against his oncoming fury. They fumble with a light switch and the screen goes black. We hear a series of calamitous crashes and howls as acts of violence that we dare not even imagine are presumably taking place, the sounds of which describe a universe being wrenched in half. With that, the film ends.

The construction of the entire film is brilliant. The early scenes with the drunk are amiable enough, and their attempts to "break into" the house are, like their similar attempts in "Night Owls," an occasion for some fun acrobatics. But it is the end sequence that so cleverly brings to the fore essential truths of the team's world: Stan and Ollie have been innocent throughout, coming into the judge's house through the kindness they showed to the drunk. In their revelry with the judge's wife, all three are transported into a joyous, childlike freedom — quite unlike that of the base debauchery of which the judge suspects them. He is the force of "moral" authority, both personally and professionally, so obsessed with suspecting and accusing others of the worst possible motives, that he never — in a thou-sand years—could conceive of the true innocent joy before him. He sees only sin. Or, perhaps, he sees freedom and must take action immediately to destroy it. He is a force of judgment, the world's justice, moving for-ward implacably to dispense punishment on the innocent. These final moments are among the greatest in the team's films.

It was shortly after the creation of this film that the two comedians left on their first extended vacation in five years. From the time of their teaming they had worked constantly, solidifying their hold on the public's affections. The characters they had created had entered into the culture, and though by this time they had made and released their first full-length film, it was through their shorts that they were welcomed, with the unreserved acceptance given to those who signify comforting familiarity, into the world's heart. Many times, these shorts were advertised and capitalized on to a far greater degree than the feature-length films they were created to support.

Their vacation, by all accounts, was a shared one purely by chance. Laurel intended to visit family in England — Hardy, never having been overseas, decided to accompany him to sample some of the famous golf courses of Scotland. MGM, the distributor of their films, seized onto the opportunity to turn the trip into a publicity tour. All pretense of a relaxing holiday was thrown out the window, as their vacation became an endless series of public appearances, interviews, and meetings with local dignitaries throughout England.[4]

The trip is relevant to this narrative in that for both men it would be a defining moment — when they realized how very much the world had taken the two characters they had created to heart. They were mobbed by crowds in Chicago, New York, England, and Paris to such a degree that at times they feared for their lives. They simply had no idea how much their films had been seen and appreciated until this time. Undoubtedly, they were moved by the passionate gratitude the public expressed for their clowning during the Depression, when carefree clowning was needed and appreciated more than ever.

The trip lasted for two months, and it was shortly after this vacation that was no vacation that the comedians were back in the studio, working on another short. Yet working conditions were somewhat different. Along with this new consciousness of their fame, there was the growing pressure to move away from the short films and into feature films. The increasing practice of programming double features by theaters was diminishing the necessity of the short film. The next three years would see their production of the shorts dwindle, as their attentions were increasingly dominated by making more features, until the shorts were phased out altogether in 1935.

Before that time, however, there were still many fine shorts to be made — 13 of them, to be exact — and one of the strangest and most memorable of them is "Their First Mistake," their first post-vacation entry. They are back in domestic mode, with Ollie married to Mae Busch, and Stan once more as the marriage-destroying friend. Ollie's wife doesn't want him seeing Stan all the time — so Stan suggests Ollie adopt a baby to keep her busy. They adopt a baby but find that the wife has moved out already and is suing Ollie for divorce — she's also suing Stan for alienation of Mr. Hardy's affections. The film ends with them stuck with the baby, attempting to tend to it.

Granted, there is in the premise something vaguely disquieting, slightly distasteful. Yet that is just the beginning of the strangeness of this film. We are made aware that we are in a world of not too sunny a disposition in the comedy's first seconds, when Ollie ventures timidly: "Good morning, honey!" and is met with a volley of abuse as blasting and as violent-sounding as a barrage of fire from a machine gun. "Don't you say good morning to me!" Mae Busch is insanely, tragically angry. "It's Stan this and Stan that! If you go out with that Laurel again we're through!" There is very little love in the hearts of the wives of Oliver Hardy. It seems that there is mostly only hatred and disgust — matched in equal measures with a perverse need to possess and control that which they profess to hate and are disgusted by. They are in a futile battle to deny what is manifestly true: Ollie is married to no one but Stan. Stan angers them, because he will not allow them total possession and total control over the subject of their hatred and disgust.

None of the wives have been as vehement as Busch is here in opposition to their partnership. She chases Ollie around and beats him with a broom. Sequestered in Stan's room, directly across the hall in the same boarding house — a rather strange living arrangement — the team discusses what they should do. In one of their most bizarre scenes, they lie back and lollygag on a bed as they exchange their dialogue, distractedly busying themselves with all manner of strange physical movements. There is an easy, unrestrained sense of intimacy in this scene, which is quite funny but also oddly affecting. It's a sort of unashamed, matter-of-fact intimacy, as children who have not yet learned to put up walls between themselves and the rest of the world. And again we see the great acting talent of the two men and the great chemistry that existed between those two talents. It is here that the dialogue takes place. Stan: "What's the matter with her?" Ollie: "Oh, she thinks I think more of you than I do of her." Stan: "Well, ya do, don't you?" Ollie: "We won't go into that."

It is here that self-consciousness begins to creep into their work. This isn't a bad thing — it's quite understandable given that they were now five years into creating and playing these characters. They are delving into the meaning and the nature of their relationship. The "We won't go into that" confirms what has long been evident: that Ollie chooses Stan above all others.

The nature of this choosing — and of what precisely is being chosen — is explored in depth in the very next scene, in which they arrive with the baby, find that Mrs. Hardy is gone, and are served with the divorce papers. They go into a very ripe melodrama parody routine, with Ollie as the discarded mother, Stan as the abandoning cad. Ollie: "You're the one that wanted me to have this baby, and now that I've got it, you want to leave me flat?" It's a type of overdone camp humor that they've never done before and would never do again, and it's all in the service of laughs, of course. But at the same time it begs the question: Are they male and female? Is their relationship a "marriage?" Are two men united so indivisibly merely a reflection of the standard heterosexual marital union? Now in possession of a baby, are they now, as the nominal parents of that baby, a "family?"

These questions are answered definitively in the final segment of film, which is merely a series of gags revolving around the baby. As unsettling as Stan and Ollie's bland assumption that they can get go out and get a baby, like any possession, and give it to Ollie's wife to stop her from interfering in their friendship, just as unsettling is the use of an infant by the creators of the film as another prop, entrusting its care to Laurel and Hardy as another project they can screw up. They smash and crash about in their usual fashion, the baby screaming all the while. They trip on electric cords, they crash through closed kitchen doors, they entangle themselves in each other's clothing — they run through all their usual business. The irrelevance of the baby to them is signified in the film's final images, as they bed down for the night. The baby cries and Ollie sleepily passes the bottle over to it, only to deposit the nipple in Stan's mouth. Ollie unwittingly feeds Stan several bottles of the milk before he realizes his mistake, leaping up from the bed angrily. Here the film, rather anticlimactically, ends.

As strange and as somewhat distasteful as the image of a grown man lying in bed and holding a bottle of milk for another grown man to suck on is, it is a telling one in defining the nature of their relationship. Here, Stan usurps the baby, hungrily nourishing himself on the nipple Ollie provides. They are not bound together by romantic love but by a bond no less intimate and strong, one more akin to that between a parent and child. Ollie is not Stan's father or mother but no one could argue that he is Stan's protector. As noted before, their films are comic depictions of our own loss of innocence, our own banishment from Eden. Many times, it is Ollie who actively seeks to lose his innocence, to eat the apple of the knowledge of good and evil. He is always on the verge of crossing over, but it is always Stan, who is innocence itself, who ensures that he will remain in Eden, ever innocent, ever a child.

As children themselves, they have no business — as this scene attests — setting out to look after a child. The insular nature of their relationship is affirmed. They have each other, but all they will ever have is each other. The film begins with their relationship being challenged and it ends with its essential nature being reconfirmed.

The self-consciousness is also a part of their next film, "Towed in a Hole." Here, they hark back to the formula of a simple, steady series of slapstick gags descending from "The Finishing Touch" and "Hog Wild." They are fishmongers, and as Ollie says, they have finally made a success for themselves. Stan, however, has the idea that they could make more money by getting a boat and catching the fish they sell themselves. They buy a boat and the rest of the film concerns their attempts to fix it up.

The gags here are simple, slow and deliberate — it really does owe a fair amount to the silent "The Finishing Touch." Yet here, each gag is absolutely grounded in the characters, and the deliberation and emphasis, with much use of close-ups for intimate facial reactions, add a sense of greater sophistication, and, yes, greater self-consciousness and self-awareness than we have seen before. The simplicity of the gags—Stan moving the rudder of the boat twice so that it whacks Ollie, resulting in him being doused with paint — is followed up with the incisive and extended reactions of the characters— Ollie sternly looking down at Stan as Stan meekly moves about the boat, attempting to avoid his gaze. The drawn-out sawing of the board as used in "The Finishing Touch"— where Stan laboriously cuts through the board Ollie was sitting on, sending him crashing to the earth — is now seen as Stan saws the mast that Ollie's ladder leans against, sending him crashing and splashing to the earth again. The sawing is just as prolonged and excruciating, but here the context and execution and the pay off are all much richer, infused as they are by the richness of their characterizations. Stan saws the mast because Ollie's imprisoned him in the hold because of his previous screw-up — he gets his head stuck between the mast and the bulkhead while amusing himself in some foolish manner and must saw himself loose. As Ollie paints above, he hears the sawing, and looks at us puzzledly. Stan adjusts himself, keeps sawing. Ollie stops his painting, looks down wonderingly, and frowns again with uneasy uncertainty. This uncertainty persists until the final moment before the mast jerks, then falls sideways, and he screams and falls out of frame.

Nowhere is this new, purposeful self-awareness more present than in the water fight they have with each other on the boat's deck. The two men pause in their work in order to pour buckets of water over each other in new and inventive ways. The "tit for tat" is now merely between the two of them —fittingly in a film that is basically another of their two-man shows (Billy Gilbert appears briefly to sell them the boat). When Stan takes the battle to another level by seizing the hose, Ollie quickly seeks to broker a truce, saying, "Wait a minute — isn't this silly? Here we are, two grown men acting like a couple of children!" Here we have it — the modus operandi of the team stated straight out for all to hear. "Why we ought to be ashamed of ourselves," Ollie laments, "throwing water at each other!" "Well, you started it," Stan points out. "No, I didn't!" "You certainly did!" And so on until Stan begins weeping, confirming their eternal babyhood.

Yet the self-awareness displayed in Ollie's encapsulation of their basic predicament, and in his further "Don't let's fight with each other — that's why we never get anywhere!" in no way impedes the further disasters and hostility to come, resulting in Stan being branded with two black eyes, his arms tied around a barrel to keep him from further trouble. It has always seemed a little brutal to this writer, and at odds with the team's essential equality, for Ollie to be giving Stan black eyes at this stage of their history. The recognition of their shared folly certainly doesn't hinder Ollie from accepting one more suggestion of Stan's in the film's final minutes — that of raising the boat's sail to help propel it when their truck proves incapable of towing it. A gust of wind sends the boat plowing into the truck and wrecking both, resulting in them not augmenting their business as planned but destroying it utterly. "Towed in a Hole" is slapstick done methodically, meditatively, more artfully than ever before — it is slapstick as character study.

The fascination with the characters continues in "Twice Two," in which they give birth to the feminine expression of these characters. The premise is that Stan and Ollie have married each other's sisters — which, one would think, would give them a better chance at happy wedlock than in the other films. The wives plan a special dinner for their shared anniversaries.

Unfortunately, Stan and Ollie fare no better in marrying the female versions of each other than in all their previous domestic arrangements. Fanny, the female Hardy, is, predictably, as bullying and short-tempered as any of their other wives. But the award for the portrayal of the most unpleasant and annoying of all the wives in the team's films must go, tellingly, to Stan Laurel. As Ollie's wife, Laurel is a screeching, backbiting, vengeful horror and is perhaps the most unabashedly hostile compendium of negative feminine qualities in their films. It's notable that as the film progresses, the wives take center stage with their petty bickering, leaving Stan and Ollie to fade ponderously into the background.

Obviously, the parallel here is "Brats," in which the team played their own sons through camera trickery. Here there is camera as well as aural trickery, in that the wives' voices are dubbed in — the female Laurel has a grating, high-pitched voice; the female Hardy, a lower, husky tone. Though it's certainly worth it to see Oliver Hardy strut gracefully around in a slip, and to see Laurel resurrect his curly wig once more, "Twice Two" is way off in its tempo and pacing, perhaps because of the need to lip-synch the voices, which presumably curtailed on the set improvising. The greatest problem is that nothing particularly happens in the film. The two couples meet for their dinner, which is ruined by the wives' increasingly hysterical jibes at each other.

In this sense, the film is one of their most scathing satires of domestic life. In playing the women themselves, the team is free to go all the way in skewering the pretenses and foibles of matrimony, all the way down to Ollie proclaiming, "I'll have you know that my family is every bit as good as your family!" In their portrayals of the catty, vicious women, the clowns come as close as they ever would to earning the accusations of misogyny that have been leveled at them unfairly through the years. But the greatest crime here is that due to its slow pace and its insufficient plotting, the film's interesting premise never really goes anywhere.

The slow pace is there in "Me and My Pal," their next film, and another experiment, though a slightly more successful one. Ollie is preparing to get married, and Stan is his best man. Stan brings his wedding present (a jigsaw puzzle) over to Ollie before the wedding, and they both become so obsessed with completing the puzzle that they miss the wedding. The film has the similar slow-simmering anxiety as a nightmare in which one knows that one is due at a crucially important event, but for some unexplainable reason, one is continually forestalled from making it to the event, as time drags inexorably on, and the decisive hour approaches and passes and we find ourselves mysteriously helpless to do anything about it. Stan sets the puzzle out on the table, Ollie regarding it with disgust as he awaits the cab that will take him to his wedding. Yet bit by bit, Ollie takes an interest in Stan's idiotic folly, venturing closer and closer, till he must draw up a chair and collaborate in putting the pieces together.

We see the sparse, consciously subtle, consciously psychological tone of the comedy here. In short order, the cab driver, a delivery man, Ollie's butler, and a cop all become enveloped in the puzzle. There are cutaway shots of Ollie's wedding party waiting at the church, with the bride weeping, and the bride's father (James Finlayson) growing ever more apoplectic. Phone calls are made, telegrams are sent to Ollie — these are ignored. The puzzle has become all — its solution is the all-consuming mission of the strength and attentions of all involved. In the end, the furious Finlayson arrives, precipitating a fight among everyone that rivals the mass chaos of some of the silent films.

There are many wonderful touches in "Me and My Pal" that make it oddly appealing, if not one of the team's strongest comedies. In the beginning scene Ollie listens, glowing with pride, as a radio announcer describes his forthcoming wedding to the daughter of oil magnate Peter Cucumber—until the focus of the news item shifts focus to "Hardy's confidante, close advisor, and sternest critic, Stan Laurel," going on further to detail Mr. Laurel's views on the motion picture industry and on technocracy (a faddish ideology of the thirties). In the final scene, after all participants in the melee are carted off in a paddy wagon, Stan and Ollie emerge from their hiding places. Stan hands Ollie a telegram that had come earlier, advising him to sell off some stock at a two million dollar profit. Before Ollie can phone his broker, news comes over the radio that the stock has crashed, "resulting in the loss of millions to its investors—now, back to The Happy Hour!" "Don't worry, prosperity's just around the corner," Stan offers, echoing wryly the common hopeful phrase of the Depression (in one of the team's few topical references—along with "One Good Turn" to that event), in which virtually everyone had lost substantially. Ollie throws Stan out and returns to furiously kick the pieces of the scattered jigsaw puzzle about.

Altogether less experimental is their next short, "The Midnight Patrol," a solid effort in the "occupation" mode—here they are employed as policemen. Sent to the scene of a break-in, they arrive and in the end arrest the apparent criminal, who happens to be their chief, trying to get into his house after losing his key. They bring him proudly down to the station, and he shows his displeasure with their mistake by borrowing a gun from one of his officers and shooting them as they try to make their escape. "Send for the coroner!" he intones as the film fades out.

It's a well-crafted if unremarkable comedy. The best scene is their attempt to break into the house—using the heavy marble seat of a bench as a battering ram, they swing it back and forth for momentum before charging ahead. Stan loses his grip, and Ollie goes flying backwards into a lily pond, the bench pinning him to its bottom under the water. For a moment, Stan can't understand why Ollie won't get up out of the water for another try at the door. We are treated to the blurry sight of Ollie on his back under the water, unable to move, his words gurgling to the surface in bubbles: "Don't just stand there lookin' at me! Do something to help me!" After an excruciating length of time, Stan gets the message and pulls the bench up off of him.

The team returns to their more unembellished slapstick roots with "Busy Bodies," a film that is in some way a sibling of the earlier "Towed in a Hole." Clothed in the same denim overalls, the team is once more driving down the road, celebrating their good fortune at being gainfully employed. Likewise, at the end, their job destroyed, Stan here finds trivial consolation in one minute aspect of their inventory that remains unafflicted by the general disaster that has overwhelmed them—to the outraged fury of Ollie. Whereas "Towed in a Hole" was openly self-conscious, "Busy Bodies" offers only a succession of slapstick gags executed with flair and grace. It is a masterful classic, a tour de force in which the clowns display their virtuoso skills in all their simple, spontaneous, and unpretentious glory.

They are workers in a sawmill. From the beginning, trying to enter the place, yet continually being struck by the plank two guys happen to be carrying by each time, notice is served that each and every slapstick possibility of the sawmill will be plumbed. And in the repeated slammings against the plank and the bodies hitting the floor, we can feel the rhythm, the music so crucial to the success of these physical hijinks. They proceed to their work, where in short order Ollie's fingers become stuck in a window frame. In Stan's attempts to free him, both men and the frame collapse on top of Charlie Hall. As a result, they engage in some fisticuffs with Mr. Hall, which ends with Stan offering him a cigar. Ollie is initially hurt by this but heartened when Stan calls over the foreman, and points to a "No Smoking" sign — thereby ensuring that Hall is immediately dispatched by the foreman.

The team returns to work. Stan planes off the posterior of Ollie's pants. Ollie bends back a saw, and lets it whip, slamming it down on Stan's head. Stan picks up a heavily shellacked brush, and shoves it hard against Ollie's chin. Ollie falls— Stan takes pity on him, and tries to remove the brush from his chin. He ends up lathering Ollie's face with soap and "shaving" it off with a plane.

It is a tribute to the film's craft, to its unassuming art, that one never notices how easily each of these preposterous events flows effortlessly from the ones before it. And the success of each of the gags here depends entirely on the skillful execution of all involved — it is entirely physical, like dance. There can be little doubt that when Stan, Ollie and Charlie Hall have their exchange of punches, we are watching three masters at work. As well, when Ollie is sent crashing into a wall as a result of Stan's shoving him, Stan goes to help but is interrupted by a man asking him to hang his coat up in the closet. Stan opens the door, hitting Ollie in the face. Ollie angrily slams the door shut, which causes a tool to fall off the wall and strike him on the head. Stan emerges from the closet, hitting Ollie in the face with the door again. Beyond the sheer skill in simulating all this violence is the rhythm, the music of it that causes it to be funny — the timing, which is so important, is here brisk, efficient, wry, musical.

As well, in the sequence immediately following this, in which Stan "shaves" the brush's bristles from Ollie's chin, we have the leisurely, inventive, seemingly improvisational spontaneity at the heart of so much of the team's best work. "Busy Bodies" has such a feeling of freedom, of uncluttered simplicity throughout its 20 minutes of purely physical comedy, that one almost does it injustice by talking about it in words. Within its tiny confines, emotions of jubilation, anger, jealousy, and remorse, a lot of what it means to be human, all pass through in a natural flow, almost without us noticing. Ollie is genuinely hurt when Stan seems to make friends with their enemy, Hall; his faith is restored when he sees what Stan's plan has been. Stan is angry enough at Ollie to shove him across the room; but he quickly takes pity on him and tries to help him. In its purity, uncontaminated by anything save the desire to arouse laughter, it is timeless and ever relevant. It is an example of their comedy at its very best — without typically ever calling attention to itself for being so.

"Dirty Work" is another "workman-like" comedy that finds them at an occupation. Here they are chimney sweeps, come to clean the chimney of a mad scientist-type. In addition to their antics as they try to do their job is the "science fiction/horror" subplot of the doctor mixing up his rejuvenation formula in his laboratory. At the end, the scientist calls them in to try it and Ollie falls into a vat of it, emerging as a monkey.

Before that are the standard creations of messes and tumbles off the roof. "Dirty Work" is probably best remembered for the scene in which Ollie lies in the fireplace after falling down the chimney. A brick falls down on his head — he shouts with pain. Another falls — he shouts again. Three bricks fall at once, in a cluster — he looks hopefully, despairingly, up. A brick falls down and hits him in the face. This could conceivably go on forever. Apparently Ollie isn't going to move until every last brick has fallen down on his head. It has something to do, we suppose, with the idea of letting fate do its worst, in hope that it will exhaust its inventory of misfortune.

"Dirty Work" is solid in the manner of "The Midnight Patrol," and it is pleasant but isn't essential in the way much of their earlier work was. As more creative energy begins to go to the making of the features, many of their last shorts are in this mode — good, even great, comedies that don't explore the characters or go to extremes to the degree that their really essential films do.

"Oliver the Eighth" is another one in this class, and it shares with "Dirty Work" the idea of bringing in a stock character from the "horror-thriller" movie genre to add to the fun. Stan and Ollie are barbers and decide to answer a personals ad by a wealthy widow looking for a companion. They both write in, with Ollie typically betraying his partner by depositing Stan's letter in the trash while mailing his own. The widow is Mae Busch, trumping her previous roles as dangerous women in "Come Clean" and "Chickens Come Home" by being both crazy and a murderess — she has married seven Olivers before and has handily slit each of their throats. Stan and

Ollie end up staying the night at her mansion, fearfully anticipating her appearance with a knife.

Like many of their films of this era, "Oliver the Eighth" is low energy and slow moving and isn't helped by its three-reel length (their last short in this format). The best part is the meal with Busch and her equally mad butler, at which imaginary food is served. Ollie gamely plays along and keeps having to convince Stan to do the same, until Stan finally exclaims bluntly to Busch: "You're nuts!" There is also some fun to be had in the team's fearful attempts to turn in for the night. They are horrified by the hand that appears to grasp the footboard of the bed and Stan shoots at it — only to find it's Ollie's foot. As well, there is Ollie's complex device to ensure that Stan will keep watch, as he dozes peacefully, but much of this is unpleasantly evocative of the night they spent in another mansion with another murderer in another substandard comedy, "The Laurel-Hardy Murder Case." "Oliver the Eighth" also shares the cop-out conclusion of that earlier film: the unsatisfying "It was all a dream!" ending.

"Going Bye-Bye!" is another one in this class of later plot-driven, rather than character-driven, shorts, though a very spirited and raucous member it is. Their testimony leads to the conviction of murderer Walter Long, and he swears revenge. They put an ad in the paper for someone to drive out of town with. Mae Busch answers, they go to her apartment, she asks if her friend can go with them — he has become locked in a trunk. The friend is Walter Long — just escaped from prison. They try to get him out of the trunk.

There are a lot of brash, violent gags here, and a lot of wonderfully observed moments: Ollie being propelled headfirst into his suitcase when Stan opens the door; Ollie's immortal quip "Excuse me a moment — my ear is full of milk"; their by-play with Mae Busch's doorbell — (and has any other comedian ever had as much interaction with doorbells as Laurel and Hardy? They're always ringing off the wall, or flying through a window, or their buttons are being pushed into the wall, or pulled out of the wall, or the ringers are exploding and falling off the wall onto Ollie's head); their exchanging back and forth of the flowers as they work on the trunk and run around during the last half of the film — a surreal running gag, somehow deeply funny on a human level, yet utterly nonsensical too. In keeping with the roughness of the film, it ends with their most repellent "freak ending" yet. Long makes good on his constant vow to "tear off their legs and tie 'em around their necks." We are given the disturbing image of them in this condition in the final shot, with the by-now expected "Another nice mess!" from Ollie and the helpless weeping of Stan.

Following swiftly on the heels of "Going Bye-Bye!" and thankfully more leisurely paced and gentler in tone is "Them Thar Hills," an unexpected gem of a comedy and perhaps their last really great short. Ollie is laid up with the gout, and the doctor prescribes mountain air and plenty of water (and lots of it). The team rents a trailer and heads for the wilderness. We see a shoot-out between bootleggers and police — the bootleggers pour their liquor down a well. The well is naturally at the very place where Stan and Ollie set up camp. They become obliviously drunk on the "water" when a couple — who could it be but Mae Busch and Charlie Hall? — come to get gas for their car. Stan and Ollie innocently get the woman drunk, much to the chagrin of her husband.

This film contains two great sequences. The first is in a long scene of the team preparing their meal in the trailer once they've set up camp. For a protracted length of time we simply see them going about mundane tasks in real time: Ollie fastidiously sets up a table, spreading out the tablecloth, with his trademark delicate gestures; Stan concerns himself with the tasks assigned him — preparing coffee, buttering bread, chopping wood. They both carry out their tasks with quiet incompetence. Stan hands Ollie the wrong utensils, he butters the bread before slicing it from the loaf, he switches around objects on the counter so that Ollie removes the top of a canister rather than a can of beans. But what is notable in this audaciously extended sequence is the subtlety of the comedy being performed, a little minuet of confusion and ineptitude. It is a scene that isn't really like anything else in movies. It's one of the scenes where their magical chemistry as partners is displayed for all to see.

As they go about their duties, Ollie hums a little song with which Stan can't resist joining in. As Ollie becomes more perturbed by his accompaniment, he gradually becomes more menacing in his singing, daring Stan to continue with his participation. Yet Stan does, as he must in the face of Ollie's authoritarian wrath, persist with defiance in his singing, adding his voice emphatically to the refrain until he's met with the dustpan Ollie clangs against his head, furnishing the climax to this extended, mesmerizing scene. "I'm singing this song!" Ollie asserts vociferously.

The other great segment occurs when Hall returns from filling his car with gas to find his wife and the team merrily singing away. Like the judge in "Scram!" he is completely outraged by the condition he finds his wife in at the hands of the team. He is infuriated, grabbing his wife and shoving her roughly out of the trailer, causing Ollie to protest "Hey — you can't treat that lady that way!" Hall punches Ollie in the snout, and here, in the last quarter of the film, our old friend — the reciprocal destruction battle — makes its appearance once again, all the more welcome and hilarious for being so unexpected. The mean, eternally resentful Hall is given a pat of butter slapped atop his head and has a hank of his hair snipped off and affixed to his chin with molasses, both courtesy of Stan as Ollie roars his delighted approval.

The sequence works so perfectly because it flows so naturally from the events we've seen unfold before us: Hall, already angry and short-tempered, already feels he has had his pride wounded by his wife and the team. Stan and Ollie, in their oblivious joyfulness, merely see a mean-spirited, hate-filled man. As always, Stan is the main angel of vengeance — with inventive exactitude, he is instantly, magically able to devise from the everyday objects around him the retribution that is the most inspiredly absurd and humiliating possible. Stan and Ollie are heroic in their imaginative defense of innocent, joyful whimsy against the enraged disapproval of Hall. If Hall is ridiculous with butter on his head and hair glued to his chin, he is doubly so with a plunger stuck to his forehead, and later, with his belt cut so that his pants fall around his ankles. Ollie is the one who absorbs most of Hall's anger, in the form of precise punches to his nose, and on whose behalf these punishments have been carried out, but he is also the one who derives the most enjoyment from them, hollering with laughter at Hall's comeuppance. In a great touch, Ollie pounds the table in his merriment, causing his plate of beans to spill into Hall's fallen pants, a happy fact duly noted by Ollie, arousing him to even greater heights of hilarity.

As it must, the jubilation comes to an end with Hall destroying their trailer, then setting Ollie afire. At Stan's suggestion, Ollie jumps into the well to put himself out but the alcohol-filled well blows him sky-high — not exactly what the doctor ordered for his recuperation.

"Them Thar Hills" benefited from its happy revisitation of the savage battles of the past — their little war with Hall is perhaps their most concentratedly hostile since their fight with Finlayson in "Big Business." "The Live Ghost" is more in the fashion of their comedies of late — it uses elements of an established genre and is more plot-driven, less spontaneous-feeling. In this, its aesthetic is more similar to that of their features, particularly in its elaborate sets and obvious care taken to create atmosphere. It is a nautical adventure — they are hired by Captain Walter Long to shanghai a crew for his ship — a boat no one will willingly sail out with since it's rumored to be haunted. Stan and Ollie are shanghaied themselves and end up at sea with a shipload of sailors united in their anger against them. A drunken Arthur Housman and a tub of whitewash allow them to "see" a ghost.

It's probably the best of their "horror comedies," although that isn't saying a lot. It's pleasant and fun, with some nice dialogue and some frantic running around in panic. The end, in what is now becoming a convention, consists of Walter Long carrying out an absurdly grotesque threat he's been making throughout the film, as he did in "Going Bye-Bye!" He has promised to reward anyone talking about ghosts on his ship by twisting their heads from back to front, and when the team attest to what they've seen at the end, he shows himself as good as his word. It seems more obligatory than inspired, by this time.

Undoubtedly, the comedians had been exhilarated by their reclaiming of their old style in "Them Thar Hills" and understandably desired to keep the resurrection going. If the reciprocal destruction seemed to sneak back in at the end of that film, it only made sense to attempt to build an entire comedy on it, like in the old days. Their blatant intention of doing just that is shown in the title of their next work — "Tit for Tat." Stan and Ollie are the owners of an electrical shop who get into a battle with the owner of the grocery store next door. If the title of the film doesn't point out its self-conscious raison d'être, the sign on the front of the store does — "Open for Big Business."

The problem is that what had seemed so naturally unplanned in "Them Thar Hills," and what had seemed a necessary emotional catharsis in "Big Business" and the other silents of its ilk, is now contrived and forced in "Tit for Tat." The beauty of its prototypes was that they allowed us to see, unfolding logically and gracefully before our eyes, how a cataclysmic, destructive war could proceed from a trifle, how emotions leading to vengeance and violence could bubble up from under the most mundane everyday events at a moment's notice and lay waste to the world. In "Tit for Tat," the main source for the hostilities that erupt are not even to be found in the film — it is a "sequel" to "Them Thar Hills." Mae Busch and Charlie Hall play the same roles as in the earlier film, with the memories of that conflict fueling the new film.

Not that "Tit for Tat" isn't a very funny film. Any comedy that allows Ollie to be propelled into Mae Busch's bedroom, then to walk down the stairs with Mae and arouse her husband's anger as he tells her "I've never been in that kind of position before!" obviously has a lot going for it. And no film can go wrong when it has Stan and Ollie exchanging ridiculous indignities with Charlie Hall as they march smartly back and forth between their respective stores, doing their best to destroy those stores — as all the while a little man is seen departing from their establishment carrying progressively larger pieces of merchandise (the topper to the running gag — he pulls up a moving van to the entrance of the store by the end). It is funny to see Stan and Ollie dump an entire canister of lard over Hall's head, as it is funny to see Hall smash the light fixtures one against the other in a domino effect across the length of their store.

It's all funny, but it isn't essential as it was in their earlier works, and the hostility doesn't point toward and satirize larger hostilities as the early battles did — it simply exists as a tradition and ritual in and of itself. The policeman and the crowd who watch the accelerating destruction are not passively complicit in that destruction as in "Big Business"— the crowd is merely dispersed by the cop at the end, who himself is the victim of what is here just another in a series of reasonably inventive gags. Again, funny, perhaps a nostalgic trip into the past, but not particularly meaningful.

They revert back to the form they had been using in "The Fixer-Uppers," another plot-driven comedy with a consciously created atmosphere — this time a distinctly Parisian one. It's a remake of one of their early pre team shorts, "Slipping Wives." The team (they are Christmas card salesmen), is engaged by a lovelorn woman (Mae Busch again) to save her marriage by making her artist husband, Pierre Gustave, jealous. It is arranged that Ollie will kiss her in view of her husband — this being Paris, the artist not only becomes jealous but also challenges Ollie to a duel to the death. There is some byplay with the eternally intoxicated Arthur Housman, and the novel setting provides some interest, but overall this is a very low energy film, with virtually no physical comedy. It's probably the best example of how the team's attentions were being siphoned away from the shorts as more time and money were being put into the features. Though the star performances are great as always, something in the construction of "The Fixer-Uppers" and several of these later shorts seems unambitious, half-hearted.

And yet, as is the case with virtually all of their Roach films, there are moments and gags that are magical, which do rise above the general innocuousness and provide something magnificent. Here, the Mae Busch character seeks to show them how her husband kissed her at their first meeting, so as to display the type of firepower to make her spouse jealous. She demonstrates on Stan, wrapping her arms around him, pressing her lips to his— he stands limply, his lips unparted, in infantile asexual stupor. His eyelids flutter weirdly, his eyeballs roll back in his head. The kiss persists. Ollie, looking on, shares with us his growing annoyance. The kiss persists. Ollie takes out his pocket watch, consults it. With rising amazement now, he holds the watch up to his ear to see if it's still ticking. The kiss persists, then Mae Busch breaks away, leaving Stan to fall thudding to the floor. Now emboldened, he leaps to his feet, pecks Mae Busch in return with a funny "pop!" sound effect, and she swoons helplessly across a couch. It's one of their most audacious "extended" routines.

It isn't that "The Fixer-Uppers" isn't enjoyable — it's just that in its restrained tone, it pales beside their earlier, more intensive work. Thankfully, with "Thicker Than Water," their final short, they return to the

brutal domestic comedies of their past and create one of their most raucous and spiritedly silly episodes. Ollie's wife here is perhaps the most furiously unpleasant since Mae Busch in "Their First Mistake"—the mood is
set in the first scene, in which Ollie kisses his finger and extends it to his
wife's lips. She responds by biting down hard on his finger.

Stan is a boarder in the Hardy household. Money is tight, and through
the participation of Stan, the funds intended for the payment of their furniture have gone astray. Moved by Ollie's lament of "creditors hounding
me at my fireside," Stan comes up with the idea of pulling out all the Hardy
savings from the bank in order to pay the bill off and own the furniture outright. They do so, then venture into an auction where a woman asks them
to hold the bidding on a grandfather clock for her; they become saddled
with the clock, all of the Hardy life savings consumed by its purchase. When
they get home, Ollie is trounced so soundly by his wife that he is taken to
the hospital and given a blood transfusion.

Once again we are in contact with the darkness that lurked at the heart
of the domestic arrangements of "Their First Mistake," or "Blotto." There
is no love or mercy in Ollie's relationship with his wife, and the whole film
has an inevitable, foredoomed quality—we know it is trouble when Stan suggests taking the money out of the bank, and we see further trouble on the
way when they enter the auction. Though "Thicker Than Water" is mainly
remembered as being the last Laurel and Hardy short, it distinguishes itself
by containing several great routines. There is first the dishwashing sequence
when Mrs. Hardy orders them into the kitchen to clean up, rather than
attend the ball game as they'd planned. It's simple stuff—Ollie washes the
dishes, hands them to Stan, who dries them, then places them back in the
tub from which Ollie extricates the dishes to wash them and pass on to Stan
to dry.... It's another of their demonic loops that threaten to go on forever
until Ollie catches on and angrily tells Stan to find another place to put the
clean dishes. Stan puts them on a functioning gas burner. When Ollie picks
them up to put them away, he shrieks with pain as they crash to the floor.

After this, the furniture store owner — James Finlayson in his valedic-
tory Laurel and Hardy short-subject appearance — arrives to collect his payment. What follows is a complex dialogue sketch the like of which wouldn't
have been out of place in an Abbott and Costello film, as Finlayson helplessly attempts to navigate the labyrinthine logic of "She gave the money
to me to give to you to give to her to give him to pay my rent." It's a great
striking out into a new realm of comedy for the team; especially for Stan,
nothing could be more self-evidently rational than the tale of the progress
of his rent money. Predictably, it's all too much for the furiously double-
taking Finlayson, who gives up: "You're all nuts!"

In addition, there is also the fine sequence in the auction, where they try to hold the bidding for the woman, not realizing for some time that they're bidding against each other. Finally Ollie says, "You're bidding against me!" "Well, you're bidding against me!" Stan reasonably replies, and continues to bid defiantly until Ollie has to grab him and physically restrain him from doing so.

At the end, Ollie is beaten with a frying pan and is given a blood transfusion. Stan is called on to donate some of the lost blood and something goes haywire in the process—Laurel ends up with too much of Hardy's blood, Hardy ends up with too much of Laurel's blood. Their final scene is of them exiting from the hospital. Stan has taken on all of Ollie's mannerisms and characteristics, including his voice, hairstyle, moustache, and necktie—he coyly waves it to the nurses in parting. Ollie now has Stan's voice and personality—he gazes blankly from his clean shaven face, scratching his thatch of unmanageable hair straight up.

After all this time, they have made the final evolution—having shown themselves to be indivisible, having walked off in the past like one organism shoved into a single pair of oversized pants, they now make the leap and actually become each other. The gag is childishly silly, of course, and freakish and disturbing to boot, but beyond this, there is something indisputably right about it—especially coming in their final entry in the form that they would forever claim to be their ideal, their authentic and ultimate artistic canvas. Economics and change were forcing them into new, larger, more respectable enterprises. But here, in the shorts, whose unpretentious freedom allowed an atmosphere in which anything could happen, something did happen which couldn't have happened anywhere else—and this they must have known well. They had come together from wildly disparate backgrounds to form this new entity: the miracle of their partnership had occurred with the creation of two characters, neither of which could have been born without the other, neither of which, once being born, could or would exist without the other—ever, through all recorded history—as the men behind those characters also had come to know full well. These two characters, so identifiable that now the fact of that identifiability is a gag, came to life and found their greatest expression in the anarchic, violent, cartoonish world of the 20-minute-long film. Knowing now that freedom was gone and would never be attained again, they go out with the nuttiest, most far-out and bizarre gag imaginable—and also, and this is by no means contradictory, the truest gag possible.

From now on, they would be the prisoners of plots. Many of the features would have great moments, equaling anything in the shorts, and several of them would be great in their entirety. But never again would their comedy flow so clear and unimpeded, never again would their vision be allowed to assert itself without restraint, as it did in the short films. By all accounts, the happiest working years of the comedians' lives were during the production of the shorts, and the joy that was taken in their creation transmits itself to us through the years. It is part of what makes these films so special, along with the great thrill of discovery within them on the part of the performers, which gives them a luminous quality. They are among the great treasures of comedy that humanity has sympathetically gifted itself with. And the great liberating sense of freedom their laughter affords us has been passed on from the freedom in which they were created, which was only possible within this humble, lowly and unpretentious art form.

6

FEATURES

Stan Laurel expressed the view that he regretted they had ever gone into features.[1] Both the comedians preferred the shorts, and one senses they both felt a little bit out of their depth in the features. Their technique consisted of following a situation as it logically and organically spiraled into utter disaster. This was ideal for the 20-minute length yet could not sustain a movie for 60 minutes.

Inevitably the need to bring in other elements to sustain the film resulted in a corruption of their comedy, leaving many to lament their impurity in comparison with the perfection of the shorts. Yet there is much greatness in the features—many of their classic scenes are contained within them.

There is a sense in many of the features of the middle period of a battle between the Laurel and Hardy world of aimless whimsy and the containing, mundane world inserted to "propel the plot," and give us normal, mediocre people "we can really care about," instead of those two idiotic, bumbling clowns. Because the features cost more money, the boss had greater say on what should be included in them to appeal to a broader audience. Though Hal Roach had no greater moneymakers than Laurel and Hardy, and their ascendancy to that status was achieved largely through the vision of Stan Laurel (and the freedom offered by Roach to pursue that vision), once the team began increasingly to work in features, a fight for control began between the producer and the artist, causing a great deal of frustration on each side. This fight exists as a constant tension behind these films and resulted in the team leaving Roach and, in so doing, terminating their artistic existence. Paradoxically, they would find less freedom at the other studios, and they must have looked back ruefully at the compromised freedom they enjoyed on the Roach lot.

If many of the stresses surrounding these films stemmed from economic forces, so the team's entry into features was at the behest of economic realities. The market for the short film was dying, owing to the Depression-era phenomenon of double features and to the growing popularity of animated cartoons. Though both of the comedians at the time expressed that they weren't in favor of making the transition to longer films, these realities ensured that it wouldn't be a question of if but when that transition would be made.

The opportunity presented itself when they were beginning a short in 1931 with a prison theme. The idea was to use the sets of the current MGM prison feature *The Big House*. When MGM insisted that Laurel and Hardy exclusively make a film for them in return for the use of the set, Roach balked and built his own sets. These sets proved so expensive that the two-reeler became a six-reeler by way of justifying the expense.

The resulting film *Pardon Us* (1931) has all the disjointed qualities one might expect of a 20-minute film extended to three times its intended length. Laurel would describe it as a "three storey building on a one story base,"[2] meaning that the film's premise — Laurel and Hardy go to jail — couldn't adequately support the added footage. What are they supposed to do when they get there? This question obviously puzzled and tormented the makers of the film, as scenes were shot, then jettisoned, then reworked, previewed, and shot again over a six-month period. All involved worked to get a handle on the new form.

For all of this, *Pardon Us* works — the grim penitentiary sets give the film a unity and are nearly another character in and of themselves. The delicate characters of Stan and Ollie seem all the more so when thrown into the belly of this beast and are surrounded by various damned gargoyles of malevolence. The film has no plot. Stan and Ollie are admitted into jail, get mixed up in an escape plan, escape, are brought back to prison, inadvertently foil a prisoner revolt, are released. The dynamic of the film is based on the essential goodness and decency of the Stan and Ollie characters in contrast to the ferocious evil of the inmates surrounding them. There is a sense of horrific, cruel despair in the backdrop of the prison scenes, against which the pure innocence and helplessness of the two friends are all the more highlighted. The film explores these qualities and contrasts between the world's brutality and their gentleness more than any other — though it had been touched upon in "Below Zero" (1930). In a way, the prison is just a heightened version of the world Laurel and Hardy usually find themselves in.

Admittedly, the unwieldiness of the construction is at times unavoidably apparent. A bathing scene is there simply to allow Ollie to slip on the soap and fall in the tub. There is a school scene, with Finlayson as the teacher, which serves no purpose other than to recycle a series of hoary jokes undoubtedly half-remembered from a dozen vaudeville schoolroom sketches. The escape interlude is more bizarre than anything else, with the team "blacking up" to blend in with a group of black cotton pickers—fittingly, it's one of the few times they find an idyllic and sympathetic home, for awhile. The film seems to lose direction in its final 20 minutes, founders, then is brought safely into harbor.

Disjointed though it is, *Pardon Us* is also quite humorous—Finlayson as a teacher presiding over a classroom of scarfaced toughs is funny, and the utter improbability of that scene gives it the absurd, loony feel one associates with British music hall. The scene in which Stan and Ollie are thrown into solitary confinement (Stan asking before he's locked into his tomblike residence: "Do you have the time?") is an essential example of the team's bleak humor, and the long dialogue sequence that ensues, with just the comedians' voices heard over a single static shot of the doors of their cells, is effective and audacious in this very early sound film by two primarily visual comics. As a running gag throughout the film, Stan is given a "buzzing tooth" which causes him to emit a "raspberry" a sound approximating a sharp burst of flatulence, after every line he speaks. The buzzing tooth causes Stan and Ollie no end of troubles with the criminals around them and the authorities above them. It's a perfect accessory to Stan's general ability to wreak havoc around him simply by serving as a reminder of the elemental truths everybody else works so assiduously to conceal.

The prime authority figure here is the warden, presiding over this bubbling cauldron of misery and hatred and overplayed with true pompous fervor by Wilfred Lucas. He is also, uniquely in the films, a father figure to the "boys"— or rather, aspires to be, as he mellifluously welcomes them to the prison with grand eloquence and virtuous admonishments at the beginning of the film and then bids them farewell in a similar fashion at the end. In both cases his attempts to effect magnanimous wisdom are destroyed by his offense at Stan's "raspberries," which leaves him shouting and gasping for breath in astonished outrage.

Pardon Us has a purity and loyalty to the "Laurel and Hardy world"—even in its messiness— which begins to become compromised in their next feature, *Pack Up Your Troubles* (1932). Evidently, someone realized that it might not be a bad idea for a feature-length film to actually have a plot, and so here they are World War I soldiers who take on the responsibility of caring for the young child of one of their fallen comrades.

The first part of the film depicts their misadventures in war, belonging to their subgenre of "military films" ("Beau Hunks," *Bonnie Scotland*, *Flying Deuces*) in which they cast the carefully ordered regiments into complete chaos simply by their very presences. In this sequence we are introduced to their colleague Eddie, a handsome young fellow who is Stan and

Ollie's pal and a character who would have been completely unthinkable to portray in any of the shorts of the time.

The second part of the film details them trying to find the child's grandparents after the war. All they know is the surname Smith, so of course they go through the phonebook investigating each person they find listed there. In the third part of the film they are on the run from the authorities that want to put the child into an orphanage.

What's interesting here is that though through most of the film Stan and Ollie are motivated by trying to protect the little girl, little is done to depict their relationship with her. There are a few stabs at sentiment, but her presence is largely to serve as a prop in a series of very unsentimental, quite adult gags—they contact a number of wrong Smiths, including a boxer who looks at the child and sneers "Blackmail, eh?" before he clobbers them, and they present the child as the offspring of a groom at his wedding, precipitating yet one more entry in the Laurel and Hardy series of marriages as farcical disasters.

The reason for this lack of sentiment can be seen in the film's best scene, a role reversal gag in which Stan is lulled to sleep by the child's story. Besides being very funny in its execution, the gag is meaningful—unlike the relationship between Charlie Chaplin and his young charge in *The Kid* (1921), in which the clown and the child are depicted as equals, Laurel and Hardy must inevitably be seen to be less mature, more childish than the actual children in their movies, in the same way they must be inferior to everyone else in their movies. Note the special care taken in the films to ensure that even animals are seen to be invariably more intelligent than the team (Suzy the horse in "The Music Box," Dinah the mule in *Way Out West*, the eponymous dog of "Laughing Gravy"). Though the driving idea behind the film is that Stan and Ollie are the girl's protectors, this is essentially at odds with the childish ineptitude by which the team is defined—just as the sentiment one would usually expect from such a situation is at odds with the Laurel and Hardy world we have come to know, which is radically unsentimental and raises our emotional expectations only to mercilessly dash them.

That is exactly what happens here. When in the final moments of the film Stan and Ollie finally succeed in uniting the girl with her grandparents, they are told gratefully by the grandfather that they can "pack up their troubles from now on" and the soundtrack swells as the butler is instructed to tell the cook there'll be two more for dinner. The chef comes scurrying out of the kitchen in a rage and turns out to be the army cook Laurel and Hardy had earlier antagonized. The film ends with him chasing the team out of the house while waving his knife.

Pack Up Your Troubles is pleasant enough, but it isn't as funny as the more homely *Pardon Us,* and it doesn't allow the team to display its art to its fullest strength. Their next film allowed them considerably more comedic scope.

Fra Diavolo, or *The Devil's Brother* (1933), is based on an 18-century opera by Auber and is the first (and the most successful) of their three "operetta" features. It must have seemed quite audacious and unique at the time, to write themselves into an opera for a feature, eschewing completely their standard costumes, and fullheartedly embracing the entire period milieu. Here, in their roles as comic servants, they make explicit their ancestry, which includes not only the fools of the British music hall pantomime but a lineage going all the way back to Shakespeare's jesters and the clowns of the Commedia de L'arte and further. There is something timeless about the costume films, and the one with the most timeless quality is *Fra Diavolo.*

The idea of doing an opera feature sprung from the team having been lent out to MGM to provide comic relief for the opera picture *The Rogue Song* (1930) — a film now lost. The original Auber opera contains two comic servants, so these parts were enlarged for the team. The appeal of the opera films is that they provide a readymade plot and music, so that the team isn't stuck with the task of advancing the plot; they need only appear frequently to perform comic routines within the context of the plot. In *Fra Dialovo,* there are some of their best routines ever — the earsie-eyesie-nosie and finger-wiggle scenes, the wine-pouring scene, the swaying-chairs scene, and one of the best of their laughing scenes.

The downside of the opera pictures is that the plot and characters providing that plot can be rather tiresome and directly at odds to the attitude of the comedy. Here there is more of a unity, in that the title character (Diavolo) is a sadistic, brilliant, sleek thief, who is working to separate a vain, frivolous woman — and her dullard, grotesque husband (played by Finlayson) — from a large sum of money. Stan and Ollie — or rather, Stanlio and Ollio — are forced to be his henchmen under duress. There is one of the team's exercises in morbidity in a scene where Stanlio is forced to hang Ollio. Later, they think they've captured Diavolo in a sheet — it's actually Finlayson — and they violently kick and beat him.

The beginning of the film where Stanlio and Ollio are robbed of their life savings by bandits, and then decide to become bandits themselves, is in keeping with the progression of many of their films, as their eager attempts to conform to society result in them rejecting it outright, overturning the tables and striking out anew. Here they are allowed to live outside the dreary reality of society yet still maintain their innocence. They are forced to assist Diavolo in his banditry at the same time as they plot to capture him. They exist in a magic no-man's-land between the confines of society and the ruthless criminality of Diavolo, belonging to neither world, floating in uncharted space, manifesting their foolishness. Notably, virtually all of their scenes involve just the two of them, reacting to each other, with few props, creating comedy in their self-contained little cocoon, as the opera and all its trappings unfold around them.

There is a sophisticated sheen to *Fra Diavolo*, and the great care taken with the costumes and sets makes it their most elaborate and attractive film so far. It's obvious that it was a very important production for the Roach studios, and its success ensured that more Laurel and Hardy operas would be made. Though the straight plotline and particularly the songs are inevitably less interesting than the comedy sequences— especially for contemporary audiences— at least here they are in keeping with the team's sensibility, and *Fra Diavolo* offers the pleasure of seeing them at the height of their powers— at the peak of their fame — performing material as great as any they would have.

Sons of the Desert (1933), their next feature, offers these pleasures as well, along with a plot into which they are entirely integrated. The film, based in part on their sound short "Be Big" (1931); (Ollie feigns illness so that they can attend a lodge function) and their silent short "We Faw Down" (1927); (their wives, unbeknownst to them, discover their ruse and grimly watch as they try to defend it) was prepared over a lengthier amount of time than usual, resulting in their most masterfully constructed feature. It is as meaningful as their best shorts, and its theme of self-deception means that just as much — or more — of the humor is resultant of psychological comedy as it is from slapstick. The concentration here is on the inner lives of the characters, the degree of their innocence versus their corruptibility, their otherworldliness versus their worldliness— these inner struggles map the arc of the action, motivate the plot, in a way they do in no other feature.

Fittingly, the world depicted in *Sons of the Desert* is more "real" than in other features— the atmosphere of the film is more similar to the "highbrow" comedy films being produced concurrently in Hollywood than to any of the team's other films, and the wives are fleshed out here more than anywhere else, given a few more emotions than just bitterness and spite. Though Stan's wife follows in the great Laurel and Hardy spousal tradition of always keeping a shotgun at the ready, at least here the predilection is given a practical underpinning — she's a duck-hunting enthusiast, after all.

If the second half of the film is basically an enlargement of the idea at the end of "We Faw Down," that of two men lying to their wives, not realizing that their alibis are only damning them further for their wives know the full breadth of their indiscretion — it's instructive to note the differences between the way the two films handle this idea. They illustrate the evolution, or the changing nature, of the Stan and Ollie characters.

In the earlier film they both took part in the elaborate lies, working with each other to maintain the deception. Not a lot is done with the idea that the wives already know they're lying. Then the idea is brought in that the theater where they claim to have spent the afternoon burned down, but not a lot is done with that.

Here, the burned theatre has become the sinking ship from Honolulu. The brilliant idea has been added to the routine whereby the wives have turned on each other and devise a morality test for their husbands. Stan and Ollie enter and begin telling outrageous lies for a while but are soon brought to the moment of truth by their wives. The film then becomes an exploration of the differences between the two characters in much the same way as many of the shorts they were making at the time were similar quiet explorations, such as "Me and My Pal" (1933), or "Towed in a Hole" (1932). Stan weeps the truth, Ollie reaps the whirlwind. "We Faw Down" concluded with them being chased from the premises by their wives wielding shotguns. Here, their individual inner natures are allowed to carry events to their logical consequences — instead of fleeing together, they are separated: Stan is rewarded for his guilelessness, Ollie is punished for his dishonesty. The films become more about the characters than what the characters do.

Sons of the Desert is as tightly controlled as any of the shorts, as well. It also benefits greatly from its cast, especially Mae Busch and Dorothy Christie as the wives, and notably, the other star Roach comedian Charley Chase. Their scenes together in the convention sequence are excellent, and certainly the great respect the comics had for each other, the pleasure they must have taken in working with each other and from noting the momentousness of the occasion of their doing so, accounts for the palpable sense of warmth and enjoyment one gets from this sequence — perfect for a party scene.

Sons of the Desert was a great success, and the team continued their winning streak with their next feature, *Babes in Toyland* (1934), based on the Victor Herbert operetta. Unique even among the opera films, it takes place entirely in a fantasy world, one that in a direct contrast to the prison setting of *Pardon Us* is as childlike and innocent as Stan and Ollie themselves. They are given less to do here than in *Fra Diavolo* — virtually all their appearances serve the purpose of advancing the plot — but their essential goodness integrates them entirely within this land of nursery rhymes and fairy tales. If *Babes in Toyland* suffers from a deficit of classic Laurel and Hardy scenes, it illustrates how pleasant it is just to spend time with the characters, especially within such an atmosphere of fancy and wonder.

Unfortunately, the atmosphere surrounding the making of this most whimsical, unpretentious film was anything but pleasant. Roach had purchased the property, which simply consisted of a series of vignettes and songs. He wrote a proposed plotline for the movie that was rejected by Laurel. They wrangled for a time, then Roach threw up his hands, leaving Laurel to do as he liked, and leaving Roach bitter about the experience forever after. This would mark the beginning of the discord that would ultimately break apart the Roach–Laurel and Hardy partnership.[3]

Undoubtedly, and understandably, the great expense involved in the production of such a film — with its elaborate children's storybook sets— meant that Roach would feel a greater need for control over its making. The plot Laurel created for the film was roundly condemned by Roach — as was the resultant film — yet it is difficult to see how the melding of the Laurel and Hardy world with that of Toyland could have been achieved better. Stannie Dum and Ollie Dee, as tenants of the Old Woman Who Lives in the Shoe, try to stop her from being evicted from her shoe by the evil Barnaby, who tries to force the woman's daughter, Little Bo Peep, to marry him. In the end, Barnaby attacks the entire land with his army of subterranean bestial demons known as the Bogeymen. The land is saved by an army of six-foot-tall wooden soldiers (the result of Stan's stupidity: he'd taken Santa Claus's order for 600 toy soldiers at one foot tall and instead made 100 soldiers six feet tall), allowing the witless innocence evinced by Laurel and Hardy to triumph over primordial evil. The climactic battle has been criticized as being too disturbing for children to watch, but it's no more frightening than much of what Disney put out in the same era.

It must have galled Roach that it was a large success, that it earned the team many of their best reviews ever, and that it would go on to become a sort of semi–Christmas classic, running perennially at the holidays on television in many areas. As his studio was producing some of the biggest spectaculars it would ever give birth to, he was anxious to maintain as much control as he could. This battle for control with Laurel would loom large behind their next feature as well. Notably, it was during this period that the shorts were being phased out, and the team was switching to making features exclusively.

Babes in Toyland is their only film made expressly for children, and though it's entirely successful and enjoyable on that level, it isn't a typical or prime Laurel and Hardy film. Neither is their next feature, *Bonnie Scotland* (1935), though here that designation is applied in an entirely negative manner. The film is the clumsiest attempt yet to insert a straight plotline: an earnest, blandly attractive romantic couple of unequalled banality whom our beloved clowns assist in their realization of their hearts' dreams (that loathsome accessory soon to become ubiquitous in the Marx Brothers' MGM films). Not only is the plotline here thoroughly uninteresting, but it also doesn't even have the decency to properly resolve itself. Even the title is a misnomer, because the team is first in Scotland, then quickly hightails it to India with the army for the rest of the film.

There is far too much footage dedicated to the straight plot, making it their most difficult Roach feature to sit through, and the routines they are given in the context of the plot are generally rather weak, contributing to the film's lack of success. In Scotland, most of their scenes take place in the claustrophobic confines of their boarding-house room and consist of pedestrian material about evading the landlady, cooking on the sly, etc. In the army, there is a routine about mirages, in which they are made fools of by the other soldiers, who stage an elaborate prank to mock their stupidity. It goes nowhere and displays a strangely inappropriate contempt for the characters of Stan and Ollie in that we are expected to laugh with their tormentors at their ignorance. It is the attitude that will emerge again in the post–Roach films, where we're invited to sympathize with the "real, normal" tax-paying citizens against the two exasperating dummies. In an authentic Laurel and Hardy film, our sympathies are entirely with Stan and Ollie and against the "real, normal" world. Once "reality" is introduced, and the audience is expected to empathize with the "real" characters, Stan and Ollie inevitably become "other," and their stupidity becomes annoying rather than endearing. Note that even Eddie, their pal in *Pack Up Your Troubles*, becomes irritated with their foolishness.

There are great moments in *Bonnie Scotland*, as there are in virtually all the Roach films. There is a classic dancing scene, a run-in with Finlayson, and a scene where Stan causes an entire regiment of soldiers to march out of step along with his skip-step. There is also one of their most bizarre and outlandish sight gags wherein Ollie sneezes an entire river of water dry. It's true that the great scenes are so great that they do, in a way, justify the existence of the film as a whole. But it is tough sledding between these scenes, and the earnest pledgings of the young lovers in the "real, normal" world are annoying and irritating indications of the film's schizophrenia, in direct violation of everything we have come to expect in the Laurel and Hardy world.

As one might divine from such a badly made, fractured film, its creation was blighted by a great deal more hostility between Roach and Laurel: at one point during story discussions Stan was fired and there was extensive re-editing of the film after its premiere. It was the first attempt to put the team into a film with an original contemporary "straight" story existing independent of them, and it doesn't appear to have been a great deal of fun for anyone involved.

It was perhaps with relief that they turned back to the readymade plot of opera with *The Bohemian Girl* (1936). It is an improvement over *Bonnie Scotland*, though it suffers in comparison with the other film it most resembles, *Fra Diavolo*. Here, Stan and Ollie are gypsies: Ollie's unfaithful wife kidnaps a Count's child and runs off with her lover; Stan and Ollie are left to raise the girl, and at the end she is reunited with her father. In between the songs, the team performs their routines, which are good, though not as good as in *Diavolo*. One is a direct remake of a scene in that earlier film: Stan's attempt to bottle wine, which results in more of the liquid being poured into his increasingly besotted self than into the bottles. Here, Stan performs the scene alone, without Hardy's reactions, so that it becomes more straightforwardly a showcase for Stan's pantomimic skills. As such, it's an impressive display of Laurel's ability to pace and imbue with uncountable subtle inflections a scene like this, which depends on his portrayal of gradual — at first oblivious, then wanton — intoxication. Yet the absence of Ollie and the concentration on Stan would seem to make it a scene that aspires to arouse our admiration as well as our laughter, somewhat in the nature of some of Chaplin's set pieces. In this sense it is a bit of a digression from the standard Laurel and Hardy style — where the masterful deployment of craft is made to seem effortless if not unnoticeable and asks of us only our amusement.

The other routines consist of them gypping the local citizenry, then trying to gyp each other. Naturally, Stan is more proficient than Ollie in these undertakings, and the ease with which he carries out his pilfering sleight of hand illustrates how much more at home he is than Ollie in these costume films. In their contemporary films, where they attempt to fit into a world not greatly unlike our own, Ollie is the leader, and much of the comedy belongs to him in his aspirations and his embarrassments. Here, and in the other period pieces, Stan is liberated from prosaic reality to become the spearhead of the team, utterly at ease in the abstract and timeless atmosphere of fancy which these films afford — with Ollie trailing cautiously behind. More finger games are introduced which are directly descendant of *Diavolo*, and, as in the earlier film, the team is displayed mining the richest laughter from simply sitting at a table together with minimal props, playing children's games with their hands as the elaborate production goes on all around them.

Where *Fra Diavolo* was light and buoyant and gay, however, *The Bohemian Girl* is dark, grim, somewhat unpleasant — as one might assume a film featuring infidelity, kidnapping, whipping and torture as its backdrop might well be. The photography itself seems dark, and the plot sequences aren't carried off with the same care and charm as in the earlier film. Mae

Busch as Ollie's wife flaunts her adultery before him, then presents him with a kidnapped child that she tells him is his ("I didn't want her to know who her father was until she was old enough to stand the shock"), then departs with her lover, taking all of Ollie's money with her. Though it's all funny enough, it all contributes to a very real sense of cruelty that permeates the film — right through to the scenes of Stan and Ollie being hauled onto and strapped into machines of torture.

As in *Pack Up Your Troubles*, there are brief stabs at sentiment in the sequences they share with the child they are given to raise. As in the earlier film, however, there is not much attempt to explore the relationship, and, also similar to *Pack Up Your Troubles*, the child — now grown up — is restored to her proper home, while the team meet a mean and nasty end, being tortured by the Count's henchmen despite the Bohemian girl's belated plea that they be released. The closing image of Stan and Ollie emerging from the Count's palace, having been crushed into dwarfish dimensions and grotesquely elongated into a spidery giant respectively, effectively reasserts the team's sensibility at the end of this rather confused film. Their bizarre malformations are an "answer" to the sentiment that has gone before, a decisive rebuke to and deflation of whatever amount of belief we had been foolish enough to invest in the straight plot over the past 60 minutes.

Yet throughout the film there have been indicators of the team's worldview chafing against the confines of the opera, most notably in the lengthy scene wherein the grown-up Arline sings "I Dreamt I Dwelt in Marble Halls" to her "Daddy" and her Uncle Stan. Her glowing face singing of marble halls is intercut with homely images of Stan obliviously scarfing his breakfast down, and after the song, Ollie, who has beamed proudly at her throughout, discovers that all the food has been consumed. In answer to Ollie's fury, Stan explains "I thought it was gonna get cold — I didn't know how long she was gonna dream!" Never before in the opera films has Stan's laconic honesty been allowed to comment on the pretensions of the form itself — as well, there is an anachronistic gag, in which Stan, working a butter churn, proclaims, "I'm making myself a malted milk!"

These incidents, along with the closing freak show gag so beloved to Laurel, are the attempts of the old Laurel and Hardy worldview to reassert itself, but when they cross paths with the alternating scenes of sentiment and torture of which this film is composed, it makes for a strange, disturbing comedy indeed. For students of Hollywood history, the darkness of the film is compounded by knowing that it had to be extensively recut and reconfigured after its first preview when the original female lead, 30-year-old Thelma Todd, was found dead (whether as a result of suicide or murder remains a matter of mystery). She remains in the finished film singing one song. For students of history in general, the weirdness of the film is compounded by the fact that this comic opera about gypsies went before the cameras just as the Nazis had passed the Nuremberg Law in Germany, disenfranchising anyone not of pure Aryan descent — with particular attention paid to Jews and Gypsies. Needless to say, the completed film was banned in Germany.

Beyond these circumstances, *The Bohemian Girl* betrays a certain weariness with the comic opera form on the part of its creators; this is seen in the lackluster settings and the uninspired framing of the musical and straight plot scenes. As good as the comedy scenes are, they can't entirely escape the tired grimness of the production as a whole.

Their next two features are identified in their credits as "Stan Laurel Productions." This designation was doubtless a result of the ongoing artistic and contractual disputes between Laurel and Roach, and it's difficult to know exactly what it meant. It's likely Laurel didn't produce the films in a conventional sense, and some have conjectured it was a meaningless title given to assuage his ego. The films themselves, however, display that greater control must have been given to Laurel at least in the story department, for they are the first features since *Sons of the Desert* to have their plots carried entirely by the characters of Stan and Ollie.

Our Relations (1936), the first Laurel production, concerns the confusion arising when Stan and Ollie come into contact with their seafaring twins, Alf and Bert. Based on a short story by W. W. Jacobs, the film returns the team to the realm of domestic difficulties seen in their shorts of the early 1930s — their panicked attempts to maintain their place in bourgeois society as wild, malevolent forces arise to pluck them from their careful perches of respectability ("Come Clean," "Chickens Come Home"). Here, the forces are themselves, or rather, the unreconstituted, unsocialized versions of themselves that arrive in their hometown to create havoc. As Stan and Ollie are reunited with their more unconstrained, honest selves in Alf and Bert during the course of the film, so do Laurel and Hardy return to the fertile comedic fields of social embarrassment, of matrimonial disharmony, of widespread confusion and chaos, from which they had lately been estranged. It's entirely fitting that their alter egos, the representatives of their own inner, truer selves, are sailors, an occupation Laurel and Hardy have undertaken in four prior films (including the classics "Two Tars" and "Men O' War") — no doubt due to Stan Laurel's lifelong fixation with the sea and all things nautical.

Alf and Bert come into town, and, among many other things, chat up a pair of prostitutes in a dive. Stan and Ollie later come in and are approached by the prostitutes in a familiar manner, infuriating their wives.

The film plays on the contrast between the two worlds, between the two sides of the Laurel and Hardy characters: the more obviously anarchic duo as seen in many of the early shorts and the more benevolent (seemingly), harmless characters seen in the last three features. At the end, the two pairs meet and "join together," to form a new, revitalized entity. Before this, of course, they have caused each other no end of trouble, but this is in accordance to sound Laurel and Hardy ritual, in which the careful peace-giving lies of society, of identity, are overturned to usher in a new order of what is, yes, chaos and destruction, but which is also truth. The scene in which Alf and Bert, pursued by Finlayson and his henchman, destroy the elaborate Pirate's Club nightclub is one of their few later scenes of mass pandemonium, echoing the savagery of their late silent and early sound shorts.

Our Relations also reunites the team with the world last seen in their short subjects, in that virtually all of the supporting characters are devious, hard-headed opportunists— there is Finlayson as Finn, the chiseling shipmate; Groagan, the rough and tumble proprietor of a waterfront dive; Alice and Lily, the two gold-digging hussies; the officious, pompous captain; the completely polluted drunk, played, naturally, by Arthur Housman; and the businesslike evil of the gangsters in the final reel. The wives, while somewhat more empathetic than their Mae Buschian predecessors, display the expected steely determination beneath their bourgeois trappings, and there is a character also seen in the early shorts ("Their Purple Moment," "Chickens Come Home")— the friend of the wives who carries to them tales of the husbands' improprieties, here known as Mrs. Addlequist.

As might be observed from the large roll call of supporting characters, the film is more complex than the standard Laurel and Hardy production — it is as if in response to the task of creating a film wholly based upon the team's characters, rather than on established plots of the operas, the creators overcompensated by frenziedly overplotting to ensure there wouldn't be a dead moment or tiniest evidence of padding in the entire production. The comedy here is farce with complicated misunderstandings executed at a lightning pace. This is pretty much the opposite of the team's usual approach, in which a simple situation provides a framework on which to hang a series of gags and routines. Here, aside from a telephone booth–crowding scene with Housman — which may owe something to the stateroom scene in the Marx Brothers' A Night at the Opera (1935), though it has its antecedents in the team's own "Our Wife"— and a brief, almost nostalgic exchange of reciprocal violence with Finlayson, the team is too busy keeping the incredibly intricate plot moving to actually stand still and simply "be" Laurel and Hardy.

That said, Our Relations, along with Babes in Toyland, is the most successful Laurel and Hardy film that is the least like a standard Laurel and Hardy film. Its themes of confusion and identity at times cause it to be rather confusing itself, though the "Cuckoo" theme is used to good effect on the soundtrack to alert us to the presence of Stan and Ollie, while a nautical ditty is played when Alf and Bert make their appearance. In the final third of the film, when both sets of twins are set loose, dressed in the standard Laurel and Hardy costumes, they are "differentiated" by the fact that Alf and Bert wear the bowtie and necktie on the opposite collars to which they are usually applied. Though the standard subtle explorations of the characters and the relationship between them are missing here — condensed and limited to the cute running gag wherein they share a little ritual each time they happen to say something in unison — the film is meaningful in that it reintroduces Laurel and Hardy to their roots: it reinstates grotesque, raucous reality into their comedy. After the brilliant climax in which Stan and Ollie teeter precariously again and again on the edge of a dock, their feet encased in crescent-bottomed clumps of cement, they are fittingly saved, pulled out of the briny deep by their nautical counterparts from the long-forgotten past.

As if in reaction to the fervid overplotting of *Our Relations*, their next film, *Way Out West* (1937) is a great film whose greatness lies in its simplicity. The second Laurel production, it is an affectionate parody of the western genre at the same time as it uses the genre as a handsome and unobtrusive framework for the best the team has to offer, all delivered within the spaciousness— so important to their comedy — allowed by the brevity of the plot. They come to town to deliver a deed; they are conned into delivering it to the wrong woman; realizing their mistake, they try to steal it back but are chased to the outskirts of the town; by night they break in and steal it back, and with the woman they set off out of the town. The film is as temporally and geographically simple as a child's stick drawing, and the world it portrays is as morally simple as well — there is the gleefully villainous chiseler, Mickey Finn (Finlayson again), and his wife, the brash, sneering Lola Marcel who passes herself off as Mary Roberts, the inheritor of the deed. In contrast, there is Mary herself, seemingly saintly and pure as the driven snow.

Mary Roberts's innocence is counterpart to Stan and Ollie's. It is the trusting guilelessness the team shares with her — their basic goodness, along with their stupidity — which causes them to be conned, yet here they are able to correct their mistake, and they are able to—for once — make good on their ineptitude. When they succeed in putting the scheming evildoers in their place (after all, planning to bilk a freshly bereaved daughter out of her birthright is pretty dastardly) and they stroll out of town, happily singing, united with Mary in their gentle goodness, it makes for one of the few genuinely happy endings to any of their films—barring Ollie's third descension into that unexpected hole in the bottom of the pond, of course. It is this that makes *Way Out West* their feature with the most soul.

This soulfulness is also reflected in the song-and-dance numbers executed by the team. In addition to the sprightly, triumphant "Way Down in Dixie" with Mary at the end, they sing a duet, "The Trail of the Lonesome Pine," for several verses straight with touching earnestness, before going into a routine with Stan's voice alternating between bass and soprano. And then there is a dance scene which is one of the most transcendent moments that they ever put on film. As they are portrayed slowly falling under the spell of the music, gracefully being moved into motion by its rhythm on the main street of this rough western town, they communicate so eloquently the freedom of the characters in the way that they are able to be carried away and in the way they remain uniquely themselves, no matter their surroundings. Their obvious joy in performing the dance and the purity of their intention in making it as elegant as it is funny make it one of the great Laurel and Hardy moments.

They dance before a ridiculously unreal process shot, facing us for most of it, and beam at us with delight. The obvious process shot does not repel us as it does in "County Hospital." In a way it serves as a curtain for the "stage" they are suddenly performing on. In addition to serving as a curtain, it also gives the impression that they are now standing in front of the film, addressing and performing directly for us. They communicate to us directly the genial bliss of simply being alive; we are transported vicariously with them away from the dreary dread of reality into sublime forgetfulness, the nirvana of surrendering to and being animated by joy. Their dancing in choreographed unison is a celebration of their unassuming unity, the satisfaction of their friendship. Their world of innocent, indolent pleasure contrasts with the feverish scheming of their adversaries, with the harsh, cutthroat world around them and us. Near the end of the dance the camera angle changes and situates them back at the doorway of the town saloon, dancing before the yodeling group of cowboys. Then, with a parting gallop through the bar-room door, they are back in banal reality again, immersed in the urgency of their mission in typical Laurel and Hardy fashion.

The beauty of the film is that the plot easily includes interludes such as these as well as an extended routine where Stan searches Ollie's body for the locket they've brought to give to Mary Roberts, as Finn and Lola Marcel wait and fume. Time seems to come to a stop as Stan and Ollie fumble with elemental reality. In addition is the classic scene where the team wrestles with Finn and Lola for the deed, climaxing when Stan is tickled into amoral hysteria, caving in to the enemy and helplessly relinquishing the gold mine. There is a scene where Stan eats a hat, where they play with a block and tackle for the first time since "The Music Box," and the scenes where Ollie is flummoxed by Stan's "lighting" of his thumb. The simple perfection of the film is in the number of rich scenes it has like these, while still maintaining an involving, Stan and Ollie–driven plot. The film is full of comic detail, yet it maintains the organic, leisurely pace of their best short films; as the critic Pauline Kael noted: "you ... come out feeling relaxed as if you've had a vacation."[4]

Contributory to the film's success is its great supporting cast. James Finlayson, here known as Mickey Finn, delivers his most definitive performance since "Big Business" eight years before. Sharon Lynne is entirely convincing as the devious, shameless Lola Marcel, and Rosina Lawrence sparkles as Mary Roberts, whose luminous goodness is never saccharine or cloying. Stan and Ollie appear out of nowhere, enter the town (society), are conned, then chased over the horizon by the corrupt sheriff. After they return and rectify the situation, they leave the town behind, escaping with one equal to them in decency, escaping—for once—society's embittered machinations rather than being victimized by them. As Ollie says: "Now that all our troubles are over, where do we go from here?"

The great strides made by *Way Out West* in terms of pace and plotting are pretty much entirely reversed in their next film, *Swiss Miss* (1938). There is no production credit for Laurel here, and as Roach reasserts his control, featuring the team in an original contemporary musical comedy, and lavishing on it a budget much larger than any of the films had had before, we return to the realm of Stan and Ollie being the comedy relief in their own movie. The straight plot is weak and uninteresting—a precious, pompous composer retires to the Swiss Alps to soak up inspiration for the writing of his new opera (the type who would soon receive his comeuppance in a standard Laurel and Hardy film), bedeviled by his prima donna wife, who furtively disguises herself as a "Swiss miss" in order to horn her way into his new creative enterprise. Stan and Ollie bumble around in Tyrolean costume until husband and wife are satisfactorily reunited.

It's possible Roach had his eye on the great success achieved by MGM with the Marx Brothers when planning this ambitious production. When the Marxes had been dropped from Paramount after producing their masterpiece, *Duck Soup* (1933)—which at the time was an unmitigated financial disaster—they were signed by MGM producer-dynamo Irving Thalberg, who reconfigured their approach to film comedy. Gone was the anything-for-a-laugh anarchic chaos of the Paramount films—enter the stately pace of the classic *A Night at the Opera* (1935), where their hijinks are in support of the handsome leading couple, where their anarchism serves the purpose of sabotaging their adversary's opera, rather than tearing everything to pieces just for the sheer hell of it. The film was the Marx Brothers' greatest success at the time, and though the method of welding their comedy to the banal dilemmas and plots of various young lovers would rapidly grow stale for them, the sudden revitalization of their careers through doing so would not have gone unnoticed by Roach.

The romantic lead in *Swiss Miss*, Walter Woolf King, played one of the leads in *A Night at the Opera*. In addition, there is character actor Eric Blore, comic relief in several Fred Astaire films and other concurrent "highbrow" comedies, now recruited to perform the same function in a Laurel and Hardy film! The tenor of these scenes, as in the opera films and in *Bonnie Scotland*, is in sharp variance to the team's comedy scenes. In contrast to the "opera" films, all the music is original; though many have bracketed *Swiss Miss* with the earlier opera films, it has more in common with contemporary Broadway musical comedies or reviews. To its credit, *Swiss Miss* gives little evidence of taking itself too seriously and mostly succeeds in its task of providing extremely light, somewhat banal entertainment. It suffers terribly, however, in comparison with the richly creative classic that preceded it.

The sense of whimsy that nearly redeems *Swiss Miss* is seen in its rationale for depositing the team high up in the Alps. As itinerant mousetrap salesmen, they have come, by virtue of Stan's sage reasoning, to the place that produces the most cheese. Their routines, in the main, are mildly amusing. Two of them depend on special effects — one in which they run frantically about as jets of fire blast through holes they've drilled in a cheese shop's store, and another in which they play with musical bubbles pumped from an organ they've spilled their scrubwater into. There is also another solo showcase for Laurel's pantomime skills (as in the wine-bottling scene in *The Bohemian Girl*). Here, Stan tricks a St. Bernard into relinquishing its brandy casket to him — by throwing feathers in the air to approximate snow. The scene is performed with exemplary skill, though in the end it is perhaps more impressive than it is amusing.

Better is the celebrated scene wherein they must transport a piano across a rickety bridge suspended between two mountains. Again dependent upon special effects to simulate height — by this time, ten years after "Liberty," there'll be no more athletic cavorting on perilous precipices — the scene is made more nightmarish, and outlandish, by the sudden appearance of a gorilla, who immediately begins to torment and bedevil them. As the frenzied gorilla begins to swing the bridge wildly from side to side, the bizarre, the whimsical, and the grotesque unite and intermingle. As such, the scene deserves its place in the team's pantheon of comic tableaux — with the horse on the piano ("Wrong Again,"), the street full of pies ("Battle of the Century"), the line of decimated autos ("Two Tars"), and the piano careening over Ollie's back ("The Music Box"). It isn't a typical Laurel and Hardy scene — in days past, such homely scenarios as putting up an aerial ("Hog Wild"), cleaning up the house ("Helpmates") or fixing up a boat ("Towed in a Hole") provided them with sufficient difficulties out of which to wring a goodly number of gags. Now mountains and demoniacal gorillas are needed. Now the world around them becomes increasingly surreal, frighteningly unpredictable, and they enter into a new phase of cartoonlike broadness, — albeit with the familiar grim undertones — which will manifest itself increasingly in their remaining Roach productions.

This increasing broadness is also seen in the segment where they belittle the waiter and chef for having no apple pie at the hotel. Their angry disgust serves the necessity of them receiving their comeuppance when the money they seek to pay their bill with is found to be false, but such outbursts would have been unthinkable in the films of just a few years before. Whereas Stan and Ollie by their natures have never fit into society, there is a growing sense on their part that they don't particularly care anymore that they don't fit in. This comes to the fore in the remaining four films in which they were able to control their artistic growth.

As they become broader, less self-effacing and less embarrassed to be who they are, so the world they inhabit becomes even more treacherous, absurd, chaotic — and more mysterious. Material reality becomes more and more malleable, less predictable, and, in contrast to their earlier world in which events proceeded in their logical manner toward devastation, everything now is illogical and chaotic. The backgrounds of the later features are more and more dream visions of a cuckoo universe.

It's ironic that Laurel began moving the team's comedy into this less comforting, more experimental realm just as Roach was plying their latest production with the largest budget they'd ever seen. Roach's desire to make big, important films directly conflicted with Laurel's growing appreciation for bleak humor based on malformations and ignominy. They fought bitterly over *Swiss Miss*, with Roach editing several comedy scenes from the film, including one in which Stan, in attempting to shave Ollie, severs both his nose and his big toe. Naturally, he re-attaches them in reverse, resulting in Ollie's foot sneezing.[5] At the end of the completed movie, when the chef shouts as he's chasing them with his knife — "I'll skin you alive!" — we get the idea that Laurel might have had at one time a different ending for the film planned.

It is well known Roach disliked Stan's occasional freak endings to the films. Now the grotesque began bleeding through all their comedy. Tellingly, *Swiss Miss* was the last attempt by Roach to put Laurel and Hardy into a "big, important picture." From then on, his attentions seem to be diverted elsewhere to making important pictures with others, and attaining some success for doing so (*Topper, Of Mice and Men*). Undoubtedly, he and Laurel must have become exhausted from their wrangling with each other, leaving less and less doubt that the producer and the team would inevitably part ways.

As much as their disputes were artistic, they were also contractual and, to some degree, resultant of Laurel's troubled personal life. As he was having well-publicized marital problems at the time, it's no wonder that the world within his films became more threatening and disturbing. By the same token, it's no wonder that Roach's patience was beginning to wear thin, that he became more wary about placing the hopes of his studio on Laurel and Hardy.

Swiss Miss, which shares *Bonnie Scotland*'s schizophrenic nature, as well as its backstage drama of bitter conflict, entertains on about the same level the earlier film does—though Swiss Miss has an affectionate edge in that it is lighter and frothier, features Stan and Ollie in Tyrolean pants, and allows Ollie to croon "Let Me Call You Sweetheart" as Stan accompanies him on tuba. It also deigns to resolve its plot, something *Bonnie Scotland* didn't bother to do. This problem is solved quite neatly in their next film, which has no discernible plot, and is all the better for it.

Block-Heads (1938) is a minor miracle, a film featuring 100 percent Laurel and Hardy, which follows the direction pointed by *Our Relations* back into the vital raucous domestic calamities of their early sound shorts, which glories in the earthy destructive roots of the team's comedy, and as such serves as an overview of their entire career. It is a slapstick tour de force, a passionate rededication to the anarchic sensibility that gave birth to their world 10 years before.

Notably, the film came about simply because Roach, applying for some refinancing, needed to have a film in production in order to procure a loan from the Bank of America. It had to be done quickly and cheaply, so Stan suggested a remake of their first sound short, "Unaccustomed As We Are." The film went into production before the script was completed.[6]

The result is a film as wholly unpretentious as their best shorts and as dedicated to their prime objective as anything the team did. It is unstinting in its quest to evoke laughter, piling on gag after ridiculous gag, making it probably their funniest feature. In addition, it is a meaningful examination of the relationship between the two characters, a taking stock of the past as well as adding a few new marvels, and pointing their direction for the future. Many of the stock gags from the Laurel and Hardy inventory are taken out, vividly enacted, then lovingly folded and tucked carefully away. Both of the comedians seem reenergized by their embracing of their raucous past, and Hardy in particular seizes upon the chance to deliver one of his best performances ever — he was always more at home in the domestic frenzied-embarrassment milieu than in the stilted opera films in any case.

The film is about Laurel and Hardy and the essential idea behind the team and their relationship with each other. In elaborating on the plot of "Unaccustomed As We Are" — Ollie brings Stan home to wife, she refuses to cook dinner for them, storms out, the team then becomes innocently involved with an attractive neighbor across the hall, then arousing the enmity of the neighbor's husband — a new beginning is added, wherein the team are World War I soldiers. Ollie is sent over the top and Stan is assigned to guard the trench until further notice. Evidently further notice never comes, for 20 years later Stan is still doggedly patrolling the trench. Meanwhile, Ollie has married and settled into bland, lifeless domesticity. The film begins by breaking up their relationship, and the rest of it consists of that relationship being reestablished and recreated anew. It is a form of resurrection, a testing of their meaning, their comic potency.

Stan without Ollie is a dumb machine, senselessly pacing back and forth in his trench, stopping for supper, emptying a can of beans onto his plate, then tossing the empty can onto a Mount Everest of cans accumulated over the past 20 years.

Ollie without Stan is perhaps worse, entirely engulfed in tepid, bourgeois connubial bondage. He is completely infantilized, divested of dignity under the rule of his wife (society). In earlier married films, Ollie at least makes a show of resistance, gives evidence of chafing under the confinement of matrimony. Here, he timidly asks his wife for an extra 50 cents with his allowance, to buy her an anniversary present. She relents: "Just this once!" she warns sternly, with an admonishing glance. We see that Ollie, without his partner, becomes swallowed entirely by the lies of society, that he becomes deadened and pathetic, without Stan to break him out of the prison of his role.

Stan is discovered in his trench and brought back to civilization. Ollie, leaving his apartment, is told by a porter about a story in the newspaper of a soldier remaining in the trenches 20 years after the war. Ollie laughs, glancing at the picture of the grinning Stan: "How in the world can anybody be so stupid? I can't imagine anybody being that dumb!" Then, executing one of the greatest takes of the Hardy career: "Oh yes, I can!"

This is parallel to the moment in "Putting Pants on Philip," identified by Laurel as their "first" film, where Hardy, as Piedmont Mumblethunder, arrives at the dock to meet his nephew from Scotland whom he's never seen before. On seeing the ungainly figure of Stan, he notes smugly to a bystander: "Imagine — someone has to meet that!" There follows a slow-burn take as Hardy is given the news that he is the someone who has to meet "that." And so the first part of the film is a reenactment of their initial "meeting," their coming together. The difference is that in the earlier film Hardy fears that Stan's unassimilatable otherness will tarnish his reputation and depose him from the vaunted position he holds in society — naturally, this is exactly what happens. In the later film, he welcomes Stan back into his life with the similar result in that Stan likewise ruins that life. Yet here there is the underlying feeling that Ollie half-expects him to, and desires him to, in order to overthrow the falsity his life has become.

As well, there is the recognition that Ollie's grandiose devotion of the ideal of friendship, and the sacrifices involved therein, is the glue that bonds the relationship and makes it a reality: it is the unfailing fixative that secures the more ephemeral Stan to the slightly more worldly Ollie and allows both of them to face the world as a single unit. This is made all the more apparent by the classic scene in which Ollie arrives to pick up his old friend at the Old Soldiers' Home. Stan is sitting in a wheelchair designed for amputees with his leg folded up under him. Ollie's face crumbles into sadness as he sees what he believes to the stump appending from Stan's waist. With firm resolve to make the best of it, he approaches Stan, grinning expectantly with his hands clasped behind, waiting for Stan to recognize him.

Predictably it takes Stan a couple of tries to contextualize Ollie. Then he gasps: "Ollie!" and half-rises from his chair. "Don't get up! You sit right back down!" Ollie hastily assures him, accommodating on account of his friend's horrible injury. And there follows, in this film that reminds us how refreshingly unsentimental the Laurel and Hardy world is, one of their most tender and sentimental scenes as they meet again after 20 years. Typically, this most nostalgic, warmly reflective scene takes place just as they are deploying a rather grotesque and borderline tasteless gag.

Yet there is no mistaking the genuine love and care Oliver Hardy has for his old pal, no mistaking the warmth radiating from him even as he says, "Wait'll you put those legs under the table — er, leg under that table." "Have ya missed me, Ollie?" Stan asks. "I certainly have!" Ollie states emphatically. "I missed you, too," says Stan. The warmth of their friendship is palpable.

Still, when the dinner bell rings, Stan allows how it's been nice to see him and all, but he has to run as it's mess time. Ollie won't hear of it — Stan's coming home to one of his wife's steak dinners. From now on he'll take care of Stan — whatever he has is his. He wheels Stan along in his wheel-chair.

Stan desires a drink of water, rising to walk over to a nearby water hose. Ollie, mortified, pats him back down into his wheelchair and rushes to get the hose for him. He returns to him, hands him the nozzle, then goes back to turn on the faucet. Stan naturally has the nozzle pointed at Ollie, so that when the water comes out Hardy is thoroughly soaked.

Ollie, his patience severely tested, merely returns and grits his teeth as he daintily takes the hose from Stan and flings it to the ground, patting Stan's back perhaps a touch too forcefully as he resumes wheeling him around the grounds.

A guy comes up and demands the chair for his friend, an idea Ollie becomes quite receptive to after he's been bopped on the nose. Again, Stan moves to get up. Ollie says, "Don't exert yourself, Stanley — I'll carry you." Ollie then lifts him from the chair and staggers along the path. At one point his hat falls off, and in his attempt to retrieve it, they fall over on the grass. As Ollie pulls himself to his feet, Stan stands up and helpfully leaps back into Ollie's arms so that he can continue carrying him down the path.

This image is beautiful in the manner by which it evokes so many of the character traits of both of them. Ollie is so immersed in his ideals of friendship and so inattentive that he does not "see" reality, will not recognize that Stan has two legs. It's symptomatic of the simplicity of his mind, its stupid tenaciousness— what registered was that Stan had one leg, so that's what's going to stay. In a way, both Stan and Ollie are more simple than stupid. It's this simplicity that also causes them to be so pure in their idealism, their innocence, their wonderful openness to life. Both men's downfall is that they are only capable of comprehending a minute part of reality, which in their ignorance they presume is the whole — it's the simplicity of their outlook versus the complexities created by a furtive and cunning world.

But don't all of us, to some degree, do the same thing as Stan and Ollie, when we block out certain realities that are unpleasant to think about or inconvenient to think about in order to focus on one particular aspect of reality so that existence might be made manageable? We must inevitably pretend to know, or tell ourselves that we know more than what we can know, because we're finite creatures in a universe that has no beginning or end. To admit this about ourselves at the same moment as we do it is possible — to focus only on our helplessness in the midst of infinity would lead to insanity and/or suicide. To deny it, to harden ourselves to the fact, or to stay willfully ignorant of it, makes us monstrous, less than human. Do we not suspect at times that what we call "reality" in our comforting manner is but an infinitesimal particle of something much larger, the totality of which is so much beyond our grasp that our attempts to understand it, to conceptualize it, are vain folly? A folly perhaps not too far removed, in the end, from the follies and misapprehensions of Stan and Ollie.

Stan's simplicity is in his bland acceptance of his friend's determination to carry him around. He has no concept of what it is Ollie's presuming, no idea why his friend is insistent on transporting him in this manner. He simply accepts it. Stan is infinitely adaptable. While Ollie remains fixed on an idea though all objective reality proves it false, Stan's ideas are ephemeral as soap bubbles, appearing and disappearing with as little fanfare, leaving as little impression. For 20 years he guarded a trench in Europe, now his friend's carrying him in his arms to his car. It's all the same to him.

It is only when they have made their way to the car, struggled into it, then fallen out the other side, that Ollie happens to notice that Stan has two perfectly healthy legs. Ollie: "Why didn't you tell me you had two legs?" Stan: "Well, you didn't ask me!"

From here, Ollie's gentle solicitousness disappears and he instantly becomes the impatient, annoyed, frustrated Ollie of old. When he can't pull his car out because of a truck blocking the way, he shoves and bullies Stan angrily out of the car to ask the truck's driver to move it. When the driver isn't there, Ollie impatiently tells Stan to move it himself. Stan climbs up into the cab, pulls a lever — we see a shot of the dump truck's back-end rising and the truck moves ahead. Stan leaps down and walks back — to where Ollie and his car are buried under a hill of sand.

This whole amazing uninterrupted segment serves as a defiant reaffirmation of what Laurel and Hardy are all about in the face of all the inevitably constrained features they had made through the mid–1930s. It sums the team up and is as great at doing so as "Big Business" or "Helpmates." All the tensions, the misapprehensions endemic to their relationship, are here writ large. Stan is dumb, Ollie suffers because of Stan's dumbness, yet he suffers even more because of his own dumbness, his intractable loyalty to unrealistic ideals, to his vision of what he believes reality should be as opposed to what it actually is.

Typically, by the next scene, Ollie has forgotten about the sand escapade, and he couldn't be more cheerfully receptive in response to Stan's request to try out Ollie's fancy new automatic garage door. Stan clambers behind the wheel, revs the engine, speeds wildly ahead, completely missing the plate and crashes through the garage door, running over Ollie and destroying the car in the process.

The humor here isn't just in the violence and destruction, but in the anticipation of it — in the fact that, in the best Laurel and Hardy fashion, we know that calamity will be the end result of Ollie's welcoming openness. From the moment Stan says, "Gee, can I try that?" we savor the disaster that is sure to come and our amusement is only multiplied by Ollie's complete unawareness of his impending doom. Undoubtedly, Ollie is foolish, but again we see here the simplicity of his devotion to the friendship, to the very concept of friendship itself. If it is dumb to entrust one's automobile to one who just hours ago submerged it completely in sand, is it not also admirable, in a way, to actually live out the phrase "what's mine is yours"— not merely mouthing the platitude but actually remaining true to it precisely when it seems most difficult to do so? Isn't this, really, the meaning of friendship, of unconditional love? Yet there is no strain about Ollie's amiability: he not only consistently forgives Stan, but even more rarely, he forgets— he all too quickly forgets the utter misery his friendship foists on him. Though he blames Stan, bullies him, cheats him if given the opportunity, Ollie remains loyal to him. He is always willing to give him another chance, always hopeful that this time Stan might miraculously do something right. If just the opposite should occur, and every earthly possession Ollie can lay claim to is destroyed by Stan's hands, Ollie will still make his stand beside him. Ollie's devotion to the ideal of friendship is simple and complete.

This is further emphasized throughout *Block-Heads*, whose plot, if it can be said in fact to have one, is concerned with Ollie's quest to ensure that Stan get the steak dinner he so emphatically promised him at their first meeting. This quest is obstructed by the dizzying, seemingly endless length of stairs they repeatedly trudge up and down, attempting to arrive at Ollie's apartment, waylaid by various obnoxious individuals, including the reliable James Finlayson with whom Ollie engages in an aborted battle of fisticuffs, and a bratty child and his brutish father. They are also waylaid by a former flame of Ollie's who, unaware that he is married, has dropped a note off at his apartment — they rush to get it before Ollie's wife sees it. Ollie's wife enters, expresses uncontained fury toward Ollie and undying contempt for Stan, and departs. In trying to fix the steak themselves, they blow up the apartment. The game hunter's wife from next door enters to help clean up the mess. Her dress gets ruined. They give her a pair of Ollie's pajamas to wear, then frenziedly attempt to hide her as Ollie's wife returns. The game hunter returns and discovers them hiding his wife. He makes use of the tools of his trade as he chases Stan and Ollie from the scene, blasting away with his shotgun — effectively ending the quest, we might assume, for Stan's steak dinner.

The course of the quest is a tour of the team's career. As "Putting Pants on Philip," is evoked earlier on, so the absurdly long flight of stairs references the one in their masterpiece "The Music Box," as well as that of the predecessor to that film, "Hats Off"—one of their first big hits. The old flame from Ollie's past threatening his present domestic bliss has been seen in "Chickens Come Home" As the film settles into being a remake of "Unaccustomed As We Are," we are treated to the old gag—also used in their seminal "Helpmates"—wherein Stan turns the gas on at the oven, is unable to find a match to light it with and comes into the next room and seeks Ollie's help. Ollie impatiently lights a match and strides into the now gas-filled kitchen and is blown back into the next room. The earlier uses of this gag, however, never afforded us the sublime and majestic sight of Ollie's body sailing regally as if in slow motion through the kitchen door as the explosion causes the entire universe to leap, writhe, and crash to the floor.

All the while, Stan amuses himself with such pastimes as pulling the shadow of a windowblind down as they make their pilgrimage up the stairs, or producing a glass of water — and ice —from his trouser pocket, and tamping tobacco into his fist and lighting it, allowing him to "smoke" his hand like a pipe. And here we see another reason for Ollie's devotion to Stan, which remains firm no matter what havoc is wreaked by his partner: where before Ollie's life was regimented, controlled, without dignity under the rule of his wife, now chaos reigns, anything is possible. Elemental rules governing material reality are transmuted, and the fathers of troublesome young urchins are dispatched, thundering to the earth like felled sequoias. Stan obliviously uproots all pretence to normal civilized life by his mere presence, leaving a trail of destruction and enmity in his wake. Yet this is infinitely preferable to the constrained deathlike existence Ollie has previously known.

The tour in which past glories are lovingly revisited and reclaimed culminates with Ollie's final rebellion against his wife, in which he defiantly states that he is leaving her with Stan to go to Honolulu — a nod to the subterfuge at the heart of the classic *Sons of the Desert*. This is swiftly followed by the reinstatement of another old Laurel and Hardy custom — the ending of a film signaled by fusillades of shotgun fire (the first since 1933's "The Midnight Patrol"). As with Anita Garvin's careful purchasing of a firearm in "Blotto," the blasting here has been methodically foreshadowed by the lengthy scene in which Billy Gilbert recounts to a group of journalists his latest hunting exploits, then departs to pick up a new shotgun he's had specially made. So Stan and Ollie once again exit a film running, with buckshot at their heels.

The original ending Stan Laurel envisioned for the film has often been noted — that after the shooting spree, we were to see, among the game hunter's other trophies mounted on the wall of his den, the heads of Stan and Ollie, the latter intoning from its frame: "Well, here's another nice mess you've gotten me into!"[7] This would have been the artistically perfect ending, though one suspects it would have been off the graph in terms of macabre humor for 1938 — its blunt brutality would be rather daring even today — even if it was all of a piece with the earlier amputee gag. Roach balked at this ending and instead substituted one from their silent short "We Faw Down": as they run, the shotgun blasts ringing out, hordes of men leap panic-stricken out of apartment windows on each side.

The substituted gag fails not only because it is from a time 10 years earlier in the Roaring Twenties when the subject of infidelity spawned an entire form of humor in and of itself, but also because the first use of the gag was in the pre–Hays Code era. Men in various states of undress were seen clambering out of windows in "We Faw Down" — just as Ollie and Stan had done earlier in that film — and so the meaning of their frenzy was explicit. In *Block-Heads*, we just see a bunch of guys in suits leaping out of windows as the stunt doubles for the team rush past — it is a limp ending to a film that is otherwise a comedic triumph. Perhaps a possible upside to the ending is that we do see Laurel and Hardy reunited again and running off to the horizon. And the truncated, "let-down" sense of the ending, after all the brilliance which has preceded it, gives it the feeling of some of the off-handed endings to the great early shorts, some of which simply collapse rather than end in a decisive fashion.

After this joyous revisitation of their comic past, it makes sense that their next feature actually "begins" with an ersatz two-reeler. *A Chump at Oxford* (1940) was made after the team had signed a new contract with Roach, for the first time in tandem, which called for the production of two features in a new "streamliner" format — in order to solve the problem of plots for the team, as well as to placate exhibitors who complained of over-long double bills, these new films were to be forty minutes long. After *Chump* had been made, however, it was decided to shoot an extra 20 minutes so that it would be standard feature-length for the European market — always an enthusiastic audience for the team's films. It is the standard length version that is generally known today. By the time the second film for the new contract, *Saps at Sea*, was made, the "streamliner" idea seems to have been forgotten, as it clocks in at around the usual 60 minutes.

The extra 20 minutes at the beginning of *Chump*—which has little to do with the rest of the film — is a remake of their silent short "From Soup to Nuts" (1927), the title of which is, typically, referenced in the film's dialogue (Ollie: "Come on in, folks, we've got everything from soup to nuts!"). Stan and Ollie are unemployed, arrive at an employment office, take a job as butler and maid at a fancy society dinner party — Stan naturally taking the role as maid, as he had in their first "team" film "Duck Soup" (1926) and its remake "Another Fine Mess" (1930)—and adopting the name "Agnes" as he did in the latter film. As before, the team arrives to wreak havoc at the party through their ineptitude. The blasting shotgun once more makes its entrance to signal the end of this sequence, with a repeat of the gag from another silent short, "Wrong Again" (1927)—where a policeman enters after the blast, posterior smoking, complaining of his brains almost being blown out.

Obviously, the retrospective element here is strong. What is different is that where Stan and Ollie were painfully aware of their blundering in the first film, greatly pained by it and at pains to attempt to hide it in their desperate quest to conform and belong in society, the team in the later film is cheerfully unaware of their ongoing incompetence (at the very least, they seem to no longer care about their incongruity). When Ollie seats the dinner party guests in the wrong chairs and is told to rectify the situation, he laughs and blithely shouts out to the diners: "You're all mixed up! The old guy wants ya all switched around!," proceeding to order the elegantly attired partygoers around the table in a chaotic game of musical chairs.

As for Stan—in his guise as Agnes—when he wanders the party with a platter of hors d'eouvres, he is given to kicking the socialites' chairs to offer them the treats, sampling them himself and attesting "They're good!" Later, when he is told to "take all these drinks," he sits down, "takes" them and ends up stuporifically drunk, providing a grotesque sight as he staggers blearily through the event, his wig askew, puffing his pipe.

Time has made them both grotesque. Both of them were now quickly approaching the age of 50—they were in their late 30s when they first teamed—and so they could no longer be "the boys" quite so convincingly. The two men who had sweated to hoist the piano up the infinite staircase in "The Music Box," or who had flitted from job to ill-fated job in countless two-reelers were now undeniably in late middle age. To see them suffer at the hands of fate now, when their ability to rebound is obviously more limited, when their age tells us their chances for happiness or even stark survival are rapidly disappearing, has the potential to be more (uncomfortably) tragic than amusing.

The increasing non conformist bent of their work is reflective of this. They are not about to go gently into that good night—if their previous comedy was about their inability to conform to societal roles in spite of all their best attempts, now their comedy is more about their inability to get a grip on reality itself—a reality that is depicted as being steadily more undependable and treacherous. They are still victims of the world, but now they are little concerned with this fact, little concerned about appeasing the world or fitting into it. As many humans experience as they reach middle age, they are less interested in what society thinks of them than in what they think of society. Their freakishness, their extrovertedness becomes more pronounced; their docility, their gentleness, their meekness fades into the background.

Their appearances are irrevocably changed. Hardy, after having embarked on a frenetic string of diets in the mid–1930 (when their fame had reached its highest), reducing so much at intervals that at times he seemed scarcely more portly than Laurel, had by 1938 either accepted, or resigned himself to, his destiny as an overweight man. It is here he settles into the girth that would define him for the rest of his life, becoming finally, spherically fat. His huge body seems to fill the tiny unemployment office at the beginning of *A Chump at Oxford*, and when he repeatedly trips over Stan's suitcase, we wince at the sheer spectacle of so much weight hitting the ground. From here on in, there are few of their films in which his weight escapes comment, though it should be noted that this excess weight seems not to diminish his grace or mobility one iota.

Laurel, for his part, is increasingly paunchy, and puffy about the face. Inevitably, he is less able to summon the jubilant innocence so intrinsic to his character. More often he must settle for expressing blank befuddlement, or obtuse stupidity, than the pixieish, otherworldly quality he had previously been able to master. In these later films, the clown-white favored as the basic makeup for the team seems to be applied more generously, seemingly to conceal the lines of age, which ineluctably began to mark their once childlike faces. The increased whiteness moves them further into the realm of the grotesque, uniting them in their pronounced clownishness as opposed to the rest of the world, uniting them in their strangeness, severing them from normal society, and, ultimately, reality itself.

These issues are all addressed as *A Chump at Oxford* begins. The team are street cleaners, an occupation which gives Ollie the chance to observe: "Well, here we are at last. Right down in the gutter. I wonder what's the matter with us? We're just as good as other people. But we never advance ourselves. We never get anyplace!" The artistic crisis—that of a middle-aged Stan and Ollie facing failure yet again, but now visibly aging, with time ticking away, so that another christening in an outsized mud puddle would seem cruel and unusual punishment rather than a corker to two reels of perfectly deployed gags—is faced head-on. Like the introspection of their dialogue in "Towed in a Hole," in which Ollie identified their failure to "get anyplace" as being the fact that they are "two grown men acting like a couple of children," Stan here notes the problem is that they aren't "illiterate enough"—that is, they haven't had enough education. They resolve to attend night school as quickly as possible.

Naturally, this all serves as the set-up for the premise of the film, which is "Laurel and Hardy Go to Oxford." It makes perfect comic sense to put the two dumbest men in the world into the milieu of the world's most revered institution of higher learning — the foremost center of refined intellectual achievement. On a deeper level, the premise enables the team's most readily identifiable and most taken-for-granted characteristic — their dumbness — to be examined in all of its implications.

A bank robber on the run slips on a banana peel Stan has thrown out on the sidewalk during lunch (his reasoning: "We'll just have to pick it up later anyway"). The bank president, to reward them for foiling the robbery, offers them a job in his bank — a job they explain they'd be little qualified for, having no education. The bank president declares they shall then have the best education money can buy — and in short order they arrive at Oxford.

This repository of all the intelligence amassed in human history proves to be a more daunting place than either Stan or Ollie are prepared for. From the moment they get there, they are roundly ridiculed by the students, subjected to cruel deceptions and pranks. Apparently these representatives of the intellectual elite have nothing better with which to occupy their massive intellects than to mislead and harass — for sport — two trusting, witless souls who are obviously far out of their depth.

They direct Stan and Ollie in a maze of hedges, confusing them with spurious, incomprehensible directions. Naturally, Ollie behaves as though their instructions are the most helpful, reasonable ones that could be proffered, thanking them for their help as the team advances into the labyrinth. The two clowns, predictably, spend a goodly amount of time traipsing around in circles in the leafy maze, with Ollie staggering under the weight of their luggage. At one point, Stan finds the Exit sign, and excitedly brings it back to Ollie. They spend some time advancing confidently through the maze, Stan triumphantly holding the arrow-shaped sign before him pointing the way, irretrievably lost, as if in some previously unknown scene of *Waiting for Godot*, or a newly discovered later act of *King Lear*.

Night descends, and still they founder exhaustedly through the serpentine passageways. One of their tormentors, not satisfied with merely confounding the team, now dons a ghost costume to frighten them out of their admittedly negligible wits. Shrieking pandemonium ensues, with a chase and a collision and the ghost disrobed and pointing at Stan and Ollie, cackling with delighted scorn at having so thoroughly outwitted and scared them. "Welcome to Oxford!" Ollie notes bitterly to Stan.

Charles Barr has noted the manner in which Stan's stupidity is carefully emphasized in order to foreshadow his transformation into the brilliant and acerbic Lord Paddington in the film's final 10 minutes. Yet more important, we see how the dumbness and innocence of both men are displayed, and the manner by which these qualities make them victims of a cruel, cynical world — this world is also accentuated here by being represented as Oxford, the pinnacle of the cerebral achievement directly opposite of Stan and Ollie's humble, unassuming simplicity.

This emphasis is present even in the first appended 20-minute segment of the film — which otherwise has nothing to do with the rest of the movie. Stan and Ollie are thumbing a ride by the side of the road. A fellow driving a street-cleaning truck stops and tells them to hop on the back. They do so, and the guy turns on the water sprinklers full force, completely soaking them. "What's the big idea?" Ollie shouts. "Aw, can't ya take a joke?" the guy retorts. "Get back on, I won't do it again!" They clamber back on, and, to noone's surprise but Stan and Ollie's, they are once again thoroughly drenched. They are pathetically foredoomed to suffer the whims of the furtive and cunning world around them.

As simple as Stan and Ollie are, they are not malicious — at least not without reason — and their innocence makes them incapable of presuming that anyone else could be malicious without reason either. "He's a swell fella, isn't he?" Stan observes of the student who doubletalks them into the maze. "He certainly is — I knew it from the moment I laid eyes on him!" Ollie asserts: "That's one thing I pride myself on — reading character!" Whether it was intended or not, the maze is a symbol of the complex thought patterns of the cerebral, canny rulers of the world within which the innocent simplicity of Stan and Ollie is forever and hopelessly lost. That they are sent into the labyrinth and tormented in it by these aspiring bastions of sophisticated intelligence, is an explicit comment on the ultimate pointlessness of the human intellect when it is divorced from love, from the basic humble decency that the characters of Stan and Ollie are so rich with. We need only look around to see the confounding, frightening maze that surrounds us to see the results of overarching human brilliance set loose without humility, without charity to guide it.

"You know, I think that guy was having a joke on you," Stan notes when their predicament becomes evident. "I thought you said you could read character!" "I can, but that guy was two-faced," Ollie explains, shooting a quick guilty look to us in the audience. "I'll never trust anybody again for as long as I live!" he declares, the hurt evident in his voice.

The students, however, have not finished in their task of misleading and bedeviling the two men, a task morally equivalent to tormenting a newborn baby. They convene a fake meeting with a spurious dean, then assign them the dean's quarters to live in. They carry Stan and Ollie on their shoulders in a mock parade, ridiculing them and intending to humiliate them. Stan and Ollie beam with delight, accepting all the clamor and attention as their due.

We see again their quickness to recover, to believe in their fellow humans. Once installed in the dean's quarters, availing themselves of his liquor cabinet, it is evident that all that exists for them now is this fine moment of high living. The dean, however, arrives and shows this to have been an elaborate ruse as well. The students are expelled for the prank, and they vow revenge on Stan and Ollie.

We have been shown forcefully the vulnerability the team's fabled lack of intelligence carries with it. They are duped and ridiculed again and again, though they do reclaim some dignity when they manage to engage the dean of Oxford University in a tit-for-tat pillow fight. When the dean comes to reclaim his quarters, Stan and Ollie note: "It's another rib." There's a very real sense of the team, Ollie particularly, becoming aware of the treacherousness of others, the falseness of the world as opposed to the straightforwardness and honesty of the team's approach. Ultimately, it is a growing awareness that the only humans they really can trust are each other.

This is underlied with Ollie's concern about character and his ability to read it, which is made into a running gag in the film. Naturally, beneath Ollie's bravado about reading character is his increasing knowledge that he in his simplicity is unable to penetrate the malicious wiliness of his fellow humans—that he really can't read character at all. In the end the result is, again, the awareness that the only person he really can trust—the only person he can really know—is Stan. They are united against a world of unknowable mystery and malevolence.

These themes of vulnerability and trust and character and unity—and of treachery and deception—are established before the arrival of Meredith, the valet who identifies Stan as Lord Paddington, "the greatest scholar and athlete Oxford has ever known." The Lord had bumped his head on a window and walked away years ago. To the team, the story is just another rib, another cruel prank—it makes perfect sense, with all that has gone before, for them to think of it as another elaborate hoax. Ollie is particularly quick to dismiss it, to scorn any idea that Stan could possibly be more intelligent than he. In Ollie's universe, he must be superior to Stan—in an increasingly confounding and confusing world, the certainty of this fact is his foundation, to which he clings ever tighter as insanity erupts around him. "Why, I've known Stan for years and he's the dumbest guy I ever knew!" he snorts. "I certainly am!" Stan agrees.

But the window falls on Stan's head and he instantly becomes Lord Paddington: brilliant, assured, debonair, athletic, poised. Even identity and character can switch in a moment here. "You're not trying to rib me, now!" Ollie exclaims hopelessly when he sees the new Lord Paddington. "Don't you know me, Stan?" Ollie asks plaintively, in a film that is about what we mean when we say we know somebody. "Who is this coarse person with the foreign accent?" Lord Paddington huffs. "Then it's not a rib, then, it's on the level," Ollie notes, becoming downcast. Suddenly and characteristically, he shakes off his sadness and becomes angry, attempting to hide his humiliation by dominating Stan physically. Lord Paddington, however, handily sends him catapulting out the window. His universe destroyed, his power usurped in every way, Oliver Hardy stares at us balefully from the hole his large body has imprinted into the earth.

In the next scene, the Laurel and Hardy relationship is inverted, as Ollie becomes the servant of Stan as Lord Paddington. Ollie is barely able to contain his fury and indignation as Lord Paddington meets with the dean, languidly attempting to find a place in his schedule for a meeting with Professor Einstein — who's evidently become somewhat confused about his theory. "Pardon my valet for being so horribly stupid," Lord Paddington notes to the dean, referring to Ollie. "Why do you keep him on?" asks the dean. "Oh, I don't know," his Lordship asserts, "he's got a jolly face, you know, breaks the monotony and helps fill up the room . . . someone to talk to, you understand." Ollie's camera looks bespeak anguished incredulity.

But this is as nothing compared to Lord Paddington's dressing down of Ollie once the dean leaves. Throughout this scene, Paddington refers to his former partner exclusively as "Fatty'"— shockingly cruel not only within the context of the film but also within the context of the knowledge that Hardy the actor deplored being overweight his entire life, was, according to his widow, very sensitive and self-conscious about it. "Fatty," Stan as Lord Paddington notes, "I notice you're looking a bit slovenly lately . . . you don't carry yourself with the dignity befitting a lackey." "Yes, your Lordship," Ollie notes.

Stan directs Ollie around the room, reprimanding him: "Lift up your feet — keep your chin up, Fatty — both of them!" In stunned, silent subservience, Ollie complies, moving about the room carrying the tea service — until he trips on a footstool and falls to the floor. Rising, he explodes with fury at his old partner: "I knew you when I had more brains in my little finger than you had in your whole body, even with your overcoat on! . . . You can take your Oxfords and your Lordships and your Paddingtons and do what you like with them!" Ollie reclaims his dignity in his anger, in his rejection of Oxford and all it stands for: its heartless, soulless intellectualism; its complex deceptions, its cruelty and snobbery.

"Really!" Lord Paddington exclaims. "Witty old stick in the mud, aren't you, Fatty?" "And don't call me 'Fatty'!" Oliver Hardy cries from the depth of his being, storming from the room. But his Lordship wanders over to the window to observe the students gathering below, vowing revenge. The window falls and once again befuddled Stan returns to the scene. "Ollie, where ya going?" he timidly asks his friend.

"Back to America for me!" Ollie shouts. Stan, inevitably, begins to cry: "Aren't ya going to take me with ya?" he weeps helplessly, and it is this weeping that signals to Ollie the return of his old partner: "Stan — you know me!" Ollie exclaims, laughing and embracing him and whooping with joy. The film ends on their ecstatic embrace.

The ultimate expression of vulnerability — Stan's tears — signals the reinstatement of their relationship in a film that is an exploration of the vulnerability of that relationship, of how the team's dumbness and innocence make them truly two babes in the woods in a malicious, cynical world. The themes established early on of Stan and Ollie's open trustingness being exploited by their intellectual superiors come to culmination in Stan's transformation into Lord Paddington, the prime exemplar of the merciless, arrogant, cold world that they suffer in. Paddington has no vulnerability — he is utterly certain in his sense of entitlement, in his right to torture his inferiors for sport. It is Stan's tears that reintroduce humanity, and the flawed, broken, vulnerable and eternally confused world of Laurel and Hardy.

Tellingly, their relationship, broken apart here and rejoined at the end of *A Chump at Oxford* as completely as it was at the beginning of *Block-Heads*, is not made whole again until after Ollie rejects the new, false order, reclaiming his own dignity in the process. In this manner, Ollie is able to instantaneously forgive and forget the barbs of the monstrous Lord Paddington and to characteristically welcome the bewildered Stan unreservedly back into his arms. His anger — so identifiable, along with his weight, as one of the chief characteristics of the Ollie character — clears the way for the flood of forgiveness and comradery (also inherent qualities within Ollie) on which the film ends. The film's message — that decency and kindness and friendship are the only real wisdom, and that any sort of purported knowledge bereft of these virtues is sterile and destructive — is given active demonstration in Ollie's quick and joyful acceptance of his old pal. If Ollie is often ridiculous in his pretensions to an impossible dignity beyond his reach, here he affirms the very real dignity of humanity in all its flawedness and foolishness, triumphing by its capacity to love over all the inhuman forces and systems that would diminish and deride it.

A Chump at Oxford may not be their greatest feature, but it is among their best and their funniest — the reactions of James Finlayson to swallowing a cork and his "take" on seeing Stan serve the salad "undressed" in the opening 20-minute segment would be worth the price of admission alone. And the film is one of their most meaningful and thoughtful. It is admirable in the way that it introduces the themes noted above in order to make Stan's transformation more forceful and wide-ranging in its implications, yet all the themes, as well as the sentiment at the end of the film, are lightly touched upon. Nothing is overdone — at no time is sentiment heavy-handed nor does it intrude on the comedy. Along with all the points it makes, *A Chump at Oxford* is still a slapstick comedy, where confused people hit and drop things on each other. In being so thoroughly and unpretentiously itself, it exemplifies the virtues it praises, in that it is more alive and edifying than all the carefully calculated creations of academia.

Much attention has been given to Laurel's astonishing turn as Lord Paddington. It is masterfully performed and all the more jarring because the character is diametrically opposed to the one he usually plays. Beyond his intelligence, Paddington is glib, arrogant, and cruel where Stan is meek, unassuming and gentle. The performance is gloriously funny in an entirely different comedic realm than that in which Laurel usually works. It might be noted that Paddington's wry, acerbic humor seems close to the humor Laurel is said to have preferred and excelled at offscreen in private life.

Yet not let us forget the demands Hardy's part makes of him in this episode, and the manner by which, typically, he fulfills them excellently and with gusto. He moves from scorn to anger to hurt to sorrow, and finally, to forgiveness and jubilation, so easily within the film's last 10 minutes that we might be forgiven for failing to notice the great skill with which he does so. Both comedians admirably rise to the challenge of their roles in *A Chump at Oxford*, perhaps their last film that requires them to do so at full force.

Their next feature, *The Flying Deuces* (1939)— made after *A Chump at Oxford*, but released before it — is an altogether more workmanlike affair. Taking advantage of their new, nonexclusive contract with Roach, the team made the film with independent producer Boris Morros; as such, it is often cited as evidence that they were able to make a decent film away from the Roach studios. It is an unambitious, pedestrian film, enjoyable without being particularly memorable. It succeeds in its goal of providing an hour of swiftly moving entertainment, but the obvious shoestring budget gives it an uncomfortably cheap, B-movie feel. Even so, some of the themes explored in the previous two features are touched on within this film's makeshift confines.

The team was presented with a script based on a French movie, *Les Aviateurs*.[8] The script required extensive rewriting by Laurel and his crew to make it suitable for the team, and much was borrowed from the 1931 four-reeler "Beau Hunks." The contrast between the two films reveals the difference in the teams' worldview, and how it changed between 1931 and 1939 — in the earlier film, they join the Foreign Legion to help Ollie forget a lost love; they enter into a battle with Arabs at their desert outpost and, comically, win (satirizing *Beau Geste* and other Foreign Legion dramas). In *The Flying Deuces* they first attempt to commit suicide over the lost love, then join the Legion, then arouse the hatred of the entire outpost, are condemned to death, escape with the troops in hot pursuit, commandeer a plane, crash it, and one of them is killed and reincarnated as a horse.

As with his infatuation with the female lead in *Swiss Miss*, Ollie's crush on the waitress Georgette here is unseemly, bizarre — a case of self-delusion to such a pitiful degree that it is difficult to empathize with him. Interestingly, the coincidences of the plot conspire to unite him with her. It is her boyfriend, François, who advises them to join the Legion to forget the lost love (not knowing they're speaking of his girlfriend). When they're escaping from the outpost later on, they meet her when she's just flown in to see François — Ollie greets her effusively, assuming she's changed her mind and come to seek him out. They are caught and thrown into jail, sentenced to death. Later when they're tunneling out of the jail, they dig up and find themselves in Georgette's house, and soon, in her bedroom. Perhaps it is also Georgette who throws them the note in jail, informing them of the tunnel beneath the floorboards (it's signed "A Friend"). Undoubtedly, it is only Ollie's death at the end of the film that prevents coincidence from uniting them again.

Running concurrent with the puzzling darkness of that element of the plot are the recurring themes of death, suicide, and reincarnation. So heartbroken is Ollie that Georgette loves another, he vows to kill himself. He heads down to the Seine (they're in Paris) with a big rock, and Stan. Their relationship, torn apart and reunited as it has been in their two previous films, is finally clarified and defined here for all time, as Ollie proclaims that if he is to kill himself, it is unthinkable that Stan should not accompany him. Ollie: "Do you realize that after I'm gone that you'd just go on living by yourself? People would stare at you and wonder what you are. And I wouldn't be there to tell them. There'd be no one to protect ya. Do you want that to happen to you?" They are a single entity. It is impossible for them to exist independently of each other. None of the paltry 'til death do us part stuff applies here — when they go, they will go together.

As grave and eerie as the dialogue above may be, it is equaled by what follows it — a meditation on reincarnation. Stan, stalling for time before taking the dive, wonders aloud about the life to come, questioning Ollie on what he might like to be reincarnated as. Ollie notes that he's always liked horses — as did his offscreen counterpart, Babe Hardy — so he'd be happy to come back as a horse. Stan allows that he himself would like to come back as himself: "I always got along fine with me."

The purpose of this dialogue is to set the stage for the film's final gag, wherein Ollie is killed in the plane crash, his robed figure ascending to heaven accompanied by the sound of harp music and by Stan's befuddled shrug to the camera. Fade out, and then we see a Chaplinesque Stan traipsing down a country lane with a bundle carried hobo-style over his shoulder. "Hey, Stan!" cries a toothbrush-moustached, derby-clad horse from a nearby field. "Ollie!" cries Stan, rushing over to embrace him. Their friendship survives not only death, but also physical transformation — their relationship remains firm, untouched, no matter what corporeal bodies they may be inhabiting at the time.

Before this, we have seen their entry into the Foreign Legion and their ability, through just being themselves, to arouse the ire of an entire outpost of legionnaires. As in their earlier military comedies, the regimented existence serves as a metaphor for society at large and their inability to conform to it. If, in *Pack Up Your Troubles*, they had manfully attempted to comply with the sergeant's orders, yet proved themselves woefully incapable of doing so, and in *Bonnie Scotland*, Stan had infested the rest of the troops with his idiosyncratic "skip-step" (as he tried to get in step but only succeeded in getting the rest of the platoon out of step), here they wander puzzledly through and around the smartly marching regiments, casting them into utter disarray. Here they are completely incapable of even approximating the regimented existence that surrounds them — they stumble around until they have reduced the entire exercise into shambling chaos. At the same time, they seem strangely unaware that they have done so. They now exist so irrevocably outside of society that they don't see the virtue of even pretending to understand or conform to it.

This is seen when they encounter François during the drill, accosting him with "Hey! How're ya doin'!" and "Where you eatin' tonight?" It is seen when they barge into the commandant's office, demanding to be set free of their duties—he is absent, so they take the trouble of writing him a rude note ("Never before in my career have I been so grossly insulted!" notes the scenery-chewing Charles Middleton, who essayed the same role in the earlier "Beau Hunks"). They are caught and sentenced to be shot at sunrise. "I hope it's cloudy tomorrow," Stan notes, before putting the bedsprings in his cell into service as an improvised harp to execute a rendition of "The World Is Waiting for the Sunrise"—a prime display of Laurel pantomime as well as, no doubt, an affectionate swipe at fellow clown Harpo Marx. They escape and are pursued by the entire outpost (society) for the last quarter of the film, during which they go on their wild plane ride and crash.

The message is clear: they are no longer assimilatable into society. In fact, society wants to destroy them. All they have are each other. The only certainty is the bond between them, which transcends death, time, and all physical manifestations of the spirit. The expression of the sublime pleasure of their bond here is seen in their neat little vaudeville song-and-dance turn to "Shine On, Harvest Moon," rendered with relaxed grace as they prepare to leave military service and are unknowingly pursued by the whole platoon.

This absence of rapprochement between them and the world continues in *Saps at Sea* (1940), a film that — unfortunately — also shares *The Flying Deuces'* low production values. If *Deuces* has a sense of being made on the cheap as a result of being an independent film (we aren't supposed to notice that the Legion grounds they're pursued through are really just the RKO backlot, or that the airplane hangars in the background are just soundstages), *Saps at Sea* has that quality — or lack thereof — as a result of it being their last film with Hal Roach. There is an air of seediness and carelessness in the production of the film that gives it the feel of being made hastily simply to fulfill a contract (which could certainly have been the point of view of both the comedians and the producer). For the team, they were looking ahead to independence and greener pastures, while Hal Roach was devoting more time to the production of serious, more "important" films. *Saps at Sea* exhibits neither the budget nor the care that had gone into the Laurel and Hardy features of the mid–1930s.

At least one source has claimed that the script originally prepared for the film was so inadequate that Stan Laurel tore it up, and the film was improvised day by day, converting whatever sets were available for the purpose.[9] Though this claim has been disputed, the film has the sort of off-the-cuff, what-the-hell quality such a practice would produce — and this quality is its greatest strength.

Stan and Ollie are workers in the testing department of a horn factory. Ollie becomes merely the latest in a succession of laborers who have succumbed to the nerve-shattering cacophony that surrounds them — the film has in fact opened with an ambulance carting away another unhinged individual. In a scene as disturbing as Chaplin's breakdown in the factory in *Modern Times* (1936), if not more so (and undoubtedly informed by it), Ollie overturns the table and goes berserk. Stan naturally remains impervious to the sonic madness around him. "It just goes in one ear and out the other," he shrugs.

It is not incompetence this time that does them out of a job, but the sheer unbearability of that job, its insanity tearing Ollie's tenuous sanity to pieces, which sends them out the door in search of recuperation. In the style of their latest films, the world is mad and reality is untrustworthy — note the increasingly discordant effects used in the background music. Ollie is sent home with Stan to restore his fractured nerves. Yet even starting their car to go home is a torturous ordeal. Beyond the car horn getting stuck and treating Ollie to a replay of the shrill ear-splitting noise that has recently sent him into a nervous breakdown, it is found that the car only works when the motor is placed in the backseat.

It's worth noting that during this segment, the team's standard decrepit Model T looks all the more ancient when compared to the 1940s cars all around them. Of course, by 1940, Model T's were ludicrously antiquated, as opposed to being the humorously quaint vehicles they were 10 years before. Also, the crowd, instead of standing around and staring at them with scorn or irritation — as they would in any other Roach film — here laughs joyously at their antics, as if we're suddenly in "reality" and people have gathered to watch Laurel and Hardy perform one of their routines. Again, the increasing freakishness of their clownish appearance and the anachronism of their car (and them?) divorce them from the common mass.

The unreality of the engine-in-the-backseat gag is matched by the disorder of the utilities at their home when they arrive there. Turn one tap, and water comes out of the other faucet. Their neighbor's radio freezes, her refrigerator plays music. For good measure, the old light-the-stove-and-engender-a-terrific-explosion gag is trotted out here as well. When they complain to the superintendent, he is found to be cross-eyed Ben Turpin, clown of Keystone vintage and last seen with Laurel and Hardy in "Our Wife" nine years before, where his oracular aberration caused him to marry Ollie to Stan rather than his intended bride. Here, he observes of the cock-eyed universe around him, reasonably enough: "Looks good to me!"

The appearance of Turpin, mastermind of this world gone awry, is matched by the entrance of other eccentrics such as Stan's music teacher Professor McGuire, inexplicably speaking with a florid Italian accent and attired in requisite cape, pencil-thin moustache and top hat, and the good Dr. Finlayson, who tends to the disturbed Mr. Hardy. The teacher, naturally enough, has come to instruct Stan on the horn, resulting in another outburst from Ollie that ends with the poor musico pummeled and thrown into the hallway. The doctor tries out an invention of his own, the lung-meter, which involves Ollie blowing up a giant balloon — it explodes, causing the apartment to shudder and collapse.

The silliness of the gags and the bizarre characters that come and go look back to the English music hall sketches at the turn of the century, which, at least in part, fathered Laurel and Hardy. They also look forward, in tone, to the team's own foray into the genre, the "birds-of-a-feather" skit they would perform in England in the 1950s. The gags are also characterized by an almost defiant infantility — when Dr. Finlayson listens to Ollie's heart with his stethoscope, Stan leans forward, pinning a child's doll under his rocking chair, causing it to shriek "Mama!" This is repeated several times, to the accompaniment of wide-eyed takes from all concerned, presumably expressing their growing concern that a voluble baby has made its home within the vast confines of the Hardy bodice. The infantility is also seen in such gags as Stan mistaking a banana for the mouthpiece of a phone, or, later, in the old reliable gag of sharing their bed with a goat. This quality is later made explicit when Stan reads Ollie to sleep —from a child's Mother Goose book.

The chaotic, nursery school surrealism of it all presents a world markedly different from that depicted in their early films, in which the team pulled the mask off a world that at least appeared reasonable and sane. Here all is zany — Ollie, seeking respite from the madness of work, comes home and is subjected to a variety of indignities that conclude with him plummeting out the window and being run over by a car. Never before have doorbells and transoms leapt so enthusiastically from their perches to bash themselves against the Hardy skull. There is no calm at the center of the storm. If Dr. Finlayson prescribes rest and relaxation on board a boat and a steady diet of goat's milk as a cure for Ollie's hornophobia — verging on hornomania — the goat will chew the rope of the boat, setting them off at sea with an escaped murderer stowing away on board. Stan may wipe his tears away as Professor O'Brien plays "Home Sweet Home," but there is no home, no rest — only a universe in a continuous flux of malevolent madness.

And in the midst of it, the team bids a final farewell to their old nemesis James Finlayson. Stan fittingly slams the door on him and on their relationship with him directly in the good doctor's face — so we hear but do not see him crash to the floor and deliver his final, anguished "Doh!"

The rest of the film concerns their prescribed ocean voyage, along with their goat and Rychard Cramer — his last major role with them being the glowering judge in "Scram!" (1932). Cramer is now perhaps the most acidically malevolent of all Laurel and Hardy villains. The boat scenes are handicapped by the cramped, low-rent feel of the ship's cabin, and the concluding wind-up featuring Ollie's pummeling of Cramer as Stan eggs him on with his trusty, though intermittently collapsing, horn is never quite as effective as it should be. Yet, as noted, *Saps at Sea's* greatness flows precisely from its leisurely offhanded quality — it is audacious in its outright silliness, it is expansive in the comic details it includes, with many of the uniquely idiosyncratic touches of humor so favored by the team over the years. Non sequiturs abound: Finlayson's dismissive "I don't give a continental!"; Charlie Hall's "The basement's downstairs"; the name of their boat, *Prickly Heat*; a goat named Narcissus; Stan and Ollie's rechristening as "Dizzy" and "Dopey" by their nemesis, who displays a similar wry humor in referring to his handgun as Nick Jr. It is a film that glories in silliness for silliness's sake. It has nothing to do with what's happening in the real world at all. Yet in a larger sense, it has everything to do with what's happening in the real world. In its sheer sense of abandon, in its no-holds-barred pursuit of frivolity, in its proud and shameless foolishness there is a purity and a display of freedom that go straight to the heart of what it means to be human. It is a poem about existence, and with all of its unexplained eccentricities, it is a world unto itself, and is their world of explosions and chaos and frustration so very different than the one we inhabit? Yet Stan and Ollie are always ready to start anew, always ready to believe. The warmth and optimism of the characters are reflected in the tone of their films, created as they were, as Laurel later said, for the sole purpose of laughter. If Laurel and Hardy never consciously set out to inject messages, philosophically or otherwise in their films, as did Chaplin —*Saps at Sea* was released in the same year as *The Great Dictator*— it could nonetheless be argued that in their single-minded commitment to pure and pointless whimsy they make an even larger statement by affirming the need for clowns to talk into bananas and to sleep with goats. They affirm the right and the necessity for humanity to utilize its freedom in the most absurd and nonsensical fashion possible.

Saps at Sea has traditionally been written off as a lesser effort, and few would agree that it shows Laurel and Hardy at the peak of their powers. It was their last film for Hal Roach and paradoxically the one that, in its carelessness and looseness, most exemplifies the freedom given them there which would soon be taken away forever. It was the same warm and amiable freedom, the same relaxed approach, devoid of pretension, which had allowed the Stan and Ollie characters to develop and grow, and as the film displays, the artistic growth continued right up until 1940. *Saps at Sea* shares much of the broad surrealism of the later W. C. Fields films, such as *The Bank Dick* (1940) and *Never Give a Sucker an Even Break* (1942), and its leisurely good humor and its genial foolishness are statements in themselves. In its perverse, homely strangeness, *Saps at Sea* is, in its own bizarre way, a celebration of human existence.

And as Stan and Ollie are taken into jail by the coast guard at the end, Ollie remonstrating about another nice mess, and Stan weeping, the soundtrack swells with a reprise of "Home Sweet Home." It's ironic because the clowns are on their way to be incarcerated with their murderous nemesis, and also because as these final frames flash, the team was leaving the home that had given birth to them, The team would never know another home like it. These saps would remain at sea for the rest of their lives.

7

NADIR

To interpret the concluding scene of *Saps at Sea* in a more literal manner, it might be more accurate to say that Stan and Ollie commenced a lengthy spell of incarceration — a time of nonfreedom. It's easy to imagine that in heading for the larger studios, the team looked forward to the larger budgets and the added prestige such a move would confer. They were soon to find themselves divested of practically everything they had created and cultivated artistically over the past 13 years.

The big movie studios were movie factories. Scripts were written by staff writers, staff directors were assigned to them, and films were made with efficient haste. Laurel and Hardy were hired as actors to perform in whatever script was handed them which was often created by writers who, since they apparently knew little about the team except that they were comedians and were from time to time expected to be funny, would give them "funny" dialogue with sweeping disregard for its unsuitability for the characters. It isn't fair to say that the big studios (Twentieth Century Fox, MGM) set out purposely to disembowel two of the greatest comedic creations of all times. This would suggest a maliciousness that was not present. The producers, writers, and directors of these films simply could not have cared less about the subtleties, the nuances, the richness of the characters so carefully and lovingly developed at Roach. Undoubtedly, they were as incapable of understanding the merit of the team's art as they were oblivious of the manner by which it was created. It was simply of no consequence to them. All that was important was to assemble vehicles that would efficiently exploit the remaining star power of the team's name and to get the resulting product shipped out to theaters in good time.

The team serves as comic relief in a series of uniformly bland B-movie plots. The films are not good Laurel and Hardy films — in a fundamental sense, they are not Laurel and Hardy films at all — and they are not good films of any kind. They are the lifeless, spiritless creations of bureaucratic mediocrities. Perhaps the most disturbing aspect of the films is the deadness at the heart of them — there is no governing vision, no purity of intention, only a glibly stitched-together quilt of banal clichés and insultingly pedestrian plotlines. There is no clarity, grace, magic or charm. The films are offensive in their self-satisfied pointlessness, in their complete and brazen lack of inner logic, of artistic essence. They are aberrations, soulless monstrosities, devoid of humanity, as though they have been entirely created by machines. They are simply not successful on any level.

In the worst of the Roach films, usually those put together with the same intrusive "straight" plots as seen in these later efforts, there was still the pleasure of seeing the team perform their routines, still the pleasure of spending time with the characters amidst the annoying plotline. Here, the team is divested of their singular characters, their warmth, their idiosyncrasies, most of all, their fervent aspirations to dignity, their ever-hopeful pursuit of human kindness. They are not in the Laurel and Hardy world any longer but in a slick, cynical, mundane approximation of the culture of brash patriotism of the 1940s. They are surrounded not by the smoldering Charlie Hall or by the shrill Mae Busch but by completely forgettable regular guy and gal types, gum-cracking smart alecks and contemptuous, tough-talking dames. The lack of respect shown by the studios for the team is reflected in the manner they are treated by their supporting casts in the films. They are treated — and it is clear that we are to think of them as such as well — as appalling simpletons, unworthy of respect or affection, only — possibly — deserving of our pity. In these films Laurel and Hardy are nothing more than a pair of sad, tired, washed-out, doddering old fools.

Their performances in these films betrays what Laurel later claimed was their attitude toward the entire experience — for a time they struggled to assert themselves artistically, but, finding themselves stymied at every turn, they simply "gave up the ghost." Inevitably, it was Laurel who suffered the most, after being relieved of his duties as writer and director, and rudely dismissed any time he attempted to make suggestions regarding the comedy; with nothing left to do he could only be the unwilling participant in the dismantling of the artistic entity whose creation had been his life's work. Since he'd apparently signed the contract with the full assumption of complete artistic control he'd known all his career, one can only imagine the utter shock and horror that must have come over him upon realizing the actuality of his situation. His performances in these films are those of a man in shock, a man in such anguish that in order to function at all he has necessarily made himself dead to all feeling, all emotion. All that comes through is the not-completely-smothered revulsion at having to mouth words, perform actions, which are antithetical to the urges of every comic instinct within him. He sleepwalks through the films, a blurry, submerged remnant of what once had been. He is an artistic nonentity, a walking shadow.

As though to add insult to injury, the decision was made by the big studios that the clown-white makeup favored by the team was to be eschewed for a more naturalistic, "real" skin tone — the better for them to fit into the more prosaic reality depicted in the films. The effect is not only to rob the characters further of their otherworldly quality, but also to age them by 10 years. Rather than the fey, magical music hall clown of the Roach films, Laurel here looks exactly like what he is: a much-married, much-divorced British expatriate in late middle age desperately trying to ride out a horrible situation. Hardy, who was no less disgusted by the whole experience, appears closer to the rough-hewn character actor he would later be in solo turns in films by his buddies Bing Crosby and John Wayne than anything resembling the Ollie of the mid–1930s. Though it's possible to say that his performance suffers less than Laurel's in these films since the Hardy character is more part of the "real world" that has overtaken them, the scope of his art has been drastically lessened as well — the nuances, the subtleties, the psychological depths that Hardy was so gifted at portraying are all gone. It is notable that the one film generally considered to be the best of a bad lot features the comedians in impersonations of other characters as part of its storyline (*Jitterbugs*, 1943) — it must have come as a relief to them to be able to play other parts as a change from continuing to desecrate their own creations over and over.

Just as the team needed to re-create themselves to meet the challenges of a new age, they became artistically handcuffed; just as they needed to appeal to a new generation, to respond to the challenge of a new, up-and-coming comedy team (Abbott and Costello), they were shown to be older-looking, more tired and uninspired than ever before. In a parade of shame the films were duly assembled and sent marching out into the world: *Great Guns* (1941); *A-Haunting We Will Go* (1942); *Air Raid Wardens* (1943); *Jitterbugs* (1943); *Tree in a Test Tube* (1943); *The Dancing Masters* (1943); *The Big Noise* (1944); *Nothing But Trouble* (1945); *The Bullfighters* (1945). Of these, *The Tree in a Test Tube* is perhaps the least offensive, being a short made for the government as part of the war effort, with the added bonus that it is their only surviving film in color.

The great irony is that all of these films made money, to the degree that the team was offered another contract with Fox when their original one ran out. By 1945, the comedians bowed out — as financially stressed as they might have been, they simply couldn't face the prospect of making more horrible films.

At this point they found themselves truly adrift. It was rapidly becoming clear that there was no longer any place for them in Hollywood. By all accounts, the most artistically fulfilling work they did in the 1940s was on stage, first in personal appearances to aid the war effort, then in their own traveling show. In 1947, they began their first performing tour of British music halls, an endeavor so successful and personally satisfying that it was repeated again in 1953 and 1954, each time utilizing sketches written by Laurel.

But before these later tours of the 1950s there was one more film to be made—fittingly enough, an offer came from overseas, where they'd lately known their greatest acceptance. It is a tale of homelessness and exile and of a search for paradise. The making of the film would be, for the comedians personally, as monumental a disaster as any that had plagued their screen counterparts.

8

UTOPIA

To see our old friends after an absence of ten years—that is, the ten years that had passed since their last Hal Roach film, since the last appearance of the *real* Laurel and Hardy—is a somewhat jarring experience. They look decidedly worse for wear, and at times they even seem to have become frighteningly extreme living caricatures of themselves, like walking Hirschfelds. Ollie is now impossibly huge, exceeding the steadily growing girth of even his Fox films, and finally, fearfully, obese. As if taking his cue from his partner, Stan is thinner than ever before — he became dangerously ill during the making of the film — and at times he looks literally cadaverous. They are Fat and Skinny to the nth degree. This is quite apart from their age — Hardy, 58, and Laurel, 60, which effectively marks them off from that pair of young sailors chatting up the ladies in "Two Tars."

But, to be honest, we are all somewhat worse for wear. The past 10 years had brought Auschwitz, Buchenwald, Stalin's purges, Hiroshima, Nagasaki. Humanity learned something about itself during that time, a type of knowledge that once put on can not be taken off nor borne easily. The world became a more uneasy place during that time, an uneasiness experienced first and more vividly in Europe — still a death-scarred battlefield, still a war-ravaged graveyard — where we find our hapless pals once again after such a long time.

Once again, they travel to a lawyer's office to collect an inheritance left to Stan by his skinflint uncle, characteristically never learning, as they should have from earlier experiences in "The Laurel-Hardy Murder Case" (1930) and *Bonnie Scotland* (1935), that such expeditions always come to naught. The team is left a yacht, an island, and a sum of money. Quite expectedly, their fortune is rapidly diminished by a variety of fees and taxes, thoughtfully and expeditiously collected with touching eagerness by the battery of lawyers, who generously remit to Stan and Ollie the few farthings left them. "I wish uncle had left me the taxes," Stan notes. They are still, thankfully, in full possession of an island and a yacht with which to sail to it.

Utopia (1951), also known by such other euphonious titles as *Atoll K* and *Robinson Crusoeland*, was shot in France as a joint production of the French, English, and Italian governments, all looking to kickstart their film industries after the war. *Utopia*'s script was written by a coalition of French, Italian, and American writers, each of whom evidently had a different vision of what the final product should be. Quite apart from their difficulties in understanding each other linguistically, the Italian writer was going for a social statement, the French writer for a surreal farce, the American writer for something in-between. Laurel's growing horror when he read the thoroughly unacceptable script that resulted, once he'd arrived in France for the expected 12-week shoot, was likely his first intimation that things were going horribly awry on the road to *Utopia*. He hurriedly contacted some old gagman friends back in Hollywood in an attempt to salvage the mess.[1]

The 12 weeks became 12 months—one full year of filming in the South of France in outrageous temperatures. The modern day Babel that the script conferences presumably were was reflected in the shooting of the film, in which all of the supporting cast was composed of French or Italian costars. Each cast member spoke his lines in his native language, to be dubbed later—or not—according to the destination of the various prints of the film. All of the actors were required to exchange dialogue and to react to dialogue that they did not comprehend. When disagreements arose, there came a cacophony of babble in an assortment of disparate tongues. "Nobody—including the director and us—knew what the hell was going on," Laurel commented later.[2]

Stan and Ollie tramp down to the docks at Marseilles in order to claim their yacht—a rather seedy-looking crate not much more impressive than the *Prickly Heat* of 11 years before. Their idea is to set sail for their new home, their island, as soon as possible. They engage in some gentle knockabout during the examination of their boat, displaying an ability to perform tasteful physical comedy even at their sexagenarian vintage.

One of the more pleasant surprises in the strange miscellany that constitutes *Utopia* is the reinstatement of the Stan and Ollie characters after they had been effectively put in mothballs for the years in which the Fox-MGM pictures were made. Evidently the loose chaos that characterized the production provided sufficient leeway, at least, for the team to practice their art. What is displayed in *Utopia* is something the many audience members in their European tours doubtless knew quite well, but which those of us only familiar with their recent output might have considerable doubt about—that Laurel and Hardy, even at their advanced age, were quite capable of being funny in their own inimitable manner if given the chance, were well equipped to bring their comedy into the decade of Elvis Presley and Jack Kerouac.

In the film, we are introduced to Antoine, a Frenchman described as a stateless refugee, a man without a country, who is in the process of attempting, for the umpteenth time, to land on soil in order to have a country claim him as its own. He is discovered hiding in a monkey cage, reduced to living like an animal in order to find a home. The captain, instructed to take him away again, instead foists him on Stan and Ollie, telling them he's qualified to be a mechanic for their ship. At the same time, Giovanni, an Italian stonemason, who seeks to go off someplace where he is allowed to build marble palaces, stows away on the team's boat. They set sail, discovering him along the way.

We see put in motion here the social commentary aspect of the film, and what's interesting is how neatly it dovetails with the team's comic sensibility, how it resonates with their recent career. Antoine, with his inability to be accepted into society, or absorbed by it, reflects Stan and Ollie's lifelong struggle — and failure — to do exactly that. His sense of being identityless, a man who doesn't belong anywhere, mirrors Laurel and Hardy's careers as of late — rejected by Hollywood, they float off to Europe, trying to find their way back to their art and perhaps a home.

Similarly, Giovanni, is a bricklayer, an "artist" who wants to build palaces but is always forced to build fences. He chooses exile to have the freedom to practice his art, freedom from those who "tell me what to do and how to do it!" as he says — shades of the team's treatment at Fox. As Stan and Ollie have done innumerable times, and as Laurel and Hardy the comedians were doing in making this film, he sets off into the unknown in order to be freed from society's constricting confines.

A sudden storm engulfs their ship, and a coral reef — an atoll — rises out of the ocean to give sanctuary to the four misfits. Inspired by a book Ollie reads about Robinson Crusoe, they begin to build themselves a home on the island — a new world, a paradise. Inevitably, as the film's narrator points out, an Eve arrives to corrupt the paradise. A young pouting woman who has left her bridegroom standing at the altar back in civilization, after he's told her that he won't allow her to continue her career as a singer after they're married, sets off in a rowboat to escape him and ends up on the island. The straight plot scenes here are in keeping with the team's sensibility, as the prospective married couple are always shown angry and bickering, a vain and petty pair of people — in yet another depiction of marriage as an absurd farce in the Laurel and Hardy canon.

The woman, Cheri Lamour, arrives on the island, and for a while the film seems, as one of the characters remarks, to be a remake of *Snow White and the Seven Dwarfs*. The men vie and compete for the woman's attention, who "civilizes" the island to some degree. At one point a gag is repeated from Disney's *Snow White*, when the men are lined up to receive a kiss from the woman, and Stan, like Dopey, races around to the end of the line to receive a second kiss.

The woman's ex-fiancé, a seaman, comes to the island as part of an expedition to discover uranium — that much desired element so crucial to the development of the bomb responsible for those recent and epoch-defining explosions in Hiroshima and Nagasaki. It is explained that it is now crucial for the island to define itself as a republic. The castaways are asked which one of them was the first to set foot on the island, in order to establish which country can make a claim of sovereignty over it. It was Antoine, who explains that he belongs to no country: "No country will have me." "Now every country will want you," notes the seaman dryly.

In order to preserve their island from being taken over by others ("They want to steal our geranium," Stan observes), Stan, Ollie and the others resolve to set up their own country — Crusoeland. Suitably, it is Ollie, always dedicated to ideals, to his vision of the way things should be, who is the spearhead of this resolution, and after they have collaborated on a constitution that specifies that there shall be no laws, no jails, no poverty, no passports, no immigration laws, it is Ollie who becomes president of Crusoeland. He assigns the other members of the group to various positions in his cabinet. All except for Stan, who asks, "What about me?" "Why Stanley — you're the people!" Ollie assures him. "But I don't want to be the people!" Stan declares. "But there's more of you than there are of us!" Ollie explains. "Oh — why didn't ya tell me?" Stan notes, comforted. Cheri Lamour designs the flag, using her skirt — on which is drawn a heart pierced through with an arrow.

Soon the news of the existence of a new country that has no laws, no jails, and no taxes floods the world, and from every corner of the globe immigrants come to overrun the tiny island. The shores are clotted with boats crammed with people, hordes dressed in every conceivable type of dress and speaking every imaginable language — stressing further the Babel–global village element of the film, and running roughshod through paradise. A mother is seen taking down the flag in order to wipe the noses of her children.

Inevitably it is found that utopia cannot exist without laws. After a scoundrel assaults Cheri in a café, Ollie, frustrated that he has no recourse, convenes his cabinet and rewrites the constitution of Crusoeland. The changes are posted to the public via a placard on a tree: "From this time on, there will now be laws in Crusoeland — P.S. — There will also be taxes." The scoundrel rips down the placard, confronts Ollie, and bashes him on the skull with it.

Revolution is declared. The masses, led on by the same rabble-rouser, pursue Ollie, Stan, Giovanni, and Antoine until they are captured. They are sentenced to death by hanging as the angry throng surrounds them. Before this can occur, another tempest announces itself with howling winds and rain — and the atoll, with all of its furious crowds, sinks biblically into the ocean and disappears just as mysteriously as it had originally arisen. Stan, Ollie, Giovanni, Antoine and Cheri survive the apocalypse, floating on the scaffold that was to have been the site of their execution. They are rescued by Cheri's seaman ex-fiancé, who happens to be floating by.

Utopia, plainly, is not a great film, but it is not bad in the sense that the Fox–MGM films are bad, nor is it bad for the same reasons they are bad films. It is interesting — even fascinating — in a way in which none of those previous efforts ever came close to being. Its plotline, which openly aspires to function as a parable, provides a relevant and audacious framework for the team's clowning. That clowning, particularly in the first half of the film, before the plotting becomes more intrusive, is of a piece with the work we had last seen in *Saps at Sea*. Their routine at mealtime, each becoming exponentially mistrustful of each other as Giovanni, unseen, steals their food, could have been seen in any of their Roach films. Their characters, and the relationship between those characters, as noted, are back at full strength, with all of their complexities, idiosyncrasies, and otherworldly charm intact. Stan has several "surreal" routines: literally "pouring oil on troubled waters," shaving with sandpaper, and communing on the island with his pet lobster, Oscar. The precarious, beautiful balance of the Laurel–Hardy relationship is back in all its glory, after having been dulled and deadened for the previous 10 years — they fight amongst themselves constantly.

Ollie explains to Stan that an inflatable raft found on their yacht is capable of containing four people. Stan, eyeing Ollie's vast girth: "What about me?" Ollie: "You don't have to be insulting. Haven't I always looked out for you? You're always the first thing I think of!" He turns away, hurt. Stan, remorseful, tries to engage him again. Ollie shakes his head resolutely, staring off into the distance. Stan proffers a handkerchief, dabbing at Ollie's eyes, then bringing it to his nose. Ollie blows his nose, then waves him away: "'What about me,'" he fumes — "What about ME?" he cries.

With all of this, *Utopia* has a number of handicaps to overcome. Though it all seems strangely relevant to the plot of the film, the obvious, utterly unconvincing dubbing of the voice of every other character in the film aside from Stan and Ollie gives it a tone that can only be described as bizarre. Even more bizarre, perhaps, is to meditate on the mind-set of the film's planners, who assumed audiences worldwide would have no problem in embracing a comedy in which the majority of the actors speak in voices not their own. Relevant maybe, because the comedy envisions a brave new world of postnationalism, a borderless world free of economic oppression, as a refuge from the cataclysms of tribal hatred lately unleashed across the globe — though hardly conducive to the pursuit of surefire laughs.

A greater handicap is the appearance of Stan Laurel in the film. As if the shoddy script, the incompetent director, the insane heat of the location, and the fact that every member of the crew spoke a language different not only from his own but also from each other were not enough, Laurel became seriously ill during the making of the film. A prostate problem was diagnosed, and he had an operation. Not fully recovered from the operation, he gamely returned to work, only to contract dysentery from the food on location. In the finished film, his health seems to wax and wane throughout, but there are several scenes in which he looks absolutely horrific — his emaciated, deathly appearance effectively killing our laughter before it can begin. It is evident at certain points that he is having real difficulty in even standing up. It is difficult to think of any other film whose star is seemingly at death's door for its entire running time.

Yet if Laurel at times is virtually unrecognizable as Stan from the peak years of the 1930s, he is, throughout, the Stan we have all known for years in spirit and in expression, as Ollie is Ollie. The premise of their final adventure — the creation and destruction of a new society — isn't at all unsuitable for these two perpetual outsiders, who despite all their best intentions, cannot belong, and whose earliest visions were of the societal breakdown they inspire by even trying to. The tragedy of *Utopia* is that it has so much working against it, that its making was consumed in so much chaos, misunderstanding, and sickness. Laurel and Hardy finally have the freedom to pursue their art, but they are threatened and thwarted at every turn by a disorder that surges forth to engulf them — in much the same way as their little paradise, the "perfect society" they create in the movie, is torn apart by violence and spite, then submerged and drowned beneath the waves of the ocean.

"This world of ours is far from a paradise," *Utopia*'s chipper narrator informs us, "but people go on living just the same." These words lead into the dénouement, in which the characters' fates are wrapped up — in true Laurel and Hardy fashion, the ends they come to are far from auspicious. Cheri Lamour and her fiancé, back in civilization, make another attempt to wed and are seen arguing back and forth over the head of the poor justice of the peace just as vociferously as in our first introduction to them. Giovanni is back stoically slapping fences together in his native Italy — "he'll never make marble palaces," the narrator confidently informs us. Antoine tries to sneak into another country via another animal's cage —

we are shown a sated lion arriving on land, pawing over a pair of empty boots.

Our old friends Stan and Ollie are shown deposited on their true and rightful island with a supply of food. Just as they seem ready to sink into peaceful, indolent retirement and ultimate exile, some authorities step forth and seize their supplies and island for nonpayment of taxes. Ollie turns to Stan balefully and delivers his signature line; Stan bursts into tears as Ollie simmers and shakes his head with frustration. Their image irises out, shrinking and receding into darkness, as the clowns themselves must inevitably fade into the oblivion of time, ever more distant from us as we move ineluctably away from them and their age, the men long gone and perished, leaving only laughter, the enduring shadows of their antics, and the memory of laughter.

What remained for the comedians was to return to America and recover from the horrendous one-year shoot — how many of their classics had been created in one week? There was also further professional neglect, ignominy, two more returns to the British music halls whose traditions had so nourished them, a partial rediscovery and rebirth with the popularity of their old films on television, and the further illnesses and indignities of old age, culminating, as always, in death. Oliver Hardy succumbed seven years after *Utopia*, and Stan Laurel survived a further eight years after that, doggedly doing his best to answer every piece of fan mail — and personally greeting any fan who happened to find their way to the door of his home. Laurel still created gags for the mythical twosome until that bright fount of gags and good humor was finally stilled in February 1965.

What remained for the rest of us was more unrest, collisions, confrontations, and disasters. There were more assaults on our dignity, more extravagant and elaborate pratfalls courtesy of diabolically well-placed banana peels — more unexpected submersions in absurdly deep mud holes. We travel in vehicles that are flayed apart and disintegrate beneath us long before we reach our destination — our empires crumble, crashing to the earth even as we bestow upon them their finishing touches. Conflicts, riots, war, humanity fighting against itself — and winning — as fate or nature never could. The long unwinding of the code of civilization, resulting in James Finlayson yelping "Doh!" and a frenzy of pants-ripping. We must lose all we have until we realize all we have is each other, though by that time no words can span the distance, so overwhelmed are we by the calamity of our misfortune, no thought can be articulated. All that remains is to weep in frightened incomprehension, or to lament, turning to our other self, and state, straight from the center of our stricken being: "Here's another nice mess you've gotten me into!"

FILMOGRAPHY

Films are listed here in the order of their release

1919

"Lucky Dog"—G. M. Anderson-Metro—Two Reels—Silent. Released December 1921 by Metro. Directed by Jess Robbins. Costarring Florence Gillet.

A chance meeting in a Stan Laurel comedy, in which Oliver Hardy plays a menacing villain.

1926

"45 Minutes from Hollywood"—Hal Roach—Two Reels—Silent. Released December 26, 1926 by Pathé Exchange. Directed by Fred Guiol. Costarring Glenn Tryon, Charlotte Mineau, Theda Bara.

Laurel and Hardy appear in the film but share no scenes together.

All films after this, unless otherwise noted, are produced by Hal Roach.

1927

"Duck Soup"—Two Reels—Silent. Released March 13, 1927, by Pathé Exchange. Directed by Fred Guiol. Based on a sketch by Arthur J. Jefferson (Laurel's father). Costarring Madeleine Hurlock, William Austin.

The first film to purposely "team" Laurel and Hardy.

"Slipping Wives"—Two Reels—Silent. Released April 3, 1927, by Pathé Exchange. Directed by Fred Guiol. Story by Hal Roach. Costarring Priscilla Dean, Herbert Rawlinson.

Laurel and Hardy share a few fleeting scenes together.

"Love 'Em and Weep"—Two Reels—Silent. Released June 12, 1927, by Pathé Exchange. Directed by Fred Guiol. Story by Hal Roach. Costarring Mae Busch, James Finlayson, Charlie Hall.

"Why Girls Love Sailors"—Two Reels—Silent. Released July 17, 1927, by Pathé Exchange. Directed by Fred Guiol. Story by Hal Roach. Costarring Malcolm Waite, Viola Richard, Anita Garvin.

"With Love and Hisses"—Two Reels—Silent. Released August 18, 1927, by Pathé Exchange. Directed by Fred Guiol. Story by Hal Roach. Costarring James Finlayson, Frank Brownlee, Anita Garvin.

"Sugar Daddies"—Two Reels—Silent. Released September 10, 1927, by MGM. Directed by Fred Guiol. Costarring James Finlayson, Noah Young, Charlotte Mineau.

"Sailors, Beware!"—Two Reels—

Silent. Released September 27, 1927, by Pathé Exchange. Directed by Hal Yates. Story by Hal Roach. Costarring Anita Garvin, Tiny Sandford, Viola Richard.

Laurel and Hardy share fleeting scenes together.

"Now I'll Tell One" — Two Reels — Silent. Released October 5, 1927, by Pathé Exchange. Directed by James Parrott. Costarring Charley Chase, Edna Marion, Lincoln Plumer.

Laurel and Hardy appear in this Charley Chase comedy but appear to share no scenes together. Only one reel survives of this film.

"The Second Hundred Years" — Two Reels — Silent. Released October 8, 1927, by MGM. Directed by Fred Guiol. Costarring James Finlayson, Eugene Pallette, Tiny Sandford, Ellinor Van Der Veer.

Laurel and Hardy are deliberately teamed.

"Call of the Cuckoos" — Two Reels — Silent. Released October 15, 1927, by MGM. Directed by Clyde Bruckman. Costarring Max Davidson, Lillian Elliott, Spec O'Donnell, Charley Chase, James Finlayson, Charlie Hall.

Laurel and Hardy make a gag cameo appearance in this Max Davidson comedy.

"Hats Off" — Two Reels — Silent. Released November 5, 1927, by MGM. Directed by Hal Yates. Supervised by Leo McCarey. Costarring James Finlayson, Anita Garvin, Dorothy Coburn.

By all contemporary accounts, this is the "breakthrough" film in terms of their teaming. The reels are now lost.

"Do Detectives Think?" — Two Reels — Silent. Released November 20, 1927, by Pathé Exchange. Directed by Fred Guiol. Story by Hal Roach. Costarring James Finlayson, Viola Richard, Noah Young.

"Putting Pants on Philip" — Two Reels — Silent. Released December 3, 1927, by MGM. Directed by Clyde Bruckman. Supervised by Leo McCarey. Costarring Harvey Clark, Dorothy Coburn, Sam Lufkin.

The film Laurel selected as the "first" Laurel and Hardy film.

"The Battle of the Century" — Two Reels — Silent. Released December 31, 1927, by MGM. Directed by Clyde Bruckman. Supervised by Leo McCarey. Costarring Noah Young, Sam Lufkin, Eugene Pallette, Anita Garvin.

The film is partially lost.

1928

"Leave 'Em Laughing" — Two Reels — Silent. Released January 28, 1928, by MGM. Directed by Clyde Bruckman. Supervised by Leo McCarey. Story by Hal Roach. Costarring Edgar Kennedy, Charlie Hall, Viola Richard.

"Flying Elephants" — Two Reels — Silent. Released February 12, 1928, by Pathé Exchange. Directed by Fred Butler. Story by Hal Roach. Costarring Dorothy Coburn, Tiny Sandford, Leo Willis.

"The Finishing Touch" — Two Reels — Silent. Released February 25, 1928, by MGM. Directed by Clyde Bruckman. Supervised by Leo McCarey. Costarring Edgar Kennedy, Dorothy Coburn, Sam Lufkin.

"From Soup to Nuts" — Two Reels — Silent. Released March 24, 1928, by MGM. Directed by Edgar Kennedy. Supervised by Leo McCarey. Story by Leo McCarey. Costarring Anita Garvin, Tiny Sandford, Otto Fires, Edna Marian.

"You're Darn Tootin'" — Two Reels — Silent. Released April 21, 1928, by MGM. Directed by Edgar Kennedy. Supervised by Leo McCarey. Costarring Otto Lederer, Agnes Steele, Chet Brandenberg.

"Their Purple Moment" — Two Reels — Silent. Released May 19, 1928, by MGM. Directed by James Parrott. Supervised by Leo McCarey. Costarring Anita Garvin, Kay Delsys, Jimmy Aubrey.

"Should Married Men Go Home?"— Two Reels— Silent. Released September 8, 1928, by MGM. Directed by James Parrott. Supervised by Leo McCarey. Story by James Parrott and Leo McCarey. Costarring Edgar Kennedy, Edna Marian, Viola Richard.
  The first film in the "Laurel and Hardy Series."

"Early to Bed"— Two Reels— Silent. Released October 6, 1928, by MGM. Directed by Emmett Flynn. Supervised by Leo McCarey.

"Two Tars"— Two Reels— Silent. Released November 3, 1928, by MGM. Directed by James Parrott. Supervised by Leo McCarey. Story by Leo McCarey. Costarring Thelma Hill, Ruby Blaine, Charlie Hall, Edgar Kennedy.

"Habeas Corpus"— Two Reels— Silent. Released December 1, 1928, by MGM. Directed by James Parrott. Supervised by Leo McCarey. Story by Leo McCarey. Costarring Richard Carle, Charles A. Bachman, Charley Rogers.

"We Faw Down"— Two Reels— Silent. Released December 29, 1928, by MGM. Directed by Leo McCarey. Costarring Vivien Oakland, Bess Flowers, Kay Delsys, Vera White, George Kotsonaros.

1929

"Liberty"— Two Reels— Silent. Released January 26, 1929, by MGM. Directed by Leo McCarey. Story by Leo McCarey. Costarring James Finlayson, Tom Kennedy, Jean Harlow.

"Wrong Again"— Two Reels— Silent. Released February 23, 1929, by MGM. Directed by Leo McCarey. Assistance by Lewis R. Foster. Story by Leo McCarey and Lewis R. Foster. Costarring Del Henderson, Harry Bernard, Charlie Hall.

"That's My Wife"— Two Reels— Silent. Released March 23, 1929, by MGM.

Directed by Lloyd French. Supervised by Leo McCarey. Story by Leo McCarey. Costarring Vivien Oakland, William Courtwright, Charlie Hall, Jimmy Aubrey.

"Big Business"— Two Reels— Silent. Released April 20, 1929, by MGM. Directed by James Horne. Supervised by Leo McCarey. Story by Leo McCarey. Costarring James Finlayson, Tiny Sandford, Lyle Tayo.

"Unaccustomed As We Are"— Two Reels— Sound. Released May 4, 1929, by MGM. Directed by Lewis R. Foster. Story by Leo McCarey. Costarring Mae Busch, Thelma Todd, Edgar Kennedy.
  Their first sound film.

"Double Whoopee"— Two Reels— Silent. Released May 18, 1929, by MGM. Directed by Lewis R. Foster. Story by Leo McCarey. Costarring Charlie Hall, Tiny Sandford, Jean Harlow, Rolfe Sedan.

"Berth Marks"— Two Reels— Sound. Released June 1, 1929, by MGM. Directed by Lewis R. Foster. Story by Leo McCarey. Costarring Pat Harmon, Silas D. Wilcox, Harry Bernard, Baldwin Cooke.

"Men O' War"— Two Reels— Sound. Released June 29, 1929, by MGM. Directed by Lewis R. Foster. Costarring James Finlayson, Harry Bernard, Anne Cornwall, Gloria Greer.

"Perfect Day"— Two Reels— Sound. Released August 10, 1929, by MGM. Directed by James Parrott. Story by Leo McCarey and Hal Roach. Costarring Edgar Kennedy, Kay Delsys, Isabelle Keith, Harry Bernard.

"They Go Boom"— Two Reels— Sound. Released September 21, 1929, by MGM. Directed by James Parrott. Story by Leo McCarey. Costarring Charlie Hall, Sam Lufkin.

"Bacon Grabbers"— Two Reels— Silent.

Released October 19, 1929, by MGM. Directed by Lewis R. Foster. Story by Leo McCarey. Costarring Edgar Kennedy, Charlie Hall, Eddie Baker, Jean Harlow.

"The Hoose-Gow"—Two Reels— Sound. Released November 16, 1929, by MGM. Directed by James Parrott. Story by Leo McCarey. Costarring James Finlayson, Tiny Sandford, Leo Willis.

The Hollywood Review of 1929—120 minutes—Sound. Produced by Harry Rapp for MGM. Released November 23, 1929, by MGM. Directed by Charles Reisner. Costarring Jack Benny, Conrad Nagel, Joan Crawford, Buster Keaton, and others.

The team contributes a "magicians" routine to this all-star review-format feature film.

"Angora Love"—Two Reels—Silent. Released December 14, 1929, by MGM. Directed by Lewis R. Foster. Story by Leo McCarey. Costarring Edgar Kennedy, Charlie Hall, Harry Bernard.

Their final silent film.

1930

"Night Owls"—Two Reels—Sound. Released January 4, 1930, by MGM. Directed by James Parrott. Story by Leo McCarey. Costarring Edgar Kennedy, James Finlayson, Anders Randolph.

"Blotto"—Three Reels—Sound. Released February 8, 1930, by MGM. Directed by James Parrott. Story by Leo McCarey. Costarring Anita Garvin, Tiny Sandford, Frank Holliday, Baldwin Cooke, Charlie Hall.

"Brats"—Two Reels—Sound. Released March 22, 1930, by MGM. Directed by James Parrott. Story by Leo McCarey and Hal Roach.

"Below Zero"—Two Reels—Sound. Released April 26, 1930, by MGM. Directed by James Parrott. Story by Leo

McCarey. Costarring Charlie Hall, Blanche Payson, Frank Holliday, Leo Willis.

The Rogue Song—115 minutes— Sound—Technicolor. Released May 10, 1930, by MGM. Produced by Lionel Barrymore for MGM. Directed by Lionel Barrymore. Laurel and Hardy sequences directed by Hal Roach. Original story by Frances Marion and John Colton. Based on the 1912 London opera *Gypsy Love, A New Musical Play in Three Acts* by Franz Lehar, A. M. Willner, and Robert Bodansky. Costarring Lawrence Tibbett, Catherine Dale Owen, Florence Lake.

Laurel and Hardy are the comic relief in this feature-length opera film—an influence on their own later opera films. The film is now lost.

"Hog Wild"—Two Reels—Sound. Released May 31, 1930, by MGM. Directed by James Parrott. Story by Leo McCarey. Costarring Fay Holderness, Dorothy Granger.

"The Laurel-Hardy Murder Case"— Three Reels—Sound. Released September 6, 1930, by MGM. Directed by James Parrott. Costarring Fred Kelsey, Tiny Sandford, Del Henderson, Robert Burns, Dorothy Granger, Frank Austin.

"Another Fine Mess"—Three Reels— Sound. Released November 29, 1930, by MGM. Directed by James Parrott. A remake of the silent "Duck Soup," based on a sketch by A. J. Jefferson (Laurel's father). Costarring Thelma Todd, James Finlayson, Eddie Dunn, Charles Gerrard, Harry Bernard.

1931

"Be Big"—Three Reels—Sound. Released February 7, 1931, by MGM. Directed by James Parrott. Costarring Anita Garvin, Isabelle Keith, Charlie Hall, Baldwin Cooke.

"Chickens Come Home"—Three Reels—Sound. Released February 21, 1931, by MGM. Directed by James W. Horne. A remake of the silent "Love 'Em and Weep" (story by Hal Roach). Costarring Mae Busch, Thelma Todd, James Finlayson, Frank Holliday, Elizabeth Forrester.

"The Stolen Jools"—Two Reels—Sound. Released April 1931 by Paramount and National Screen Service. Produced by Pat Casey. Presented by National Variety Artists in cooperation with Chesterfield cigarettes. Directed by William McGann. Costarring Wallace Beery, Norma Shearer, Eddie Kane, Buster Keaton, and others.

A cameo by the team in a star-studded short to raise funds for the relief work of the National Variety Artists' tuberculosis sanitarium.

"Laughing Gravy"—Two Reels—Sound. Released April 4, 1931, by MGM. Directed by James W. Horne. A reworking of the silent "Angora Love." Costarring Charlie Hall, Harry Bernard, Laughing Gravy (a dog).

"Our Wife"—Two Reels—Sound. Released May 16, 1931, by MGM. Directed by James W. Horne. Costarring James Finlayson, Babe London, Ben Turpin, Charley Rogers, Blanche Payson.

Pardon Us—56 minutes—Sound. Released August 15, 1931, by MGM. Directed by James Parrott. Photographed by George Stevens. Costarring Walter Long, James Finlayson, Wilfred Lucas, June Marlowe, Tiny Sandford.

Their first feature-length film.

"Come Clean"—Two Reels—Sound. Released September 19, 1931, by MGM. Directed by James W. Horne. Costarring Mae Busch, Gertrude Astor, Linda Loredo, Charlie Hall.

"One Good Turn"—Two Reels—Sound. Released October 31, 1931, by MGM. Directed by James W. Horne. Costarring Mary Carr, James Finlayson, Billy Gilbert.

"Beau Hunks"—Four Reels—Sound. Released December 12, 1931, by MGM. Directed by James W. Horne. Costarring Charles Middleton, Charlie Hall, Tiny Sandford, James W. Horne.

"On the Loose"—Two Reels—Sound. Released December 26, 1931, by MGM. Directed by Hal Roach. Story by Hal Roach. Costarring Thelma Todd, Zasu Pitts, Claud Allister, John Loder.

The team makes a gag cameo appearance in this Thelma Todd—Zasu Pitts short.

1932

"Helpmates"—Two Reels—Sound. Released January 23, 1932, by MGM. Directed by James Parrott. Costarring Blanche Payson, Robert Callahan.

"Any Old Port"—Two Reels—Sound. Released March 5, 1932, by MGM. Directed by James W. Horne. Costarring Walter Long, Jacqueline Wells, Harry Bernard, Robert Burns.

"The Music Box"—Three Reels—Sound. Released April 16, 1932, by MGM. Directed by James Parrott. Based in part on the silent "Hats Off." Costarring Billy Gilbert, Charlie Hall, Gladys Gale.

Winner of the Best Live-Action Short Subject Academy Award of 1932.

"The Chimp"—Three Reels—Sound. Released May 21, 1932, by MGM. Directed by James Parrott. Costarring Billy Gilbert, James Finlayson, Tiny Sandford, Charles Gamora.

"County Hospital"—Two Reels—Sound. Released June 25, 1932, by MGM. Directed by James Parrott. Costarring Billy Gilbert, May Wallace, William Austin.

"Scram!"—Two Reels—Sound. Released September 10, 1932, by MGM. Directed by Raymond McCarey. Costarring Arthur Housman, Rychard Cramer, Vivien Oakland.

Pack Up Your Troubles— 68 minutes— Sound. Released September 17, 1932, by MGM. Directed by George Marshall and Raymond McCarey. Music by Le Roy Shield and Marvin Hatley. Photographed by Art Lloyd. Costarring Jacquie Lyn, Donald Dillaway, James Finlayson, Billy Gilbert, Frank Brownlee, George Marshall, Rychard Cramer.

"Their First Mistake"—Two Reels— Sound. Released November 5, 1932, by MGM. Directed by George Marshall. Costarring Mae Busch, Billy Gilbert, George Marshall.

"Towed in a Hole"—Two Reels— Sound. Released December 31, 1932, by MGM. Directed by George Marshall. Costarring Billy Gilbert.

1933

"Twice Two"—Two Reels—Sound. Released February 25, 1933, by MGM. Directed by James Parrott. Costarring Baldwin Cooke, Charlie Hall.

"Me and My Pal"—Two Reels—Sound. Released April 22, 1933, by MGM. Directed by Charles Rogers and Lloyd French. Costarring James Finlayson, James C. Morton, Eddie Dunn, Charles Plinge, Charlie Hall.

Fra Diavolo (a.k.a. *The Devil's Brother*, a.k.a *Bogus Bandits*)— 90 minutes— Sound. Released May 5, 1933, by MGM. Directed by Hal Roach and Charles Rogers. Based on the 1830 comic opera *Fra Diavolo* by Daniel F. Auber. Adaptation by Jeanie McPherson. Music by Auber. Musical direction by Le Roy Shield. Photographed by Art Lloyd and Hap Depew. Costarring Dennis King, Thelma Todd, James Finlayson, Henry

Armetta, Lane Chandler, Arthur Pierson, Lucille Browne.

"The Midnight Patrol"—Two Reels— Sound. Released August 3, 1933, by MGM. Directed by Lloyd French. Costarring Walter Plinge, Frank Brownlee, Charlie Hall, Robert Kortman.

"Busy Bodies"—Two Reels—Sound. Released October 7, 1933, by MGM. Directed by Lloyd French. Costarring Tiny Sandford, Charlie Hall.

"Wild Poses"—Two Reels—Sound. Released October 28, 1933, by MGM. Produced by Robert F. McGowan for Hal Roach. Directed by Robert F. McGowan. Costarring Hal Roach's Rascals: George (Spanky) McFarland, Matthew (Stymie) Beard, Tommy Bond, with Franklin Pangborn and Emerson Treacy.

The team contributes a gag cameo to this "Our Gang" comedy.

"Dirty Work"—Two Reels—Sound. Released November 25, 1933, by MGM. Directed by Lloyd French. Costarring Lucien Littlefield, Sam Adams.

Sons of the Desert— 68 minutes— Sound. Released December 29, 1933, by MGM. Directed by William A. Seiter. Associate direction by Lloyd French. Story by Frank Craven. Dance direction by Dave Bennett. Original music by Marvin Hatley and Le Roy Shield. Photographed by Kenneth Peach. Costarring Mae Busch, Dorothy Christie, Charley Chase, Lucien Littlefield.

1934

"Oliver the Eighth"—Three Reels— Sound. Released January 13, 1934, by MGM. Directed by Lloyd French. Costarring Mae Busch, Jack Barty.

Hollywood Party— 68 minutes— Sound. Released June 1, 1934, by MGM.

Produced by Harry Rapf and Howard Dietz for MGM. Directed by Richard Boleslawski, Allan Dwan, and Roy Bowland. Original screenplay by Howard Dietz and Arthur Kober. Costarring Lupe Velez, Jimmy Durante, Ted Healey and his Stooges, Charles Butterworth, Patsy Moran, Tom Kennedy, and others.

The team contributes a classic routine with Lupe Velez to this star-studded feature length review picture.

"Going Bye-Bye!" — Two Reels — Sound. Released June 23, 1934 by MGM. Directed by Charles Rogers. Costarring Mae Busch, Walter Long, Sam Lufkin.

"Them Thar Hills" — Two Reels — Sound. Released July 21, 1934 by MGM. Directed by Charles Rogers. Costarring Mae Busch, Charlie Hall, Billy Gilbert.

Babes in Toyland (a.k.a *March of the Wooden Soldiers*) — 79 minutes — Sound. Released November 30, 1934, by MGM. Directed by Charles Rogers and Gus Meins. Screenplay by Nick Grinde and Frank Butler. Adapted from the musical comedy by Victor Herbert. Book and music by Glen MacDonough. Musical direction by Harry Jackson. Photographed by Art Lloyd and Francis Corby. Costarring Charlotte Henry, Felix Knight, Henry Brandon, Florence Roberts, Virginia Karns, William Burress.

"The Live Ghost" — Two Reels — Sound. Released December 8, 1934, by MGM. Directed by Charles Rogers. Costarring Walter Long, Mae Busch, Charlie Hall, Arthur Housman.

1935

"Tit for Tat" — Two Reels — Sound. Released January 5, 1935, by MGM. Directed by Charles Rogers. Costarring Charlie Hall, Mae Busch, James C. Morton, Bobby Dunn. Nominated for Best Live-Action Short Subject Academy Award of 1935.

"The Fixer-Uppers" — Two Reels — Sound. Released February 9, 1935, by MGM. Directed by Charles Rogers. Costarring Mae Busch, Charles Middleton, Arthur Housman.

"Thicker Than Water" — Two Reels — Sound. Released March 16, 1935, by MGM. Directed by James W. Horne. Costarring Daphne Pollard, James Finlayson, Gladys Gale.

Their final short.

Bonnie Scotland (a.k.a *Heroes of the Regiment*) — 80 minutes — Sound. Released August 23, 1935, by MGM. Directed by James W. Horne. Screenplay by Frank Butler and Jefferson Moffitt. Technical advice by Colonel W. E. Wynn. Music by Le Roy Shield and Marvin Hatley. Photographed by Art Lloyd and Walter Lundin. Costarring June Lang, William Janney, Anne Grey, James Finlayson, David Torrence, Daphne Pollard.

1936

The Bohemian Girl — 70 minutes — Sound. Released February 14, 1936, by MGM. Directed by James W. Horne and Charles Rogers. Based on the 1843 opera by Michael W. Balfe. Book by Alfred Bunn. Art direction by Arthur I. Royce and William L. Stevens. Musical direction by Nathaniel Shilkret. Photographed by Art Lloyd and Francis Corby. Costarring Jacqueline Wells, Mae Busch, Darla Hood, Antonio Moreno, Thelma Todd, James Finlayson.

"On the Wrong Trek" — Two Reels — Sound. Released April 16, 1936, by MGM. Directed by Charles Parrott and Harold Law. Costarring Charley Chase, Rosina Lawrence, Bonita Weber, Gertrude Sutton.

The team does a gag cameo in this next-to-last Charley Chase short for Hal Roach.

Our Relations— 74 minutes— Sound. Released October 30, 1936. Produced by Stan Laurel for Hal Roach. Directed by Harry Lachman. Based on the short story "The Money Box" by William Wymark Jacobs. Screenplay by Richard Connell and Felix Adler. Adapted by Charles Rogers and Jack Jevne. Musical score and direction by Le Roy Shield. Settings by Arthur I. Royce and William L. Stevens. Photographed by Rudolph Mate. Costarring Daphne Pollard, Betty Healy, Sidney Toler, Alan Hale Sr., Iris Adrian, Lona Andre, James Finlayson, Arthur Housman.

1937

Way Out West— 65 minutes— Sound. Released April 16, 1937, by MGM. Produced by Stan Laurel for Hal Roach. Directed by James W. Horne. Original story by Jack Jevne and Charles Rogers. Screenplay by Charles Rogers, Felix Adler, and James Parrott. Art direction by Arthur I. Royce. Settings by William L. Stevens. Musical direction by Marvin Hatley. Photographed by Art Lloyd and Walter Lundin. Costarring James Finlayson, Sharon Lynne, Stanley Fields, Rosina Lawrence, Vivien Oakland, Chill Wills and the Avalon Boys Quartet.

Pick a Star— 70 minutes— Sound. Released May 21, 1937, by MGM. Directed by Edward Sedgwick. Screenplay by Richard Flournoy, Arthur Vernon Jones, and Thomas J. Dugan. Art direction by Arthur I. Royce. Musical score by Arthur Morton and Marvin Hatley. Costarring Patsy Kelly, Jack Haley, Rosina Lawrence, Mischa Auer, Lyda Roberti.

The team contributes two routines to this full-length musical.

1938

Swiss Miss— 72 minutes— Sound. Released May 20, 1938, by MGM. Directed by John G. Blystone. Original story by Jean Negulesco and Charles Rogers. Screenplay by James Parrott, Felix Adler, and Charles Melson. Art direction by Charles D. Hall. Musical direction by Marvin Hatley. Photographed by Norbert Brodine and Art Lloyd. Costarring Walter Woolf King, Della Lind, Ludovico Tomarchio, Eric Blore, Adia Kuznetzoff, Charles Judels, Anita Garvin, Charles Gamora.

Block-Heads— 58 minutes— Sound. Released August 19, 1938, by MGM. Directed by John G. Blystone. Original story and screenplay by Charles Rogers, Felix Adler, James Parrott, Harry Langdon and Arnold Belgard. Musical direction by Marvin Hatley. Photographed by Art Lloyd. Costarring Minna Gombell, Billy Gilbert, Patricia Ellis, James Finlayson, Harry Woods, Tommy Bond.

1939

Flying Deuces— 69 minutes— Sound. Released October 20, 1939, by RKO-Radio Pictures. Produced by Boris Morros for RKO-Radio Pictures. Directed by A. Edward Sutherland. Original story and screenplay by Ralph Spence, Alfred Schiller, Charles Rogers and Harry Langdon. Art direction by Boris Leven. Musical direction by Edward Paul. Photographed by Art Lloyd. Costarring Jean Parker, Reginald Gardiner, James Finlayson, Charles Middleton, Rychard Cramer.

1940

"A Chump at Oxford"— 63 minutes (European release and most-known version now); 42 minutes (American release)—Sound. Released February 16, 1940, by United Artists. Directed by Alfred Goulding. Original story and screenplay by Charles Rogers, Felix Adler, and Harry Langdon. Art direction by Charles D. Hall. Musical direction by Marvin Hatley. Photographed by Art Lloyd. Costarring Forrester Harvey, Wilfred Lucas, Forbes Murray, James Finlayson, Anita Garvin, Charlie Hall.

Saps at Sea—57 minutes—Sound. Released May 30, 1940, by United Artists. Directed by Gordon Douglas. Original story and screenplay by Charles Rogers, Felix Adler, Gil Pratt, and Harry Langdon. Art direction by Charles D. Hall. Musical direction by Marvin Hatley. Photographed by Art Lloyd. Costarring Rychard Cramer, James Finlayson, Eddie Conrad, Ben Turpin, Charlie Hall, Patsy Moran.
   Their final film for Hal Roach.

1941

Great Guns—74 minutes—Sound. Released October 10, 1941, by Twentieth Century Fox. Produced by Sol M. Wurtzel for Twentieth Century Fox. Directed by Monty Banks. Original screenplay by Lou Breslow. Art direction by Richard Day and Albert Hogsett. Musical direction by Emil Newman. Photographed by Glen MacWilliams. Costarring Dick Nelson, Sheila Ryan, Edmund MacDonald, Russell Hicks, Ludwig Stossel.

1942

A-Haunting We Will Go—67 minutes—Sound. Released August 7, 1942, by Twentieth Century Fox. Produced by Sol M. Wurtzel for Twentieth Century Fox. Directed by Alfred Werker. Original story by Lou Breslow and Stanley Rauh. Screenplay by Lou Bres-

low. Art direction by Richard Day and Lewis Creber. Musical direction by Emil Newman. Photographed by Glen MacWilliams. Costarring Harry A. Jansen (Dante the Magician), John Shelton, Sheila Ryan, Don Costello, Elisha Cook, Jr.

1943

The Tree in a Test Tube—One Reel—Silent, with narration—Color. Released early in 1943. Produced by the U.S. Department of Agriculture, Forest Service. Directed by Charles McDonald. Music by Edward Craig. Narrated by Pete Smith. Their only surviving color film.

Air Raid Wardens—67 minutes—Sound. Released circa April 4, 1943, by MGM. Produced by B. F. Zeidman for MGM. Directed by Edward Sedgwick. Original screenplay by Martin Rackin, Jack Jevne, Charles Rogers, and Harry Crane. Art direction by Cedric Gibbons. Musical score by Nathaniel Shilkret. Photographed by Walter Lundin. Costarring Edgar Kennedy, Jacqueline White, Horace McNally, Nella Walker, Howard Freeman, Donald Meek.

Jitterbugs—74 minutes—Sound. Released June 11, 1943, by Twentieth Century Fox. Produced by Sol M. Wurtzler for Twentieth Century Fox. Directed by Malcolm St. Clair. Screenplay by Scott Darling. Art direction by James Basevi and Chester Gore. Musical direction by Emil Newman. Lyrics and music by Charles Newman and Lew Pollack. Photographed by Lucien Andriot. Costarring Vivian Blaine, Robert Bailey, Lee Patrick, Francis Ford, Noel Madison.

The Dancing Masters—63 minutes—Sound. Released November 19, 1943, by Twentieth Century Fox. Produced by

Lee Marcus for Twentieth Century Fox. Directed by Malcolm St. Clair. Screenplay by Scott Darling. Based on a story by George Bricker. Art direction by James Basevi and Chester Gore. Musical direction by Emil Newman. Music by Arthur Lange. Photographed by Norbert Brodine. Costarring Trudy Marshall, Robert Bailey, Matt Briggs, Margaret Dumont, Charles Rogers, Daphne Pollard.

1944

The Big Noise— 74 minutes— Sound. Released September 1944 by Twentieth Century Fox. Produced by Sol M. Wurtzel for Twentieth Century Fox. Directed by Malcolm St. Clair. Screenplay by Scott Darling. Art direction by Lyle Wheeler and John Ewing. Musical direction by Emil Newman. Photographed by Joe MacDonald. Costarring Arthur Space, Doris Merrick, Veda Ann Borg, Robert Dudley, Bobby Blake.

1945

Nothing but Trouble— 70 minutes— Sound. Released March 1945 by MGM. Produced by B. F. Zeidman for MGM. Directed by Sam Taylor. Original screenplay by Russell Rouse and Ray Golden. Additional dialogue by Bradford Ropes and Margaret Gruen. Art direction by Cedric Gibbons and Harry McAfee. Musical score by Nathaniel Shilkret. Photographed by Charles Salerno Jr. Costarring Henry O'Neill, Mary Boland, David Leland, John Warburton.

The Bullfighters— 69 minutes— Sound. Released May 18, 1945, by Twentieth Century Fox. Produced by William Girard for Twentieth Century Fox. Directed by Malcolm St. Clair. Original screenplay by Scott Darling. Art direction by Lyle Wheeler and Chester Gore.

Musical direction by Emil Newman. Photographed by Norbert Brodine. Costarring Richard Lane, Ralph Sanford, Margo Woode, Carol Andrews, Diosa Costello, Edward Gargan.

1951

Utopia (a.k.a. *Atoll* K, a.k.a. *Robinson Crusoeland*)— 98 minutes (European release); 82 minutes (American release)— Sound. Released November 21, 1951, by Les Films Sirius. A French — Italian coproduction by Les Films Sirius (Paris), Franco-London Films S.A. (Paris), and Fortezza Film (Rome). Directed by Leo Joannon and John Berry. Screenplay by John Klorer, Frederick Kohner, Rene Wheeler, and Pierro Tellini, based on an idea by Leo Joannon. Art direction by Roland Quignon. Original music by Paul Misraki. Photographed by Armand Thirard. Costarring Suzy Delair, Max Elloy, Adriano Rimoldi, Luigi Tosi, Robert Murzeau.

The silent films have been available on VHS and DVD through a company called Image Entertainment. Though this company does not produce anymore, their products are still available. The individual silent shorts can be purchased on separate VHS tapes or on compilations on VHS and DVD. These can be ordered at moviesunlimited.com

The sound Roach films haven't been available for some time on VHS, though the website mentioned above does offer *Heroes of the Regiment* and *Bogus Bandits* (*Bonnie Scotland* and *Fra Diavolo*, respectively) as well as *Pardon Us* and *Pack Up Your Troubles* on VHS. Also offered is perhaps the only truly appropriate instance of a digitally colored black-and-white film, *The March of the Wooden Soldiers* (*Babes in Toyland*), in which the surreally vivid hues approximate the fanciful colors of a children's storybook.

Two of the team's lesser films have always been readily available on VHS and DVD. *Flying Deuces* and *Utopia,* having long ago fallen into the public domain, circulate heavily in prints of wildly varying quality. Kino Films has put out a superior restored version of *Flying Deuces,* which can be ordered at kino.com. This same company also sells a two-DVD set of restored Stan Laurel solo comedies.

In North America, the rights to Laurel and Hardy's sound Roach films are held by the Hallmark company, which released a DVD compilation in 2003 containing *Sons of the Desert,* "Busy Bodies," "The Music Box" and "Helpmates." This was followed in 2005 by another volume composed of *Way Out West, Block-Heads,* and "Chickens Come Home." While one can't argue with the selection, fans have been disappointed to find that the source materials used were often television prints, with no care taken in terms of restoration. That being said, the second volume is a marked improvement in terms of image quality over the first volume — with *Block-Heads* in particular looking as good as it ever has.

The substandard versions of the films offered in the land of the films' birth are all the more lamentable when compared to the releases to be had elsewhere. England, Germany, and the Netherlands all offer DVD box sets containing virtually the entire Laurel and Hardy — Roach output in restored versions. The Benelux set from Holland offers the output in its entirety. Kinowelt in Germany and Universal Video in England are missing *Babes in Toyland, Bonnie Scotland,* and *Fra Diavolo.* Each set has unique assorted extras and special features— Benelux offers the films in chronological order, the other sets group them according to theme. The Universal set includes computerized color versions of many of the films, as well as phonetic foreign-language versions.

All of the European DVD sets are in PAL format, which means they can't be played on North American equipment. Some fans, however, have found the purchase of all-region DVD players to be well worth the investment.

Laurel and Hardy are two of the few movie stars of three quarters of a century ago to have a worldwide appreciation society numbering in the thousands. For information on the Sons of the Desert, go to sotd.org, or write Roger Gordon, 2230 Country Club Drive, Huntingdon Valley, PA, 19006.

CHAPTER NOTES

1. Stan (1890–1965)

1. McCabe, *Mr. Laurel and Mr. Hardy*, p. 153.
2. McCabe, *Comedy World of Stan Laurel*, p. 200.
3. McCabe, *Babe: The Life of Oliver Hardy*, p. 58.
4. Skretvedt, *Laurel and Hardy*, p.346.
5. Walker, *Peter Sellers*, p. 203. Sellers was known to carry Laurel's picture with him everywhere he worked, and he shared Laurel's veneration of legendary British music hall comic Dan Leno (1860–1904). Sellers believed that Leno spoke to him from the dead and "guided" Sellers's career.
6. McCabe, *Mr. Laurel and Mr. Hardy*, p. 78.
7. Skretvedt, *Laurel and Hardy*, p. 220.

2. Ollie (1892–1957)

1. McCabe, *Babe: The Life of Oliver Hardy*, p. 117.
2. Ibid., p. 118.
3. McCabe, *Mr. Laurel and Mr. Hardy*, p.47.
4. McCabe, *Babe: The Life of Oliver Hardy*, p. 22.
5. Ibid., p. 4.
6. McCabe, *Mr. Laurel and Mr. Hardy*, p. 47.
7. Ibid.
8. Ibid., p. 42.
9. Ibid., p. 11.
10. McCabe, *Babe: The Life of Oliver Hardy*, p. 97.
11. From Carl Reiner, another satirist of human nature, in an interview on the TVO program "Saturday Night at the Movies."

12. Quoted in Skretvedt, *Laurel and Hardy*, p. 56.
13. McCabe, *Mr. Laurel and Mr. Hardy*, p. 86.
14. Skretvedt, *Laurel and Hardy*, p. 108.
15. Brando quote from Lawrence Grobel, *Conversations with Brando*, p. 80.
16. McCabe, *Mr. Laurel and Mr. Hardy*, p. 96.

3. Films

1. McCabe, *The Comedy World of Stan Laurel*, Introduction.
2. Idea from Robin Cook, from his writing about the films of Leo McCarey, program book for the Cinematheque Ontario (Winter 2003).
3. Fred Lawrence Guiles, *Stan*, p. 15.
4. McCabe, *Mr. Laurel and Mr. Hardy*, p. 29.

4. Silents

1. Quoted in Skretvedt, *Laurel and Hardy*, p. 155.
2. McCabe, *Mr. Laurel and Mr. Hardy*, p. 91.
3. Skretvedt, *Laurel and Hardy*, p. 64.
4. Review quoted in Skretvedt, *Laurel and Hardy*, p. 102.
5. Quoted in McCabe, *Babe: The Life of Oliver Hardy*, p. 71.
6. McCabe, *The Comedy World of Stan Laurel*, p. 64.
7. Skretvedt, *Laurel and Hardy*, p. 104.
8. Henry Miller, *The Cosmological Eye.*
9. McCarey quoted in Leonard Maltin, *The Great Movie Comedians*, p. 109.

10. McCabe, *Mr. Laurel and Mr. Hardy*, p. 42.

11. Skretvedt, *Laurel and Hardy.*

5. Sound

1. Basil Wright, quoted in McCabe, *Mr. Laurel and Mr. Hardy*, p. 113.

2. Skretvedt, *Laurel and Hardy*, p. 224.

3. Ibid., p. 230.

4. McCabe, *Mr. Laurel and Mr. Hardy*, p. 125.

6. Features

1. McCabe, *Mr. Laurel and Mr. Hardy*, p. 121.

2. Ibid.

3. McCabe, *Babe: The Life of Oliver Hardy*, p. 129.

4. Kael, *5001 Nights at the Movies*, p. 824–5.

5. McCabe, Kilgore, and Bann, *Laurel and Hardy*, p. 363.

6. Skretvedt, *Laurel and Hardy*, p. 343.

7. McCabe, Kilgore, and Bann, *Laurel and Hardy*, p. 370.

8. Skretvedt, *Laurel and Hardy*, p. 359.

9. Guiles, *Stan: The Life of Stan Laurel*, p. 198.

7. Nadir

The pain and frustration of the comedians at the larger studios has been well documented by McCabe and Skretvedt and remains onscreen for all to see. Some fans may object to the harsh dismissal of the films here, but as per the title of the book, the concern in these pages is the team's art, which can't exist in films where they were not allowed to practice that art. The closest parallel to the team's work in this period is the movie work of Elvis Presley in the 1960s—another tragic case of a unique, inimitable talent put to work in bland mediocre films. Just as one wouldn't introduce a novice to the phenomenon that was Elvis Presley by showing him or her *Roustabout*, one couldn't expect a newcomer to appreciate the magic of Laurel and Hardy by showing him or her anything they produced at MGM or Twentieth Century Fox.

8. Utopia

1. Skretvedt, *Laurel and Hardy*, p. 419.

2. "Quoted in McCabe, *Mr. Laurel and Mr. Hardy*, p. 145.

BIBLIOGRAPHY

Barr, Charles, *Laurel and Hardy,* London: Studio Vista, 1967.

Grobel, Lawrence, *Conversations with Brando,* Hyperion, 1991.

Guiles, Fred Lawrence, *Stan: The Life of Stan Laurel,* Michael Joseph, 1980.

Kael, Pauline. *5001 Nights at the Movies.* New York: Henry Holt/Owl, 1991.

Kerr, Walter, *The Silent Clowns,* Knopf, New York, 1980.

Maltin, Leonard, *The Great Movie Comedians,* Crown Publisher, Inc., 1978

McCabe, John, *Mr. Laurel and Mr. Hardy,* Doubleday, New York, 1961

_____. *The Comedy World of Stan Laurel,* Robson Books, 1975

_____. *Charlie Chaplin,* Doubleday, 1978

_____. *Babe: The Life of Oliver Hardy,* Robson Books, 1990

_____, with Al Kilgore and Richard Bann, *Laurel and Hardy,* W. H. Allen, 1975

Miller, Henry, *The Cosmological Eye,* New York: New Directions, 1939

Skretvedt, Randy, *Laurel and Hardy: The Magic Behind the Movies,* Moonstone Press, 1987.

Walker, Alexander, *Peter Sellers: The Authorized Biography,* Weidenfeld and Nicolson, 1991.

INDEX